Defective and Unsafe Products: Law and Practice

Defective and Unsafe Products:
Law and Practice

Barry Cotter LL.B (Hons), Barrister, Old Square Chambers

Consultant editor
The Hon John Melville Williams QC

Butterworths
London, Dublin, Edinburgh
1996

United Kingdom	Butterworths a Division of Reed Elsevier (UK) Ltd, Halsbury House, 35 Chancery Lane, London WC2A 1EL and 4 Hill Street, Edinburgh EH2 3JZ
Australia	Butterworths, Sydney, Melbourne, Brisbane, Adelaide, Perth, Canberra and Hobart
Canada	Butterworths Canada Ltd, Toronto and Vancouver
Ireland	Butterworth (Ireland) Ltd, Dublin
Malaysia	Malayan Law Journal Sdn Bhd, Kuala Lumpur
New Zealand	Butterworths of New Zealand Ltd, Wellington and Auckland
Puerto Rico	Butterworth of Puerto Rico, Inc, San Juan
Singapore	Reed Elsevier (Singapore) Pte Ltd, Singapore
South Africa	Butterworths Publishers (Pty) Ltd, Durban
USA	Michie, Charlottesville, Virginia

A CIP Catalogue record for this book is available from the British Library.

ISBN 0 406 00248 7

Printed and bound in Great Britain by Clays Ltd, St Ives plc

PREFACE

The Consumer Protection Act 1987 is now well embedded as domestic legislation, and the European Directive[1] upon which it is based approaches its tenth Anniversary. This text covers both civil liability for defective products and criminal liability for unsafe products. Neither substantive food law nor the sections of the 1987 Act relating to misleading price applications will be considered. In practice these areas are quite discrete and are covered comprehensively in other texts.

Since it entered the statute book use of the Act has proved to be lopsided in that whilst prosecutions are being heard on a daily basis throughout England and Wales under the criminal provisions within the Act, there are very few reported decisions concerning its civil liability provisions. It may be that whereas the service of a summons upon a client produces an immediate requirement for familiarisation with the criminal provisions of the Act many practitioners still prefer to run cases concerning personal injury and damage by virtue of defective products upon the basis of ordinary principles of contract or negligence. Whilst at first blush it may seem that there are an alarming number of qualifications to the supposed strict liability under the Act which mean that the prospects of successfully pursuing an action are little better under the Act than if the action were framed solely in negligence or tort, this is in fact misconceived. The Act and the 1985 Directive upon which it is based provide a streamline cause of action to the plaintiff consumer and huge advantages during the course of litigation. Use of the Act is therefore to be encouraged, and hopefully this text will prove to be a useful guide.

Further, final agreement on the 1992 Directive (after years of negotiations) has now resulted in the 1994 General Product Safety Regulations. These Regulations substantially alter the position of producers or distributors of consumer products. New duties are imposed and existing duties under the 1987 Act widened. The nature and extent of these duties are likely to be the subject of lively debate in the courtroom in due course and this text can only serve to highlight potential areas of difficulty, and seek to give some guidance.

I would like to express my thanks to Richard Port, for his considerable assistance over the last year, to Tony Hill, my clerk, for his patience, and to Philip Alden for his encouragement and support.

Barry Cotter
Bristol
November 1995

1 85/374/EEC; see Part 4 below.

CONTENTS

TABLE OF STATUTES

References in this Table to *Statutes* are to Halsbury's Statutes of England (Fourth Edition) showing the volume and page number at which the annotated text of the Act will be found.

Page references printed in **bold** type indicate where the material is set out in part or in full.

AUSTRALIA

SOUTH AUSTRALIA

TABLE OF STATUTORY INSTRUMENTS

Page references in **bold** type indicate where the material is set out in part or in full.

TABLE OF CASES

E

F

Decisions of the European Court of Justice are listed below numerically. These decisions are also included in the preceeding alphabetical list.

Part 1

CIVIL LIABILITY

INTRODUCTION

The enactment of the 1987 Consumer Protection Act was the culmination of a considerable amount of debate and research within various forums in the United Kingdom and the European Community as a whole concerning the introduction of strict liability in law for damage caused by defective products. Whilst the 1987 Act, as section 1(1) states, was intended to have the effect of complying with Council Directive (85/374/EEC) upon the approximation of the Laws, Regulations and Administrative Provisions of the Member States concerning liability for defective products, there had already been domestic consideration of the subject. The Pearson Commission (the Royal Commission on Civil Liability and Compensation for Personal Injury under the Chairmanship of Lord Pearson) published a report in 1974.[1] One of the recommendations was that 'producers should be strictly liable in tort for death or personal injury caused by defective products', and further, that 'defect' should be defined in accordance with Article 2 of the Strasbourg Convention, which stated that a 'product has a defect when it does not provide the safety which a person is entitled to expect, having regard to all the circumstances including the presentation of the product'. Whilst it was the view of the Commission that producers of finished products and component producers should be strictly liable in tort for defective products, it felt that distributors should not be so liable but instead should have an obligation to disclose to any person injured by a product either the name of the producer of the goods or the name of the relevant supplier to the distributor. It was also recommended that there should be liability in respect of 'own brand' products in relation to 'those who brand them' as well as their producers. Importers into the European Community were to be treated as producers for the purposes of product liability.

The Commission also felt that there should be defences for the producer by way of proving that he did not put those products into circulation, or that the product was not defective when he did so, or that he did not put it into circulation in the course of 'a business'. Interestingly it was the Commission's view that 'the producers should not be allowed a defence of development risk'. A defence of contributory negligence was recommended but it was proposed that there should be no financial limits on the producer's liability.

Although it was to take 13 years, many of the recommendations were eventually included within the Consumer Protection Act 1987. The European Community first published a draft Directive for strict liability in August 1974, the same year that the Pearson Commission published its report. Further, a

1 Cmnd 7054.

number of countries signed the Strasbourg Convention in September 1976, and hence in the mid to late 1970s many of them were optimistic about progress towards the implementation upon a European basis of laws relating to strict liability. In fact, reflecting the many problems of producing an agreement between Member States, the Final Directive was not agreed until 25 July 1985.[2]

Parliament chose to implement the Directive in an Act which also consolidated many of the provisions then in existence concerning criminal liability for unsafe products and misleading price indications. The resulting Act is therefore of primary importance for those involved in the manufacture, importation, distribution, or retail sale of products. However, unlike the Provisions relating to criminal law, the sections relating to strict liability for defective products have been, it appears, sadly under used and certainly have not received a great deal of judicial consideration. There is a belief in some quarters (including the Department of Trade and Industry) that the lack of judicial consideration merely reflects the success of the Act in that those potentially liable are forced to settle claims without recourse to the Courts. However it is this author's experience that many practitioners still favour remedies in contract against the retailer. Further, many practitioners still believe, (it is submitted erroneously), that the requirements of the proof of a defect mean that many claims under the Act will still be very difficult to pursue.

Several aspects of the practical working of the Directive are being investigated by the Commission, as it appears that the experience within the United Kingdom may well reflect that faced within other Member States. Nevertheless, it is submitted that the Act does provide a substantial if not comprehensive armoury for the practitioner, particularly if the correct tactical approach is employed. It provides a very significant advancement upon the position faced in the early 1980s.

There are still some large grey areas of interpretation including those where the Act does not truly reflect the wording of the Directive. This aspect will be considered in greater detail later within the text and it is submitted that in practice judicial interpretation of the divergence in wording is likely to always favour the Directive (not the least of the arguments for which is simple reliance upon section 1(1)).

Reference will be made within the first chapter to the key concepts and definitions within the Act. Thereafter there will be an analysis of potential liability under the Act, defences, the European perspective, and also of the interaction between civil and criminal liability. There is consideration of residual liability outside the Act, principally under the laws of contract and tort. Finally there are examples of how cases can work in practice.

NORTHERN IRELAND

Although Part 1 of the 1987 Act does not apply to Northern Ireland[3], the Consumer Protection (Northern Ireland) Order 1987 (SI 1987/2049; NI 20) contains the provisions implementing the EEC Council Directive on Liability for Defective Products in Northern Ireland. Further, regard can be had to the interpretation and commentary upon the equivalent provisions in Part 1 of the 1987 Act. The Order itself is set out later.[4]

2 A full copy of the Directive is set out in Part 4.
3 See chapter 4.
4 See Part 4.

Chapter 1

KEY CONCEPTS

1.1 PRODUCT

The starting point for the consideration of potential liability under the Act and a prerequisite for a claim is the existence of a relevant product. At the outset it is vital to note that *services* are not products so the provision of instruction, information or advice without any relevant product is not covered by the Act[1]. It is therefore necessary to first consider the definition of relevant product.

1.1.1 Definitions

Article 2 of the Directive defines relevant products as 'all movables, even though incorporated into another moveable or into an immovable'. The preamble refers to 'movables which are used in the construction of immoveables or are installed in immoveables'. The definition within the Act is contained within section 1 and states that 'product' means any goods or electricity and, subject to section 1(3), includes a product which is comprised in another product, whether by virtue of being a component part or raw material or otherwise. The word 'goods' is further defined in section 45(1) to include 'substances, growing crops and things comprised in land by virtue of being attached to it and any ship, aircraft or vehicle'[2]. It is important to note the position of components and raw materials within the definition of a product[3]. It is the intention of both the Directive and

1 Warnings, instructions or labels accompanying or comprised within a product are relevant when considering the meaning of 'defect'; s 3(2)(a).

2 Section 10(7) of the Act produces a further defined category of 'consumer goods' which is stated to be goods ordinarily intended for private use or consumption but excluding certain items including growing crops, water, food, gas, aircraft, licensed medicinal products or controlled drugs, and tobacco. By Regulation 2 of the General Product Safety Regulations 1994 a new definition of 'product' is put in place for the purposes of criminal liability for the supply of unsafe goods (in line with Council Directive 92/59/EEC on General Product Safety). 'Product' is defined as 'any product intended for consumers or likely to be used by consumers, supplied whether for consideration or not in the course of a commercial activity and whether new, used or reconditioned; provided, however, a product which is used exclusively in the context of a commercial activity even if it is used for or by a consumer shall not be regarded as a product for the purposes of these Regulations provided always and for the avoidance of doubt this exception shall not extend to the supply of such a product to the consumer'. Hence the definition under Section 10 has been considerably widened.

3 See Arts 2, 3, 5, 7 and 9; ss 1, 2(5), 4(1)(f), and 5(2).

the Act that if a defective component or piece of raw material is used within the production of a product that both the producer of the final product and the producer of the relevant 'ingredient' should be jointly and severally liable to the end-user. However both the Directive and the Act recognise the difficulty faced by the manufacturer of a component where the defect in the end product is really attributable to the design of the product in which the component has been fitted or to instructions given by the 'final' manufacturer of the product. To this end Article 7(f) of the Directive and section 4(1)(f) contain defences for the component manufacturer (or raw material producer). Unfortunately both the European Provision and the Domestic Section seem capable of a strangely restricted interpretation. Under the Article it appears that the component has to be fitted into or in the end item and section 4(1)(f) makes reference to a defect 'in a product in which the product in question (the component) had been comprised'. During the debate of the Consumer Protection Bill[4] it was stated that 'the Article is clearly aimed where components such as nuts and bolts are made to the order of the finished product manufacturer, who then uses them for purposes for which they were not designed. That is to say that the component manufacturer is acting upon instructions given by the manufacturer of the finished product'. This has led to a potential overlap with the definition of a 'defect'[5], as it is difficult to see how a component can be said to be defective if a subsequent product only failed because of an improper use of that component. In such circumstances it would be extremely difficult in any event to pursue the component manufacturer.

Significantly, those producers who provide packaging or labelling may well fall outside the restricted scope of the defence in both the Directive and the Act[6]. However, in practice if labelling or packaging is solely in compliance with instructions given by another producer there is likely to be an indemnity as to liability by virtue of either contractual provisions or the duty of care owed.

1.1.2 Agricultural products

Primary agricultural products also receive special attention under the Directive by way of exemption. Such products are defined as 'the products of soil, of stock-farming and of fisheries, excluding products which have undergone initial processing'[7]. As is often the case within the Community the subject of agricultural produce has lead to radically differing views, (the Pearson Commission recommended no exemption). Whilst there can be sympathy with the primary agricultural producer who has little or no control over many of the chemicals present in the environment, and frequently produces items which by their very nature are of variable quality and can have a short 'shelf life', this must be balanced against the increasingly widespread, intensive, and sophisticated methods used in modern farming. Such is the sophistication of some of the systems in operation it will frequently be difficult in practice to state exactly what is a 'primary' agricultural product. The preamble to the Directive states that it is appropriate to exclude liability for agricultural products and game except where they have undergone a processing of an industrial nature

4 House of Commons Reports, Vol 483.
5 See s 3.
6 See s 4(1)(f)(i).
7 See Art 2.

which could cause a defect in these products. Many types of agricultural produce are now not only treated with fertilisers or pesticides but with other chemicals often after harvest, in order to enhance or preserve 'shelf life'. Additionally there is the difficulty of the extent of the boundary of 'initial processing' in so far as it extends into treatment and preparation for sale (eg the filleting of fish or the 'gutting' of animals)[8]. Although primary agricultural produce and game have been excluded from the main force of the Directive provision has been made by way of Article 15 (derogation from Article 2) to provide for their inclusion. However the Consumer Protection Act 1987 follows the Directive and the exemption applies.

1.1.3 Building materials[9]

The position of building materials under the Act also requires special consideration. Section 46(4) states that references within the Act to supplying goods shall not include references to supplying goods comprised in land where the supply is effected by the creation or disposal of an interest in land. Further, the definition of 'product' within the Article clearly excludes 'immoveables' ie buildings themselves. Nevertheless the builder who incorporates products into a building without creating or disposing an interest therein does not have any immunity under the Act. Building materials are 'products' for the purposes of the Act[10]. An example often cited is that of a bag of defective cement purchased and used in building work on a house. Where the defect causes subsequent personal injury there will be strict liability. There may of course be complicated issues upon the nature of the 'defect' and causation but the prima-facie liability remains.

1.1.4 Drugs and other medical products

Neither the Directive nor the Consumer Protection Act 1987 provide any special provision for pharmaceuticals or other medical products[11]. Arguments were put forward that by the very nature of many 'drugs' damage may be caused to the system and strict liability could induce conservative practices which would in due course be to the disadvantage of the population as a whole. This view did not find favour. The position of such products will however be very different from the vast majority of other products and the questions as to whether a 'defect'[12] existed[13] and also the defence concerning the state of scientific and technical knowledge at the relevant time[14] are likely in some cases to be extremely complicated[15].

8 See generally ss 1 and 2(4).
9 See s 1.
10 The Pearson Commission also recommended that movable products incorporated into immoveables should be regarded as 'products' for the purpose of product liability.
11 The Pearson Commission did not recommend special treatment for drugs.
12 Questions concerning the extent to which drugs should cater for biological conditions which are extremely rare within the population as a whole, likely prescription and the interaction with other pharmaceutical products.
13 See generally s 3.
14 Section 4(1)(e).
15 Further, having regard to the conduct of recent group actions such as the Benzodiazepine litigation cases may well be vigorously defended by manufacturers, distributors and prescribers and subject to considerable problems in terms of funding.

1.2 DEFECT

The Strasbourg Convention provided[16] that 'a product has a 'defect' when it does not provide the safety which a person is entitled to expect, having regard to all the circumstances including the presentation of the product'. The Pearson Committee Report[17] stated that a product should be considered as defective:

> 'When it does not provide the safety which a person is entitled to expect, taking all circumstances into account, including:
> (b) the presentation of the product;
> (c) the use to which it could reasonably be expected that the product would be put;
> (d) the time when the product was put into circulation.
> The product shall not be considered defective for the sole reason that a better product is subsequently put into circulation.'

Section 3 of the Act sets out the definition to be applied within domestic legislation, implementing and expanding upon these earlier definitions. It is to be noted that the relevant definition of 'defect' relates to the safety of the product as opposed to its general quality, fitness for purpose or merchantability. Clearly, absolute safety is not required and the question is one of fact and degree in every case having regard to the objective test as to what persons generally are entitled to expect in relation to a product having regard to all the circumstances. The Section itself specifies within sub-sections specific matters which must[18] be considered, and these are:

(a) The manner in which, and purposes for which, the product has been marketed, its get-up, the use of any mark in relation to the product and any instructions for or warnings with respect to, doing or refraining from doing anything with or in relation to the product;

(b) What might reasonably be expected to be done with or in relation to the product; and

(c) The time when the product was supplied by its producer to another.

However it is likely that other matters will play a prominent part in assessing whether a defect exists[19]. Section 10 of the Act, which sets out specific considerations to be taken into account when assessing whether an item is reasonably safe[20], has now been largely superseded by the General Product Safety Regulations 1994 which define[1] a 'safe product' as –

> '...any product which, under normal or reasonably foreseeable conditions of use, including duration, does not present any risk or only the minimum risks compatible with the product's use, considered as acceptable and consistent

16 Article 2(c).
17 Article 6.
18 'Shall be taken into account', s 3(2).
19 See s 3(2).
20 See chapter 8 below. The section states that goods are not reasonably safe having regard to all the circumstances including, (a) the manner in which, and purposes for which, the goods are being or would be marketed, the get-up of the goods, the use of any mark in relation to the goods and any instruction or warnings which are given or would be given with respect to the keeping, use or consumption of the goods; (b) any standards of safety published by any person either for goods of a description which applies to the goods in question or for matters relating to goods of that description; and, (c) the existence of any means by which it would have been reasonable (taking into account the cost, likelihood and extent of any improvement) for the goods to have been made safe.
1 Regulation 2.

with a high level of protection for the safety and health of persons, taking into account in particular –

(a) the characteristics of the product, including its composition, packaging, instructions for assembly and maintenance;

(b) the effect on other products, where it is reasonably foreseeable that it would be used with other products;

(c) the presentation of the product, the labelling, any instructions for its use and disposal and any other indication or information provided by the producer; and

(d) the categories of consumers at serious risk when using the product, in particular children.

Clearly as the definition of 'defect' contained within section 3 refers to the safety of the product, regard should be had to the definition under the General Product Safety Regulations 1994, or any other specific Regulations covering the product in question.

It is important to note that in assessing whether an item was 'reasonably safe having regard to all the circumstances' under section 10 of the Act Courts have on occasions made two separate errors[2]. Firstly, in relation to 'risk' and 'hazard'. Section 3 makes reference to the'risks' of damage or injury[3], and this must not be confused with a 'hazard'. A hazard is a potential source of harm or a 'method' of damage or injury whereas the risk is the assessment of the likelihood of injury or damage occurring by virtue of the 'hazard'. Hence, the existence of a hazard does not mean that a product is to be axiomatically considered defective. The vital consideration is the possibility or probability of the hazard causing death or personal injury[4].

Second, the courts have been led into misleading and unfavourable comparisons with other products. The fact that higher levels of safety may be obtained or that other products presenting a lesser degree of risk are available should not necessarily mean that a product is defective. It is stated within section 3 that 'nothing in this section shall require a defect to be inferred from the fact alone that the safety of a product which is supplied *after* that time is greater than the safety of the product in question. However this expressly refers to a *subsequently* produced and safer item. It does not specifically refer to the fact that other items on the market at the same time produce a higher level of safety. However, when considering many products a Court should not ordinarily hold that persons are generally entitled to expect all consumer products to produce

2 Whereas the definition of 'defect' under s 3 has not received judicial consideration, s 10 has regularly been considered in Magistrates' Courts by virtue of Local Authority prosecutions. Whilst the new test for a 'safe product' within the General Product Safety Regulations 1994 now addresses one of these features, s 3 does not possess an express reference to either;

3 Risk (defined in ISO/IEC Guide 31) is the probable rate of occurrence of a hazard and the degree of severity of the harm. See also s 10, and the General Product Safety Regulations 1994, reg 2.

4 An example is the pipe-cleaner. In two Trials over eight days the London Borough of Barking and Dagenham sought to establish that the presence of pipe-cleaners within craft kits constituted an unreasonable risk of injury. The hazard was stated to be children using the pipe-cleaner as a weapon to cause, inter alia, occular injury. The manufacturer of the craft kit pointed to sales of many millions of pipe-cleaners per year and the fact that there had been no recorded injury caused in this fashion over 30 years. Hence it was argued whilst the hazard may exist the risk was negligible. On Appeal from the Magistrates who found no realistic risk existed it was found that there was a reasonable risk and hence the products were not safe; *Barking and Dagenham London Borough v Acorn Hobby* (1993), unreported, Swindon Crown Court, HHJ Fanner. The decision has been the subject of criticism as wrongly 'merging' the concepts of risk and hazard.

the same level of safety regardless of cost and quality[5]. Nevertheless, in some circumstances, particularly warnings and instructions, straightforward comparisons are very helpful in assessing possible defects as there can be little excuse for not 'matching' the safety levels of other similar items on the market.

1.2.1 Misuse[6]

Section 3(2)(b) when making reference to 'what might reasonably be expected to be done with or in relation to the product', incorporates a reasonably foreseeable degree of 'misuse'[7]. The duty to guard against such 'misuse' is potentially an onerous one and is the subject of considerable debate within some areas of product manufacture and importation[8]. Frequently much reliance is placed upon appropriate warning labels or instructions. However, such solutions are open to the criticism that under normal and foreseeable conditions of use packaging is quickly discarded and 'small-print' often missed. Unfortunately alternative designs or other methods of securing safety may be very expensive. In practice the balance can be very difficult to achieve and a requirement to anticipate and cater for possible methods of use by each and every individual impracticable[9]. When considering misuse regard should be had for the possibility of alleging contributory negligence pursuant to section 6(4) of the Act.

1.2.2 Warnings and instruction

Warnings and instruction both receive express mention within section 3 when the assessment is made as to whether the safety of a product is such as persons are generally entitled to expect. Whilst in relation to certain items there is specific regulation of the nature and extent of warnings to be attached to the products[10]. The adequacy of instructions or warnings is frequently in issue before

5 A common consumer item which produces very great variance within safety features is the motorcar. Some new models will possess steel superstructures, impact resistance design, air bags and a number of other features combining to give a much safer ride with a higher price than the average and seemingly 'basic' model. This does not mean that the basic model is necessarily defective. However there may well come a point when the absence of such features cannot be excused upon the grounds of cost and consumer expectation within the marketplace. It is again a question of fact and degree in each case.

6 See s 3.

7 The General Product Safety Regulations 1994 refer within the definition of 'safe product' in s 2 to 'normal or reasonably foreseeable conditions of use, including duration'.

8 See s 2 and the 'Toy-Box' argument as applied to the toy industry.

9 For example, the manufacture of one type of bottle top designed to prevent easy opening by a child which was then criticised on the basis that some elderly, weak or infirm individuals were having considerable difficulty in taking the top off. See also the Child Resistant Packaging (Safety) (Amendment) Regulations 1993.

10 For example, see Sch 4 of the Toys (Safety) Regulations 1989 'Warnings and Indications of Precautions to be taken when using Toys', and the European Harmonised Standard for Toys, EN71. Specific references are made as to the nature, extent, content, and even deemed effect of warnings. For example, a warning 'Not for Children under 36 Months' when applied to a 'soft' toy is deemed in certain circumstances to be of no effect and the toy must be considered for its safety when given to children under that age. Further, in respect of other toys which are not suitable for children under 36 months there must be a warning ' Not Suitable for Children under 3 Years' together with a brief indication, which may also appear in the instructions for use, of the specific risks calling for this restriction (eg small parts a choking hazard). See also the Chemicals (Hazard Information and Packaging) Regulations 1993.

the Courts[11]. Whilst a particularly careful approach would require prominent, comprehensive and permanent types of warning and instruction such an approach will rarely find favour with those charged with the marketing of a product. In specific cases reluctance to address concerns has led directly to onerous regulations governing and requiring warnings (as in the case of the Tobacco Products Labelling (Safety) Regulations 1991 (as amended by the 1993 Regulations)). Further, ergonomic experts and other safety consultants are now regularly used by Local Authorities to assess the likely adequacy or effect of specific warnings on consumer products when considering possible prosecutions. Clearly each individual warning must be considered in the light of its contents, prominence and likely duration. Manufacturers and importers are now clearly aware that the simple presence somewhere on an item of a warning or label will not necessarily be seen as adequately drawing the attention of consumers to the existence of a hazard. It is certainly arguable that the more unusual or unexpected the particular hazard the higher will be the degree of notice required for the end-user to provide reasonable safety[12].

1.2.3 Types of defect

There are generally thought to be four generic types of defect: (i) a lack of safety in design, (ii) a lack of safety in construction, (iii) inadequate warnings or instructions, and (iv) a failure to conform to express warranty. It is necessary to consider each in detail.

1.2.3.1 Safety in design

This type of defect relates to the 'intentional' make-up of the product. It may be that the hazard in question has been appreciated and ignored as not posing a reasonable foreseeable risk or that the hazard has not been appreciated at all. In the latter case the manufacturer or importer may be on considerably weaker ground in justifying the design. This type of defect is, in practical terms, likely to be the most difficult to prove. Whilst it is unlikely that there will be issues over supply or the intervening actions of third parties (so far as they may affect the condition of the item) a manufacturer or importer is not likely to readily concede a design defect as this may lead to a requirement to withdraw all like examples of the product (or indeed other similar products containing the same defect) from the market[13], and change the design.

Clearly comparison with national voluntary standards (including the standards of any Community member) or standards or guidelines of Trade or Manufacturers Associations will be relevant[14].

11 By virtue of prosecutions in relation to safety of goods historically under s 10 of the Consumer Protection Act 1987 but in the future under the 1994 Regulations.

12 Comparisons have been made to Exemption Clauses and to the fact that the more unusual or unexpected a particualr term is, the higher the degree of notice required to incorporate it and the requirement in certain circumstances to 'make it conspicuous' as highlighted by Denning LJ 'Some Clauses I have seen would need to be printed in red ink on the face of the document with a red hand pointing to it before the notice could be held to be sufficient'; *J Spurling Ltd v Bradshaw* [1956] 1 WLR 461, CA.

13 See Reg 8(b) of the General Product Safety Regulations 1994.

14 It should be noted that the approval of the Safety Standards Regulations 1987 has been revoked by the General Product Safety Regulations 1994 but by Regulation 10(2) the voluntary national standards, community technical specifications or other standards may be considered.

Further, consideration will be given to the fact that the objective test for a defect requires safety to be such as persons *generally* are entitled to expect. Thus if a design causes a hazard for a tiny and idiosyncratic proportion of the population it may well be argued that this does not constitute a design defect[15].

Expert evidence is likely to be a necessity in cases concerning this type of defect and little other than general guidelines can be drawn from previous cases[16].

1.2.3.2 Defect in construction or assembly

These types of defects can be loosely termed 'unintentional' in that usually if the particular item had been brought to the specific attention of the producer it would have been considered (unlike the category above) to be defective. There are two common categories:

(i) the foreign body ie some substance or object which should not ordinarily be present, a classical example being the case of *Donoghue v Stevenson*[17].

(ii) a failure in 'finishing off' or completing the production process, examples being the sharp wire left to protrude or the failure to tighten up internal nuts or bolts.

This type of case may on occasions contain considerable difficulties for the person pursuing the action in proving that the defect was present at the time of relevant supply by a manufacturer or importer and hence to overcome the specific defence set out at paragraph 4(1)(d)[18]. For example, if it is the potential Plaintiff's case that an injury has been caused by a protruding wire on a bicycle there may be considerable difficulty in pursuing the manufacturer alone if it is alleged that the construction process means that such wires have a cap on the end and the cap must have been 'knocked off' in the wholesalers or retailer's premises. Much may turn upon a detailed examination of the production methods and the extent to which the same are capable of malfunction and also of theinspection and testing systems in operation[19]. It is however likely that a manufacturer or importer will have to produce internal documentation and possibly independent expert evidence to support and justify the production, sampling and testing methods in operation if it is to be claimed that it is highly improbable that the item was defective at the relevant time of supply. Naturally, the evidence of intermediates within the supply chain may also be very important in establishing when the defect arose. (Indeed, there may well be proceedings based upon alternative possibilities as to how and when the defect arose.)

15 The argument will depend upon the foreseeability and nature and extent of the population susceptible to the hazard. Examples may be found in the area of unusual or complex allergies.

16 See for example, *Grant v Cooper* [1940] NZLR 947 (Sheep dip); *Wyngrove's Executrix v Scottish Omnibuses Ltd* 1965 SLT 286 (Bus); *Lambert v Lewis* [1978] 1 Lloyd's Rep 610 (towing coupling on vehicle); *Vacwell Engineering Co Ltd v BDH Chemicals Ltd* [1971] 1 QB 88; *Adelaide Chemical and Fertilizer Co Ltd v Carlyne* (1940) 64 CLR 514, (acid in unsuitable container); *Hawkins v Coulsdon and Purley UDC* [1954] 1 QB 319, CA; *Mason v Williams* [1955] 1 All ER 808 (chisel); *Davie v New Merton Board Mills* [1959] AC 604, HL; *Hindustan SS Co v Siemans Bros & Co Ltd* [1955] 1 Lloyd's Rep 167.

17 [1932] AC 562, HL (the snail in the ginger beer bottle).

18 See *Evans v Triplex Safety Glass Co Ltd* [1936] 1 All ER 283.

19 A system as envisaged within BS5750 (and now BSEN ISO 9000) will frequently enable a manufacturer to locate the production batch and assess the possibility of an isolated defect. See also *P & M Supplies (Essex) Ltd v Devon County Council* (1991) 156 JP 328 (concerning 'hand made' toys), chapter 10 and the defence of due diligence.

As with the first category cases are likely to be somewhat specific to their own facts[20].

1.2.3.3 *Inadequate warnings and instructions*

Warnings and instructions for use will often have a vital role to play in the overall safety of a product. This will particularly be the case where the hazard is not readily apparent, for example, where the product will readily catch fire[1]. As stated above[2], comparisons can be made with products on the market producing a similar type of hazard. A failure to provide warnings or instruction where other producers deem it necessary will often prove difficult to justify. In some areas there are mandatory requirements and the Chemicals (Hazard Information and Packaging) Regulations 1993 cover a wide range of substances[3]. It must be stressed that as appropriate warnings and instructions often add little to the production cost of a product absence frequently attracts considerable criticism[4]. Recently Courts have tended to be less impressed with warnings or labels attached to 'packaging' as opposed to those printed upon the product itself. This tends to reflect the fact that packaging is quickly discarded and any warning or instruction contained thereon quickly forgotten. Also there is a tendency towards favouring an indication of the hazard involved with the use of an item as opposed to merely stating 'Not Suitable' for a particular class of individual[5]. Yet again case law has produced a diverse number of examples of this type of defect[6].

1.2.3.4 *Lack of conformity to express statement*

If an express statement is made with or upon a product whether it be by way of warning, instruction, direction or claim as to safety generally, and there is a failure to comply or match up to the statement, the product may well be defective. Often the defect is due to the consumer being lulled into a false sense of security. Frequently phrases such as non-toxic and hypo-allergenic are used as a marketing tool and there must be great care taken by manufacturers or importers that the product does in fact comply with such express statements.

20 See for example *Barnett v H & J Packer& Co Ltd* [1940] 3 All ER 575; *Escola v Coca-Cola Bottling* 150 P 2d 436 (1944); *Herschtal v Stewart & Arden Ltd* [1940] 1 KB 155; *Lockett v A & M Charles Ltd* [1938] 4 All ER 170; *Malfroot v Noxal Ltd* (1935) 51 TLR 551; *Geddling v Marsh* [1920] 1 KB 668; *Chaproniere v Mason* (1905) 21 TLR 633; *Preist v Last* [1903] 2 KB 148, CA; *Clarke v Army and Navy Co-operative Society* [1903] 1 KB 155; *Daniels and Daniels v R White & Sons* [1938] 4 All ER 258; *Barnett v H & J Packer & Co Ltd* [1940] 3 All ER 575; *Read v Croydon Corpn* [1938] 4 All ER 631; *Watson v Buckley* [1940] 1 All ER 174; *Mason v Williams* [1955] 1 All ER 808; *Steer v Durable Rubber Manufacturing* (1958) Times, 20 November; *Andrews v Hopkinson* [1957] 1 QB 229; *Howard v Furness Houlder Argentine Lines Ltd* [1936] 2 All ER 781; *Dominion Natural Gas Co v Collins* [1909] AC 640, PC.

1 See for example the Nightwear (Safety) Regulations 1985.

2 See '*Defect*', at 1.2 *ante*.

3 See also *Vacwell Engineering Co Ltd v BDH Chemicals Ltd* [1971] 1 QB 88 for common law consideration of the issue.

4 The argument that such a warning or instruction boldly displayed may unduly alarm or 'put off' consumers rarely finds much favour with a Court.

5 See for example the Toys (Safety) Regulations 1989.

6 See for example, *British South Africa Co v Lennon Ltd* (1915) 113 LT 925 (cattle dip); *Watson v Buckley* [1940] 1 All ER 174 (hair dye); *Shanklin Pier Ltd v Detel Products Ltd* [1951] 2 KB 854; *Heil v Hedges* [1951] 1 TLR 512; *Hurley v Dyke* [1979] RTR 265; *Devilez v Boots Pure Drug Co Ltd* (1962) 106 Sol Jo 552 (corn solvent); *Parker v Oloxo Ltd* [1937] 3 All ER 524.

In many respects this type of defect is more serious than a simple failure to give appropriate warnings or instructions for use. When considering the area of implied exclusion this area of defect merges into a failure to appropriately warn (for example a warning not suitable for children under 3 impliedly asserts that the item is suitable for 4 year olds). Very often it is the desire of those involved in the sale of a potential product to increase the market size that leads to difficulties with express statements or claims. Great caution is always required to ensure that all statements upon a product are factually correct[7].

1.3 DAMAGE

Article 9 of the Directive defines 'damage' as:

(a) Damage caused by death or personal injuries;
(b) Damage to, or destruction of, any item of property other than the defective product itself, with a lower threshold of 500 ECU, provided that the item of property:
 (i) is of a type ordinarily intended for private use or consumption, and
 (ii) was used by the injured person mainly for his own private use or consumption.

Section 5 of the Consumer Protection Act sets out the provisions relating to damage giving rise to liability. It defines damage as meaning death or personal injury (to include pre-natal injury and nervous shock) or any loss or damage to any property[8] including land.

The provisions differ from those within the Directive in two respects, but the divergence has not yet given rise to an issue before the Courts.

The first divergence from the wording of the Directive can be seen in the phrase 'any loss or damage to' which contrasts with the phrase 'damage to, or destruction of' contained within Article 9. This is however unlikely to cause any practical problems and the difference is likely to be of little more than academic interest[9]. The second is more significant and lies within the first of the five separate categories of loss of or damage to property which are excluded;

(a) Damage to the product itself or the loss of or any damage to the whole or any part of any product which has been supplied with the product in question and comprised within it[10]. Whilst the damage to the product itself is excluded by Article 9(b) as set out above, the balance of this exclusion creates an extra restriction to and significant departure from the definition of relevant damage as set out under the Directive[11]. Not only is this extension somewhat difficult to justify it also produces a peculiar anomaly by reason of its reference to supply with the product comprised in it as opposed to subsequent incorporation or replacement.
 The other categories are:

7 Examples are *British South Africa v Lennon*, *Watson v Buckley* and *Shanklin Pier Ltd v Detel*, *supra*.
8 Property is not specifically defined within the Act.
9 During the debate of the Consumer Protection Bill it was stated that the word 'loss' has the same meaning as 'destruction' but that the use of the word 'loss' would reduce some uncertainty, ie prevent a different or narrower construction than that intended.
10 See s 5.
11 See chapter 4, *European Perspective*.

(b) Destruction and/or loss of or any damage to commercial property. This exclusion is set out in paragraph 5(3). An issue may occasionally arise as to whether a particular product is in fact a private or consumer item in which case the test is part objective (Section 3(2)(a)) and part subjective (sub-section 3(2)(b)), with the requirement that both parts be satisfied;

(c) Destruction and/or loss of and/or damage to any property resulting in an award that would not exceed £275 (500 ECU within the Article);

(d) Economic loss[12];

(e) A failure to provide a benefit or enhancement. The fact that a positive advantage is not gained, which may ordinarily give rise to a claim for breach of contract, should be distinguished from the objectively negative effect of destruction, loss or damage to property.

With the obvious exception of economic loss any of the above forms of loss or damage may be the subject of a straightforward claim in contract and/or negligence. Further there will be no liability under the Act where a product is of inadequate quality in that it does not meet a contractual specification, (in other words, lack of merchantable quality). Liability will ordinarily lie in contract[13].

12 See chapter 3 on *Residual Liability*.
13 See chapter 3.

Chapter 2

LIABILITY

2.1 PRODUCERS AND SUPPLIERS

As stated within its preamble the intention of the Directive is the approximation of the laws of Member States concerning the liability of the *producer* for damage caused by the defectiveness of his products. This is also plainly set out within Article 1 which states that '[t]he Producer shall be liable for damage caused by a defect in his product'.

The Consumer Protection Act 1987[1] in implementing the Directive seeks also to place primary liability at the door of the producer[2]. Article 3 of the Directive defines a producer as 'the manufacturer of a finished product, the producer of any raw material or the manufacturer of a component part and any person who, by putting his name, trade mark or other distinguishing feature on the product presents himself as a producer'. In a somewhat complicated fashion the Consumer Protection Act produces essentially the same result within sections 1 and 2. The combined effect of these sections is to treat as a 'producer' those within the following categories:

(a) the manufacturer[3];
(b) an abstractor eg of minerals[4];
(c) 'processors' eg of agricultural produce[5];
(d) the component or raw material producer[6];
(e) the 'own brand' producer or person holding themselves out to be the producer of the product[7];
(f) the commercial importer into the Community[8].

It should of course be remembered that by reason of section 2(5), where two or more 'persons' are liable for the same damage, liability under the Act can be joint and several. This means that more than one individual within the categories above can be liable in respect of the same damage.

To the first and major category of producer there is a second category of persons potentially liable under the Act; suppliers who were the subject of a

1 The Act is without prejudice to liability in contract or in negligence. See s 2(6).
2 This is subject to s 2(3) in relation to suppliers.
3 See s 1(2)(a).
4 See s 1(2)(b).
5 See s 1(2)(c).
6 See s 1(2)(a) and the definition of 'product' within s 1.
7 See s 2(2)(b).
8 See s 2(2)(c) and Art 3(2).

relevant request under section 2(3) of the Act[9]. However this liability is provisional in that if the relevant request is satisfactorily dealt with there will be no liability. This liability should now be seen in light of the duties imposed upon distributors and suppliers under the General Product Safety Regulations 1994. Most reasonable and prudent suppliers will be able to avoid liability under this Section although they may still face an action based upon contractual liability.

2.2 THOSE NOT COVERED

By virtue of section 2(3) a product must have been supplied[10]. This means that an employee will not ordinarily have the benefit of the Act when considering a potential action against his employer. However the provisions of the Employers Liability (Defective Equipment) Act 1969[11] means that in practical terms little advantage is lost. Under that Act, where an employee suffers personal injury in the course of his employment in consequence of a defect in equipment provided by his employer for the purposes of the employer's business, and the defect is attributable wholly or partly to the fault of a Third Party (whether identified or not) the injury shall be deemed to also be attributable to negligence on the part of the employer. 'Equipment' includes any plant and machinery, vehicle, aircraft and clothing[12] and has been given a wide interpretation[13].

Further, the Provision and Use of Work Equipment Regulations 1992 (SI 1992/2932) (intended to implement the Work Equipment Directive 89/655) now apply. The Regulations apply not only to employers, but also to the self-employed, to occupiers of factories as defined by the Factories Act 1961 and to any person who has a degree of control of non-domestic premises made available to persons at a place of work[14].

2.3 DEFENCES

The first and most obvious defence to a potential claim is that of the relevant provisions of sections 1, 2, 3, 5 and 6[15] having not been satisfied[16]. Only if there is prima facie liability should regard then be had to the specific statutory defences set out in section 4[17]. It is only when a person seeks to rely upon one of the statutory defences that the burden of proof will swing away from the person who asserts primary liability. There are six specific statutory defences:

9 Implementing Art 3(3) of the Directive.
10 See ss 2 and 46.
11 Section 1.
12 Section 1(3).
13 See *Coltman v Bibby Tankers Ltd* [1988] AC 276, HL, and *Knowles v Liverpool City Council* [1993] ICR 21, CA.
14 Further, regard should be had to the provisions of the Health and Safety at Work Act 1974.
15 In relation to s 6 see Sch 1 in respect of limitation and 'cut off'.
16 It should also be noted that if there would be liability under the Directive but not under the Act the Court will favour the interpretations set out in the Directive. See European Perspective at chapter 3 (3.8.).
17 There may be overlap on some issues such as the ability to assess a potential defect at the time of the supply. See s 3 and the interaction with s 4(1)(e).

(a) *Compliance with Requirement or Enactment*
For all practical purposes this defence can be ignored, on the ground that it is very unlikely that it will ever be relevant[18];

(b) *No Relevant Supply*[19]
This defence is based upon Article 7(a) of the Directive which provides a defence if the producer proves that he did not put the product into circulation. It is possible to argue that the defence within the Directive encompasses a wider number of situations than those envisaged by the defence under the Act. However, this specific defence is again only likely to apply in rare and particular circumstances;

(c) *Private Transactions*[20]
There are two cumulative limbs of the section which require satisfying before this defence can be made out;

(d) *Subsequently Acquired Defect*[1]
This defence is likely to be relevant when concerned with defects in the 'make-up' or individual construction as opposed to defects in general design. Reliance will be placed upon the life history of the product after the relevant supply, and reference may be made to improper or inadequate installation or assembly or damage due to transportation, storage, testing, misuse or 'wear and tear'[2]. In appropriate circumstances the end-users' recourse may be to look to join the supplier by virtue of liability under the contract;

(e) *The Development Risks Defence*[3]
This defence will be relevant in the case of an alleged design defect and relates to the assertion that at the time of the supply of the product the state of scientific and technical knowledge was such that the defect which subsequently caused the personal injury or damage could not have been discovered. Section 4(1)(e) does not mirror the defence set out in Article 7(e) of the 1985 Directive, and is somewhat less restrictive[4]. This is likely to be a difficult and onerous defence to establish particularly having regard to the wording in Article 7(e). It is also likely to require expert evidence in support of the assertion.
Under Article 15 of the Directive the inclusion of a 'state of the art' defence was left as a matter for the individual Member States themselves. The consumer protection lobby strenuously resisted its inclusion, but the UK government preferred the views of the business community. The provision was included, and the UK government justified that inclusion on three grounds: first, that to impose liability without recourse to such a defence as provided by the Directive would stifle innovation; secondly, that businesses with any reliance upon research and development would face increased insurance premiums; and thirdly, that British industry would face a potential competitive disadvantage *vis-à-vis* its European counterparts in as much as other States would include the defence.

18 See s 4(1)(a).
19 See ss 4(1)(b) and 46.
20 See s 4(1)(c).
1 See s 4(1)(d).
2 See, for example, *Evans v Triplex Safety Glass Co Ltd* [1936] 1 All ER 283.
3 See s 4(1)(e).
4 See s 1(1) and chapter 4 (*European Perspective*) post.

It is important to note that the relevant time for consideration of the state of scientific and technical knowledge is the time when the product was supplied by the producer, and not when it was manufactured. A problem could therefore arise where there is a delay between manufacture and the supply and in that intervening period new scientific knowledge has become available.

However, perhaps the most significant point to consider is that the wording of the Act does appear to be wider than that of the Directive, the latter providing a defence only if the state of scientific and technical knowledge at the relevant time 'was not such as to enable the existence of the defect to be discovered'. This despite the fact that the UK government did state that it was determined that the defence would not be an easy one to invoke. It is true that large financial outlay or economic impracticability in discovering the defect will not serve as a defence for the Defendant, nor will it suffice to demonstrate that the product in question met existing and accepted industrial standards for similar products. 'Only if the producer can prove to the court that he took all the steps that a producer of products of that kind might reasonably be expected to take, and that the state of scientific and technical knowledge would have allowed him to take, will this defence be of any value'[5]. Nevertheless, the British producer would appear to have recourse to this defence when under the wording of the Directive he would not necessarily do so. Fortunately for the injured consumer the courts are not bound by the views of government and the courts may well interpret the legislation in a stricter fashion than was hoped by those who produced its wording.

(f) *Components, Raw Materials and the Subsequent Product*[6]

This defence is specifically aimed at the producer of a component or raw material which is then used within the manufacture of a 'subsequent product'. In order to rely upon the defence the two separate and cumulative limbs are to be satisfied. It is to be noted that the defect has to be 'wholly attributable' to the design of the subsequent product or to compliance by the producer of the components or raw material with instructions given by the producer of the subsequent product.

2.4 CAUSATION

Further to the statutory defences set out above, and in any event, any person who brings a claim under the Act will have to satisfy the normal tests as to causation, in other words that personal injury or damage was truly caused by the specific defect. As an example, cases have been brought concerning defective retractable dog-leads on the basis that the metal clip which attached to the collar was of inadequate strength to restrain a large dog (and broke under the strain). However, if the method of operation of the mechanism was not otherwise defective and an individual failed to place the dog on the lead properly with the effect that it subsequently recoiled at speed causing an eye injury to that person, the cause of the accident would not be the defective nature of the clip

5 As per Lord Lucas of Chilworth, the Government spokesman in the House of Lords; Hansard (HL) 20 January, 1987, col 841.

6 Section 4(1)(f).

but failure to properly apply the same to the dog[7]. The issue of causation has produced considerable difficulties in cases concerning drugs and other medical products, and has often required detailed expert evidence as to the state of the Plaintiff's health before he or she had contact with the relevant product and also to what the prognosis would have been had there been no contact.

2.5 CONTRIBUTORY NEGLIGENCE

The ability to claim that the end-user, or such other person who has suffered death, personal injury or damage, has been guilty of contributory negligence is enshrined within section 6(4) of the Act[8]. This will, in appropriate cases, allow the reduction of damages in line with the Plaintiff's own contributory fault[9].

2.6 JOINT AND SEVERAL LIABILITY

Section 2(5) allows joint and several liability in appropriate circumstances. Further, in appropriate cases, the producer may be able to seek a contribution under ordinary principles of the law of contract or negligence. Certainly producers of components or raw materials may seek contractual indemnities from producers of 'subsequent products' within which the components or raw materials are to be incorporated. The prohibition upon exclusions for liability under section 7 of the Act relates only to liability to a person who has suffered damage and not between producers *inter se*.

7 It is often difficult for those defending a civil action under the Act to gainsay factual evidence as to the incident in question. This is usually the case because by the very nature of the claim there will be little or no access to primary evidence concerning the material incident. Nevertheless careful and expert examination of the mechanics of the incident are required. It should, however, not be forgotten that a reasonable degree of misuse is to be foreseen by the producer.

8 See Art 8(2) of the Directive.

9 See s 6.

Chapter 3

RESIDUAL LIABILITY

3.1 CAUSES OF ACTION OUTSIDE THE ACT

Although this text is largely concerned with liability under the Consumer Protection Act 1987 it is necessary to consider how liability may be established in circumstances where the Act does not provide assistance. This usually entails falling back upon the pre-existing remedies in contract or tort (negligence).

3.1.1 Contract

Contractual liability arises primarily through implied terms and has the advantage of being strict, in other words there is no requirement of proof of fault (or negligence)[1]. However, this major advantage is subject to the considerable restriction of establishing privity of contract (confining potential liability under a contract to the contracting parties). In the case of defective goods a contractual claim will normally arise under the contract of sale and hence is likely to be against a retailer[2]. The doctrine of privity shuts out a claim in contract where the injury or damage is suffered by a third party (such as a relative or a person who has received the product as a gift[3]).

3.1.2 Tort

The liability in tort of a manufacturer for personal injury or damage to property caused as a result of a defective product supplied to consumers has been well-established since *Donoghue v Stevenson*. The usual prerequisite of potential liability in negligence is that the goods in question are not only defective but have in fact caused damage or personal injury. A lack of merchantable quality or failure to correspond with description is insufficient (although a claim in contract may lie). The absence of a requirement of privity means that the

1 See *H Parsons (Livestock) Ltd v Uttley Ingham & Co* [1978] 1 All ER 525, CA.

2 The retailer may well then have a right of action in contract or negligence against either the wholesaler or the producer.

3 An argument on the basis of agency may on occasions be run. See in this regard cases concerning 'holidays'; *Jarvis v Swans Tours Ltd* [1973] QB 233 and *Jackson v Horizon Holidays* [1975] 3 All ER 92; *Woodar Investment Development Ltd v Wimpey Construction (UK) Ltd* [1980] 1 All ER 571, HL.

ultimate consumer may have the ability to claim notwithstanding non-involvement with the contract of supply by virtue of the 'neighbour principle'[4]. Further, a wide range of individuals may fall within the 'neighbour' principle when applied to the perspective of the producer. In many cases the use of the product will be open to or involve a number of parties and a duty will be owed to each[5] of them. Also the class of persons who owe a duty may well include suppliers of many forms and those who assemble or install goods or repair or service them[6].

3.1.3 Other statutes

As stated above[7] employees will not ordinarily have the benefit of an action based on the Act when injured by products belonging to their employer, due to the lack of a relevant supply. However, the Employers' Liability (Defective Equipment) Act 1969, the Provision and Use of the Work Equipment Regulations 1992, and the Health and Safety at Work etc Act 1974, provide considerable assistance, and frequently produce a relevant breach of statutory duty.

3.2 ESTABLISHING LIABILITY

The general principles relating to a claim in negligence are well established and relatively easily ascertained[8], and they are therefore not set out within this text. In essence it is necessary to prove a duty to take care, a breach of that duty, and consequential damage. The area of remoteness of damage and also that of contributory negligence have been examined in a large number of cases. However, the situation with regard to economic or financial loss is somewhat problematic and is examined in a little detail below. The position with regard to potential liability in contract is far more complicated and has been the subject of a number of widespread and recent changes. These are set out later within this chapter[9].

4 Lord Atkin in *Donoghue v Stevenson* stated 'You must take reasonable care to avoid acts or omissions which you can reasonably foresee would be likely to injure your neighbour. Who, then, in law is my neighbour? The answer seems to be persons who are so closely and directly affected by my act that I ought reasonably to have them in contemplation as being so affected when I am directing my mind to the acts or omissions which are called in question'; [1932] AC 562 at 580. Further,'a manufacturer of products, which he sells in such a form as to show that he intends them to reach the ultimate consumer in the form in which they left him with no reasonable possibility of intermediate examination, and with the knowledge that the absence of reasonable care in the preparation of the products will result in an injury to the consumer's life or property, owes a duty to the consumer to take reasonable care'. (Ibid at 559).

5 For example, a duty to those who are carried in motor vehicles as well as to those who drive them; see *Malfroot v Noxall Ltd* (1935) 51 TLR 551.

6 See *Watson v Buckley, Osborne, Garrett & Co Ltd* [1940] 1 All ER 174; *Kubach v Hollands* [1937] 3 All ER 907; *Herschtal v Stewart & Ardern Ltd* [1940] 1 KB 155; *Stennett v Hancock & Peters* [1939] 2 All ER 578. For further reference see those cases cited at chapter 10 regarding s 39, the duty of retailers and wholesalers to exercise reasonable care and take due diligence; cf *Gordon v M'Hardy* (1903) 6 F 210, and *Hurley v Dyke* [1979] RTR 265, HL.

7 See chapter 2, para 2.2 above.

8 With the exception of economic/financial loss.

9 See para 3.4 above.

An aggrieved end-user may of course have a cause of action in both contract and tort[10]. Apart from the different requirements for the establishment of liability it is frequently necessary to consider the effect of an overlap upon the issue of damages[11].

3.3 CLAIMS OUTSIDE THE ACT

As the Consumer Protection Act by section 2(6) expressly enshrines residual liability otherwise than by virtue of the Act, it is necessary to consider examples of circumstances where a claim in contract and tort is likely to be the only effective remedy:

(a) **claims against the retailer**[12]; there will be potential liability in contract (express or implied terms) within the contract of sale. Further there will be a duty of care which may be relevant when considering negligent storage or assembly. It may be particularly important where the producer seeks to rely upon a Defence under section 4(1)(d)[13]. Further, it may occur if there has been a failure to pass on a relevant warning or instruction which originally accompanied the product;

(b) **those who repair or alter products**; many individuals may affect the safety of a product, by repair, alteration, servicing or assembly. Under section 1(2)(a) liability extends only to a person who manufactured an item[14]. This definition is unlikely to cover running repairs or the mere installation of an item. The failure to take reasonable care whilst engaged in such activities may well give rise to liability in negligence[15];

(c) **those who analyse or test a product**; there will be no relevant 'supplier' for the purposes of the Act within those involved in the inspection, testing or certification of products. This may include Government bodies and such individuals as Public Analysts[16];

(d) **those who supply primary (unprocessed) agricultural produce**; such individuals are excluded from the provisions of the Act[17];

(e) **those given access to and suffer injury or damage as a result of exposure to a product other than by virtue of relevant supply**; for example employees[18].

(f) **When a specific Defence is raised by the Producer under section 4(1)(e)**; (the state of scientific and technical knowledge at the relevant time was such that the defect would not be discovered[19]), a claim in contract may lie as no such Defence will avoid the strict liability;

10 See *Esso Petroleum Co Ltd v Mardon* [1976] QB 801, CA; *H Parsons (Lifestock) Ltd v Uttley Ingham & Co Ltd* [1978] 1 All ER 525.

11 See *H Parsons (Lifestock) Ltd v Uttley Ingham & Co Ltd*, above.

12 Remembering the provisional liability under s 2(3) of the Act.

13 The defect did not exist in the product at the relevant time (ie the time of supply to the wholesaler, retailer or customer).

14 See s 1.

15 See for example *Malfroot v Noxal Ltd* (1935) 51 TLR 551; *Power v Bedford Motor Co Ltd* [1959] IR 391; *Stennett v Hancock and Peters* [1939] 2 All ER 578.

16 See *Driver v William Willett (Contractors) Ltd* [1969] 1 All ER 665; *Candler v Crane Christmas & Co* [1951] 1 All ER 426 at 433 per Lord Denning.

17 See ss 1(2)(c) and 2(4).

18 See s 4(1)(b). See also the Employers Liability (Defective Equipment) Act 1969.

19 See s 4(1)(e), and chapter 4 (*European Perspective*).

(g) **where the damage is to a product itself** (or to a product in which it was a component at the time of supply)[20] a claim in contract or negligence may lie;

(h) **a claim for any loss of or damage to commercial property**; such property being excluded from the operation of the Act[1];

(i) **where any award for loss of or damage to property would be less than £275**[2];

(j) **importers into a Member State from another Member State** (ie not caught by section 2(1)(c)) and other distributors; there may be a liability under contract law but the most likely liability will be by virtue of a breach of duty of care[3]. Regard should be given to the requirements under Regulation 9 of the General Product Safety Regulations 1994[4]. Due to the practical and procedural difficulties involved in proceeding against a foreign company this type of residual liability in negligence has considerable significance;

(k) **where the claim relates to inadequate quality**; (lack of merchantable quality) also in some circumstances a lack of fitness for purpose or failure to comply with the contractual description;

(l) **claims where there has not in fact been damage but a failure to provide enhancement or an expected benefit**; such as the failure of a fertiliser or other agricultural chemical to enhance a crop[5];

(m) **where the damage is by way of economic or financial loss**; There has been a gradual clarification of the law of negligence in cases concerning claims in respect of pure economic loss. In such cases the courts have shown a marked difference in attitude depending on whether the economic loss was attributable to negligent acts or negligent statements. It is therefore necessary to outline the current position.

The House of Lords' decision in *Hedley Byrne v Heller*[6] established that under certain circumstances there was a duty of care not to cause economic loss through making a negligent statement. However, with respect to negligent acts it was still the case that no duty of care existed as far as pure economic loss was concerned, though *Spartan Steel and Alloys Ltd v Martin*[7] allowed recovery where the economic loss was consequent upon physical damage. However, that principle was not considered to be cast in stone[8] and was subject to considerable erosion until the decision in *Murphy v Brentwood District Council*[9] which saw a complete shift back

20 See s 5(2).
1 See s 5(3).
2 See s 5(4).
3 See *Watson v Buckley* [1940] 1 All ER 174 and *Goodchild v Vaclight* (1965) Times, 22 May.
4 See also chapter 10 and the defence under s 39.
5 As an example, in *Matford Arable Systems Ltd v Hortag Chemicals Ltd* (Exeter County Court) H H Overend, (October 1994, unreported), boron concentrate was applied to swedes, yet failed to enhance growth. The claim was made under breach of contract.
6 [1964] AC 465.
7 [1973] QB 27, CA.
8 In *Dutton v Bognor Regis UDC* [1972] 1 QB 373, Lord Denning MR (at 396) rejected the argument that liability was limited to those who suffered bodily harm and could not extend to those who only suffered economic loss. He said that if the submission were right it would mean that if the Inspector negligently passes the house as properly built and it collapses and injures a person the Council are liable; but if the owner discovers a defect in time to repair it and does repair it, the Council are not liable. That was 'an impossible distinction'.
9 [1990] 2 All ER 908, HL. Prior to *Murphy* was the decision in *Anns v Merton London Borough Council* [1978] AC 728, which held that a Local Authority could be held liable for negligent inspection of a building if this meant that the building concerned in its present state amounted to a threat to health and safety. Any application of the *Anns* doctrine to private defendants (such as builders), enabling recovery of anticipatory repair costs in spite

to the traditional idea that damages are not recoverable in the tort of negligence for pure economic loss.

In *Murphy* the House of Lords considered the question of whether the Council owed a duty to safeguard the Plaintiff against pure economic loss[10]. Lord Bridge observed that if 'a dangerous defect in a chattel is discovered before it causes any personal injury or damage to property, because the danger is now known and the chattel cannot be safely used unless the defect is repaired, the defect becomes merely a defect in quality'[11]. The facts in the case of *Anns* revealed no damage whatsoever and thus amounted to pure economic loss. The law at the time of that decision did not extend a duty of care to such cases[12] and so it was that Lord Keith came to the inevitable conclusion that *Anns* had been wrongly decided on the grounds that it '...introduced a new species of liability governed by a principle indeterminate in character but having the potentiality of covering a wide range of situations, involving chattels as well as real property, in which it has never hitherto been thought that the law of negligence had any proper place'[13].

The law of contract would appear the most likely arena in which to seek redress for pure economic loss, but the cause of action is dependant upon there being privity between the parties. In circumstances similar to those

of an accident not having occurred, was rejected in the case of *D & F Estates v Church Comrs for England* [1989] AC 177, HL. But Lord Wilberforce, like Lord Denning MR and Sachs LJ in *Dutton v Bognor Regis UDC*, was of the view that this type of damage is properly classified as physical (and not purely economic). In *Junior Books Ltd v Veitchi Co Ltd* [1982] 3 All ER 201, HL, economic loss was recoverable in a situation bordering on contract. There was a duty not only to avoid laying a factory floor that would cause damage, but also not to lay a floor that was itself defective, even if the now defective floor did not constitute a danger.

In *D & F Estates v Church Comrs for England* the House of Lords embraced the traditional approach to economic loss, and held that recovery was only possible in situations where the defects caused damage to things other than the defective product itself, (any other type of loss would be purely economic and could not therefore form the basis of a successful claim). Further, a dangerous defect once discovered could no longer constitute a danger (see Lord Bridge at 365).

The approach to those cases where the economic loss has been caused by negligent statements is also restrictive, and especially so after the House of Lords' decision in *Caparo v Dickman* [1990] 1 All ER 568. In *Spring v Guardian Assurance plc* [1994] 3 All ER 129, it was found that the Defendant owed a duty of care to the Plaintiff in respect of the preparation of a reference. Lord Lowry stated that '...a liability based on negligent misstatement can exist only if (1) damage is foreseeable (and damage occurs) and (2) there is such proximity between the maker and the subject of the misstatement as will impose a duty of care on the former for the protection of the latter' (at 152c).

10 In *Murphy* the design of the Plaintiff's house was defective in that the soil conditions at the site were not properly inspected, and therefore the foundations that were subsequently laid were not adequate or fit for the task required of them. Those same designs were negligently approved by consultant engineers, and the Defendant Council subsequently relied on their advice. The Judge at first instance held that defects in the house were brought about by the inadequate foundations, and that their being inadequate constituted a hazard to the health and safety of the Plaintiff. The Judge further considered that there was substantial risk of the main gas pipe breaking, and that the water pipes too might be damaged at some stage hence, and with that the distinct possibility of water leaking into electrical fittings. This potential threat to his health and safety gave the Plaintiff a cause of action under the principle of *Anns*. The Council relied on negligent advice in passing the plans and thus it was liable to the Plaintiff for the resultant loss in value of the house and the associated expenses incurred because of that damage.

11 *Murphy* at 435H.

12 At 919-920.

13 At 922: see also *White v Jones* [1995] 1 All ER 691, HL.

found in *Murphy* then the Plaintiff may have recourse against the builders and not the Local Authority.

(n) **where the claim is caught by the cut-off period or limitation provisions within the Act**[14]. Section 6(6) and Schedule 1 operate to amend the Limitation Act 1980 by way of the introduction of a specific time limit for actions under Part 1 of the Act. There is a cut-off point which is ten years after the 'relevant time'[15]. Section 4(c) defines the relevant time as:

> '(a) in relation to electricity at the time at which it was generated (being a time before it was transmitted or distributed);
> (b) in relation to any other product if the person proceeded against is the producer of the product, or any person who has held himself out to be the producer of the product, or any person who has imported the product into a Member State from a place outside Member States (section 2(2)), then the time when he supplied the product to another;
> (c) if section 2(2) does not apply ie in other cases the time when the product was last supplied by a person to whom sub-section (ii) does apply in relation to the product[16].'

A right of action under the Act is therefore lost after ten years. Hence those potentially subject to liability know that it is not 'potentially open ended' in terms of time. However, it does mean that a plaintiff may lose the right of action before he knows that it even exists. Usually in such cases there would still be the possibility of an action in tort[17], subject to the proviso that claims for personal injury or property damage cannot be brought more than three years after the later of:

(a) the date on which the cause of action accrued; and
(b) the date of knowledge of the injured party or, in the case of loss or damage to property, the date of knowledge of the Plaintiff or (if earlier) of any person in whom his cause of action was previously vested[18].

Hence, if the Plaintiff is aware of damage or loss then time will begin to run, but if he is not aware then the alternative time period (ie ten years from the 'relevant time') provides some protection for those with a potential liability.

3.4 CLAIMS IN CONTRACT

Liability for defective goods can be based in contract law, the law of tort, or indeed a combination of both. English Law has taken a number of years to develop protection within the law of contract for buyers, and the law has recently changed again[19]. It is necessary to outline the development of this area of redress.

One need not look back into the too distant past of English legal history to see a very different picture than that which exists today with regard to product liability and consumer protection. Product liability once stood by the maxim

14 See s 6(6), Sch 1 of the Act.
15 Schedule 1, para 1; Limitation Act 1980, s 11A(c).
16 Therefore in relation to a retailer the relevant time is the time when the product was last supplied by a producer, 'own brander' or importer.
17 Limitation Act 1980, s 14.
18 Schedule 1; Limitation Act 1980, s 11 A(4).
19 See Sale and Supply of Goods Act 1994, below at para 3.6, and Unfair Terms in Consumer Contracts Regulations 1994 (No 3159), which came into force on 1 July 1995, below at para 3.7.

caveat emptor, and so it was that the buyer was expected to be cautious and mindful of potential problems. At this time the vendor was only liable insofar as express undertakings had been made in relation to the goods. However, this common law rule was tempered over the decades by the development of an implied condition that merchandise sold in accordance with a description shall be of a merchantable quality (though where the contract was for particular and specific goods the purchaser would not have had the benefit of this implied term). As will be seen below English law has further moved on to the extent that contracts are deemed to be subject to a variety of implied terms as well as express terms.

The distinct advantage of a claim under contract law over one under the law of tort is that liability based upon the former is strict, although it must be conceded that such advantages as this provides are somewhat curtailed by the requirements of privity (which ensures that the benefits and liabilities of contracts are limited to the contracting parties themselves).

3.4.1 Misrepresentation

Before considering the terms of the contract it is necessary to consider the pre-agreement picture. The purchaser's attention at the time of the formation of the contract is likely to be attracted to statements concerning the quality and the capability of the goods in question. If such a statement is deemed nothing more than a mere 'puff' or a matter of opinion then usually no liability will ensue should those goods fail to match the comments made about them. However, if there has been a misrepresentation of fact capable of having induced the representee into the contract then there may be a remedy under the Misrepresentation Act 1967 which creates a statutory liability for misrepresentation.

3.4.2 Implied terms

From the nineteenth century onwards the law has been such that contracts for the sale of goods have required the seller to ensure that those products he was attempting to supply in fact complied with the contract description, were of merchantable quality, and were fit for the purpose for which they were apparently sold[20]. If the vendor knew that the purchaser wanted the goods for a specific purpose and that the circumstances surrounding the sale gave grounds for believing that he had relied on the judgement of the vendor then the purchaser might benefit from the implied condition that the goods be reasonably fit for that purpose[1]:

> '... where a manufacturer or a dealer contracts to supply an article which he manufactures or produces, or in which he deals, to be applied to a particular purpose, so that the buyer necessarily trusts to the judgement or skill of the manufacturer or dealer, there is in that case an implied term or warranty that it shall be reasonably fit for the purpose for which it is to be applied'[2].

20 See, inter alia, *Chanter v Hopkins* (1838) 4 M&W 399 and *Randall v Newson* (1877) 2 QBD 102.

1 See *Jones v Just* (1868) LR 3 QB 197 at 201-203 per Mellor J.

2 Ibid at 202.

More recently these implied terms were found in the Sale of Goods Act 1979[3], along with the implied term of sales by sample[4]. However, the Sale and Supply of Goods Act 1994 has made important amendments.

3.5 SALE OF GOODS ACT 1979

Sections 13, 14 and 15 of the Sale of Goods Act 1979 make provision with regard to implied terms in contracts for the sale of goods[5]. Unlike section 14, sections 13 and 15 are not limited to the vendor who sells goods in the course of business; they encompass the private seller as well). By section 55 of the Sale of Goods Act 1893 all such terms were in principle capable of being excluded provided that there were appropriate provisions. Under the 1979 Act if such conditions are breached then the purchaser is at liberty to end the contract and demand the return of his purchase money.

3.5.1 Section 13 – Sale by description

'(1) Where there is a contract for the sale of goods by description, there is an implied condition that the goods will correspond with the description.

(2) If the sale is by sample as well as by description it is not sufficient that the bulk of the goods corresponds with the sample if the goods do not also correspond with the description.

(3) A sale of goods is not prevented from being a sale by description by reason only that, being exposed for sale or hire, they are selected by the buyer.'

Sale by description is not a concept which is easy to define, and the Act itself provides no assistance. What is clear is that all contracts for the sale of unascertained goods fall within the scope of sales by description[6]. What is more, most 'future goods' will also be deemed to fall within the category[7]. However, in *Varley v Whipp*[8], it was held that the term could equally apply 'to all cases where the purchaser has not seen the goods, but is relying on the description alone'[9]. In that case the seller sold a 'second-hand self-binder reaping machine', which goods were specific though they were not present before the contracting parties at the time of the contract.

Even where it has been deemed that there has been a sale by description it remains that not all descriptive words will necessarily constitute conditions. In *Ashington Piggeries Ltd v Christopher Hill Ltd*[10] certain animal foodstuff

3 Sections 13 and 14. Equivalent provisions were found in hire purchase agreements (Supply of Goods (Implied Terms) Act 1973, ss 9, 10(2) and 10(3)).

4 Section 15 Sale of Goods Act 1979.

5 Other implied terms might include custom, eg Trade Protocols.

6 *Wallis, Son and Wells v Pratt and Haynes* [1911] AC 394, where the respondents sold seed to the appellants as 'common English sainfoin', which turned out to be 'giant sainfoin' (an inferior variety of seed).

7 *Grant v Australian Knitting Mills Ltd* [1936] AC 85 at 100. This case, along with many others, is actually on s 14(2) of the South Australian Sale of Goods Act 1895 (which is identical with s 14 of the English Sale of Goods Act 1893), in that it imposes a condition as to 'merchantable quality' (see below), and which prior to the Supply of Goods (Implied Terms) Act 1973 was restricted to cases of goods 'bought by description'.

8 [1900] 1 QB 513.

9 Ibid at 516.

10 [1972] AC 441.

containing herring meal was held to comply with its description notwithstanding that it was toxic[11] to mink which it was intended to feed.

> 'The "description" by which unascertained goods are sold is ... confined to those words in the contract which were intended by the parties to identify the kind of goods which were to be supplied ... Ultimately the test is whether the buyer could fairly and reasonably refuse to accept the physical goods proffered to him on the ground that their failure to correspond with that part of what was said about them in the contract makes them goods of a different kind from those he had agreed to buy. The key to section 13 is identification.'[12]

Where there has been a sale by description it is then for the courts to conclude one way or the other whether those goods match the description given of them. Precision in the types of words used to describe the goods may of course vary considerably, and the courts may or may not take those descriptions in their strictest sense. The case of *Re Moore & Co and Landauer & Co's Arbitration*[13] provides an extreme example. There a seller supplied three thousand tins of Australian canned fruit, which were supposed to be packed in cases containing thirty cans apiece. Three thousand cans were duly delivered, but in cases containing either thirty cans or twenty-four. It was held that the buyer was entitled to reject the whole consignment, under section 30(3) of the Sale of Goods Act 1893, on the ground that the goods so delivered failed to correspond with the contract description[14].

3.5.2 Section 14 – Implied terms about quality or fitness[15]

> '(1) Except as provided by this section and section 5 below and subject to any other enactment, there is no implied condition or warranty about the quality or fitness for any particular purpose of goods supplied under a contact of sale.
>
> (2) Where the seller sells goods in the course of a business, there is an implied condition that the goods supplied under the contract are of merchantable quality[16], except that there is no such condition –

11 Unknown to any of the parties the foodstuff was contaminated on account of there having been a chemical reaction caused by a preservative added to it, which rendered it potentially harmful to most animals, and particularly to mink.

12 Ibid, at 503-504, per Lord Diplock.

13 [1921] 2 KB 519, CA.

14 Defects in actual quantity are now dealt with separately (s 30 of the Act), and do not involve the application of s 13.

15 Applies only to the seller who sells goods in the course of a business. Section 61(1) makes it clear that professions and government departments (including local or public authorities) are to fall within the ambit of 'business' so as to include bodies which would not naturally fall within the scope of s 14.

16 'Merchantable quality' is a difficult concept to define; see *Cehave NV v Bremer Handelsgesellschaft mbH* [1975] 3 All ER 739 at 763-764 per Ormrod LJ, who defined it as '...a composite quality comprising elements of description, purpose, condition and price. The relative significance of each of these elements will vary from case to case according to the nature of the goods in question and the characteristics of the market which exists for them.'

See also *Kendall v Lillico* [1969] 2 AC 31, regarding feeding stuff for pheasants which was contaminated. Little consideration was given to the price element in this case because ground nuts contaminated with the poison aflatoxin can still be fed to cattle (provided that the amount does not exceed a certain level), thereby retaining a market value on account of it being animal feed. On the other hand, if the ground nut extraction had been sold as feed for poultry then it would have been 'unmerchantable' on the ground that feed which is poisonous to pheasants cannot be classed as poultry feed.

(a) as regards defects specifically drawn to the buyer's attention before the contract is made; or
(b) if the buyer examines the goods before the contract is made, as regards defects which that examination ought to reveal.

(3) Where the seller sells goods in the course of a business and the buyer, expressly or by implication, makes known –
(a) to the seller, or
(b) where the purchase price or part of it is payable by instalments and the goods were previously sold by a credit-broker to the seller, to that credit-broker.

any particular purpose for which the goods are being brought, there is an implied condition that the goods supplied under the contract are reasonably fit for that purpose, whether or not that is a purpose for which such goods are commonly supplied, except where the circumstances show that the buyer does not rely, or that it is unreasonable for him to rely, on the skill or judgement of the seller or credit-broker.

(4) An implied condition or warranty about quality or fitness for a particular purpose may be annexed to a contract of sale by usage.

(5) The preceding provisions of this section apply to a sale by a person who in the course of a business is acting as agent for another as they apply to a sale by a principal in the course of a business, except where that other is not selling in the course of a business and either the buyer knows that fact or reasonable steps are taken to bring it to the notice of the buyer before the contract is made.

(6) Goods of any kind are of merchantable quality within the meaning of subsection (2) above if they are as fit for the purpose or purposes for which goods of that kind are commonly bought as it is reasonable to expect having regard to any description applied to them, the price (if relevant) and all the other relevant circumstances.

(7) Paragraph 5 of Schedule 1 below applies in relation to a contract made on or after 18 May 1973.'

By section 14(2) of the 1979 Act examination does *not* exclude liability for defects which would not ordinarily be discovered by careful examination. The purchaser is *not* required to examine the goods prior to purchase, but the danger exists when goods are duly examined, and defects which should have been discovered had the examination been thorough enough, are not so discovered.

By section 14(3) of the Sale of Goods Act 1979 the purchaser has to show reliance upon the skill and judgement of the vendor in order to establish liability, (though there is *no* such obligation under section 14(2)). Where the goods are ordinarily produced for a single purpose that purpose will be readily known and readily established. However, it will be more difficult for the courts to infer the specific purpose where the goods themselves are capable of being used for a whole range of activities.

A good example of the application of this subsection is *Bristol Tramways &c, Carriage Co Ltd v Fiat Motors Ltd*[17]. In that case the Plaintiffs had ordered particular buses which would have the capacity to cope with the challenging gradients encountered in the city of Bristol. The buses were found to be unsuitable[18] and the seller was thus held to be liable. Another example is the

17 [1910] 2 KB 831, CA.

18 The seller does not have to promise that the goods will be absolutely suitable, and nor is he expected to guarantee against peculiarities. In *Griffiths v Peter Conway Ltd* [1939] 1 All ER 685 the purchaser of a coat contracted dermatitis on account of her having particularly sensitive skin. The seller was not liable because the product that he was selling would not

case of *Godley v Perry*[19], where a plastic catapult broke and caused serious injury to the eye of the user (a boy of six).

3.5.3 Section 15 – Sale by sample[20]

(1) A contract of sale is a contract for sale by sample where there is an express or implied term to that effect in the contract.

(2) In the case of a contract for sale by sample there is an implied condition –
   (a) that the bulk will correspond with the sample in quality;
   (b) that the buyer will have a reasonable opportunity of comparing the bulk with the sample;
   (c) that the goods will be free from any defect, rendering them unmerchantable, which would not be apparent on reasonable examination of the sample.

(3) In subsection (2) above 'unmerchantable' is to be construed in accordance with section 14 (6) above.

(4) Paragraph 7 of Schedule 1 below applies in relation to a contract made before 18 May 1973.

By section 15(2)(b) the seller had a duty, unless otherwise agreed between the parties, to allow the buyer reasonable opportunity to examine the goods so as to determine in his own mind whether or not the goods conformed with the contract. Thus it was held in *Lorymer v Smith*[1] that a purchaser was entitled to repudiate a contract and not take delivery of goods when he had been denied an opportunity to examine those goods prior to delivery.

3.6 SALE AND SUPPLY OF GOODS ACT 1994

The Sale and Supply of Goods Act 1994 ('the Act') received the Royal Assent on 3 November 1994 and came into force on 3 January 1995. In 1983 the Law Commission(s) had produced a consultative document followed by a report in 1987[2] which considered the law relating to sales and how that law could best be reformed. The Act implements some of the recommendations.

Section 1, which is the main modernising provision of the Act, amends section 14 of the Sale of Goods Act 1979. Where the implied term once stated quality and fitness for purpose there is now an implied term 'that the goods supplied under the contract are of satisfactory quality'. 'Merchantable quality', as found in the Sale of Goods Act 1979, the Supply of Goods (Implied Terms) Act 1973 and the Supply of Goods and Services Act 1982, has fallen from grace and its replacement is the rather uninspiring 'satisfactory quality'. This differs from the recommendation laid down by the English and Scottish Law Commissions which had recommended the phrase 'acceptable quality'. At first glance one is tempted to think that one awkward and difficult to define phrase has been replaced by another, but the Act goes on to qualify section 1(2):

have caused harm to the vast majority of people. See also *Ashford Shire Council v Dependable Motors Pty Ltd* [1961] AC 336, PC.

19 [1960] 1 WLR 9.

20 This section provides no adequate definition of 'sample'.

1 (1822) 1 B&C 1.

2 Report on the Sale and Supply of Goods (Cm 137, May 1987).

'(1) In section 14 of the Sale of Goods Act 1979 (implied terms about quality or fitness) for subsection (2) there is substituted–

....

(2B) For the purpose of this Act, the quality of goods includes their state and condition and the following (among others) are in appropriate cases aspects of the quality of goods-
- (a) fitness for all the purposes for which goods of the kind in question are commonly supplied[3],
- (b) appearance and finish,
- (c) freedom from minor defects,
- (d) safety, and
- (e) durability.'

Thus a number of questions found wanting under the 1979 Act are to some extent addressed. And so it is that goods which previously might have been considered fit for their purpose despite the evidence of some scratches and dents would clearly fall within the ambit of section 1(2B) of the 1994 Act. The same can be said of the concept of durability which will now be tested in accordance with 'the purposes for which goods of the kind in question are commonly supplied'. (In some instances this is already set out, as for example with the Protocol on Shoes). Previously the idea of durability, though an important consideration, was only found in case law[4].

Section 14(2C)(c) retains the effect of pre-purchase examinations already found in section 14(2) of the Sale of Goods Act 1979.

So the term 'unmerchantable' as is found in the Sale of Goods Act 1979 is now changed to 'unsatisfactory quality'. The old concept of merchantability seemed to focus entirely upon the fitness of the goods to perform the function for which they were acquired, and ignore the cosmetic value or cosmetic quality. This has now been remedied by the new section 14(2B)(b) and (c), which gave statutory effect to the approach already being witnessed in the courts[5].

Section 14(6) has been amended. The new standard is that of what a reasonable person would regard as satisfactory, as opposed to the standard 'as is reasonable to expect'.

The new section 15A is inserted into the 1979 Act by way of section 4(1) of the 1994 Act. It is now the position that where there is a breach by the vendor of an implied term as set out in sections 13, 14 or 15 of the 1979 Act, and where that 'breach is so slight that it would be unreasonable for him to reject them, then, if the buyer does not deal as a consumer, the breach is not to be treated as a breach of condition but may be treated as a breach of warranty'[6]. In such a scenario the buyer is prevented from rejecting the goods outright, instead his course of action is limited to a claim for damages.

Section 35 of the Sale of Goods Act 1979 has also been amended. This section deals with the concept of acceptance. Section 11(4) of the 1979 Act states that 'where a contract of sale is not severable and the buyer has accepted the

3 Compare with: '...the goods did not have to be suitable for every purpose within a range of purposes for which goods were normally bought under that description. It was sufficient that they were suitable for one or more such purposes ...since ...they were commercially saleable under that description'. (*Kendall v Lillico* [1969] 2 AC 31) above.

4 Eg *Lexmead (Basingstoke) Ltd v Lewis* [1982] AC 225, where Lord Reid argued that it was 'a continuing warranty that the goods will continue to be fit for that purpose for a reasonable time after delivery'.

5 Eg *Rogers v Parish* [1987] 2 All ER 232, and *Business Application Specialists v Nationwide Credit Corpn* [1988] RTR 332.

6 Section 15A(1)(b).

goods or part of them, the breach of a condition to be fulfilled by the seller [cannot] be treated ... as a ground for rejecting the goods and treating the contract as repudiated'. Section 35 defined acceptance as being one of three things: (i) when the buyer expressly intimates to that effect, (ii) when the buyer does an act to the goods which is inconsistent with the ownership of the seller, and (iii) after the lapse of reasonable time. Under the Sale and Supply of Goods Act 1994 the buyer is not deemed to have accepted the goods if 'he has not previously examined them, he is not deemed to have accepted them ... until he has had a reasonable opportunity of examining them for the purpose'. Further, where the buyer is a consumer the right of examination cannot be lost by agreement, waiver or otherwise. The method of acceptance of goods through their retention after the lapse of reasonable time is now associated with, but not dependent upon, the right to examine the goods. With regard to this potential method of acceptance notice must be taken of the reasonable time the buyer might require to examine the goods. In *Bernstein v Pamson Motors*[7] it was held that three weeks (and 140 miles) constituted too long a period ie greater than a reasonable time in the case of a buyer who had bought a car, and who then sought to reject it soon after the Christmas period.

The right of partial rejection, which existed by virtue of section 30(4) of the 1979 Act, has effectively been extended by way of new section 35A under the 1994 Act. The position is now as follows:

> **'3 Right of partial rejection**
> (1) After section 35 of the Sale of Goods Act 1979 there is inserted the following section –
> '35A Right of partial rejection
> (1) If the buyer –
> (a) has the right to reject the goods by reason of a breach on the part of the seller that affects some or all of them, but
> (b) accepts some of the goods, including, where there are any goods unaffected by the breach, all such goods,
> he does not by accepting them lose his right to reject the rest.'

In order to avoid situations where buyers could effectively 'break up' goods that constituted a single item (such as a pair of shoes) the 1994 Act introduces the new concept:

> '(7) Where the contact is for the sale of goods making one or more commercial units, a buyer accepting any goods included in a unit is deemed to have accepted all the goods making the unit; and in this subsection 'commercial unit' means a unit division of which would materially impair the value of the goods or the character of the unit'.

Acceptance of any goods within the unit then is acceptance of all.

3.7 UNFAIR TERMS IN CONSUMER CONTRACTS REGULATIONS 1994

The law concerning unfair contract terms had until recently been largely contained within the Unfair Contract Terms Act 1977. However, once again a Directive has produced a significant change. The Unfair Contract Terms

7 *Bernstein v Pamson Motors (Golders Green) Ltd* [1987] 2 All ER 220; see also *Rogers v Parish (Scarborough) Ltd.* [1987] 2 All ER 232.

Directive (93/13/EEC)[8] was required to be implemented by 1 January 1995. The United Kingdom's implementing Regulations state that they only take effect as of 1 July 1995. Due to the concept of vertical direct effect[9] the delayed implementation date is not likely to afford any protection to businesses deemed to be subject to State control (such as the Health Service) or with special powers (such as British Gas). There is no horizontal effect in the case of private businesses, which would therefore appear to be protected by this period of delay in implementation.

The Regulations are to give effect, so far as is possible, to European Union obligations[10]. If any consumers are considered to have suffered by virtue of the Government's delay in implementing the Directive, then the Government will be in danger of being held liable under the principles expressed in *Francovich*[11].

The 1994 Regulations only apply with certain exceptions to terms struck between a consumer, (being 'a natural person who...is acting for purposes which are outside his business'), and a seller or supplier, (being one who sells or supplies goods respectively, and who is 'acting for purposes relating to his business'). 'Business' is defined as including 'a trade or profession and the activities of any government department or local or public authority'. This would seem to indicate that the contractual provision of public services may well fall within the ambit of the Regulations and include such utilities as energy, water and transport.

Regulation 3(5) expressly excludes terms which have been individually negotiated. Terms which have been drafted in advance and thus beyond the influence of the consumer are obviously not terms which have been individually negotiated. The onus is upon the seller or supplier to prove that a term was indeed individually negotiated.

By Regulation 4(1) an unfair term is defined as one 'which contrary to the requirement of good faith causes a significant imbalance in the parties' rights and obligations under the contract to the detriment of the consumer'. Regulation 4(2) states that an assessment of the potential unfair nature of a term shall take into account the nature of the goods or services for which the contract was concluded, and to all the attendant circumstances of the contract's conclusion, 'and to all other terms of the contract or of another contract on which it is dependent'. In determining whether or not a term satisfies the requirement of good faith, regard shall be had in particular to matters specified in schedule 2[12] of the Regulations (Regulation 4(3)). Schedule 3 to the Regulations is an illustrative though non-exhaustive list of the terms which may be regarded as being unfair.

A term deemed to be unfair will not be binding upon the consumer. However, by Regulation 5(1) and (2), the parties will still be bound should the contract be capable of existing in the absence of the unfair term. Equally, by Regulation 3, in a contract where some of the terms have been individually negotiated the Regulations are still capable of applying to the rest of the contract where an overall assessment of the contract indicates that it is a pre-formulated standard contract.

8 OJ 1993 L. 95/29.

9 See chapter 4, *European Perspective*.

10 Case C-106/89: *Marleasing* [1990] ECR I-4135.

11 Case C-6/90: *Francovich v Italy* [1992] IRLR 84.

12 Particular attention should be made to the relative strength of bargaining positions of the parties concerned, as well as to whether the consumer had an inducement to agree to the terms; whether the goods or services were sold or supplied to the special order of the consumer, and the extent to which the seller or supplier has dealt fairly and equitably with the consumer.

The Regulations require all contract terms to be in 'plain intelligible language' and if there is any doubt as to the meaning of a given term then that term will be construed in favour of the consumer. In conjunction with the provision as to individually negotiated terms it is incumbent upon the seller or supplier to clearly indicate the basis upon which the bargain is struck, and that if there are individually negotiated terms that those terms are readily understood by the consumer.

Regulation 8 of the 1994 Regulations is designed to implement Article 7 of the Directive, which makes provision for adequate and effective means to exist to prevent the continued use of unfair terms in consumer contracts. The Regulations provide for an action for breach of statutory duty. It is for the Director General of Fair Trading to 'consider any complaint made to him ... unless the complaint appears to the Director to be frivolous or vexatious'. The Director has the power to grant injunctive relief against any person using or recommending the use of unfair terms. The Regulations do not fully implement the Directive in as much as they fail to provide for action being taken by consumer groups.

3.7.1 Problems with interaction of Unfair Contract Terms Act 1977

Unfair Contract Terms Act only covers exclusion clauses, and therefore its ambit is narrow. It is now the preserve of the new regulations to cover unfair terms which do not fall into the 'exclusions' category. The cunundrum that has come about is that unfair terms which amount to exclusions will now be affected by the Regulations *and* by the Act itself.

In some ways the Act has stronger provisions than those of the Directive[13], but there is scope for the Act to be amended such that it would conform with the Directive as regards consumer contracts, and thus leave the Regulations to cover all other exclusion clauses as well as those unfair terms which do not amount to exclusion clauses.

3.8 CONCLUSION

It is therefore necessary when considering a potential claim for breach of contract to consider the effect of the new statutory regulation on the nature, extent and enforceability of implied and express terms. As the legislation is progressively the subject of judicial interpretation certain aspects will become clearer and it may be advisable to consult future specialist texts.

13 For example, it disallows reliance on certain types of clause altogether.

Chapter 4

THE EUROPEAN PERSPECTIVE

Since the foundation of the Economic Community the influence of European law on national legal systems has expanded in two ways. Firstly there has been a growth in the volume and scope of substantive law emanating from the legislative institutions of the European Union[1]. Secondly there now appears to be a readiness by the courts of Member States to enforce and give practical effect to those laws.

The doctrine of 'direct effect' has been essential to the enforceability of Community law in national courts. According to this doctrine, which has been evolved by the ECJ, provisions of Community law may confer rights upon individuals provided that they satisfy certain criteria of form and substance. These rights are in turn to be directly applied by national courts at the suit of individual litigants, without the need for domestic legislation[2]. To this extent direct effect strengthens the relationship between the individual and the Community.

The doctrine of direct effect is one of the main pillars of EU law alongside the supremacy of EU law over national law, and Article 177 of the EC Treaty. The role of Article 177 is to secure authoritative interpretation of Community law by the ECJ, and that the interpretation is uniform throughout the Community. Article 177 provides both a procedural and substantive framework by which cases can be referred to the ECJ for a ruling on the interpretation or validity of a provision of EU law. The ECJ's role under the Article relates to Community law only. Whether it is necessary to obtain a decision on a particular question of EU law is very much a matter for the national court concerned. With regard to the doctrine of direct effect the ECJ has laid down three criteria all of which must be satisfied for a provision of EU law to have direct effect.[3] First, such a provision must be sufficiently clear and precise. Second, it must be unconditional (in other words the right itself must be independent of the discretion of any body such as an institution of the Community, or even a Member State itself), and thirdly, it must not require any further legislative intervention either by the Community or else by national authorities. The criteria for direct effect were developed on the basis that the national court had to be in a position to identify the right of the particular EC law in question without jeopardising the uniformity of it.

1 So named after the Treaty of European Union 1992.

2 Article 189 of the EEC Treaty, and s 2(1) European Communities Act 1972 which enacts this requirement into UK law.

3 This was first laid down in Case 26/62: *Van Gend en Loos* [1963] ECR 1, with regard to Art 12 of the Treaty of Rome. The test has been refined by subsequent case law.

The supremacy of EU law over national law was established early on in the life of the EEC by the ECJ in *Costa*, (Case 6/64) [1964] ECR 585. The effect is to subordinate national law to directly applicable EC law and to require national tribunals to give weight to non-applicable EC law when considering the interpretation of construction of national legislation. Needless to say the principle of supremacy only has effect in areas covered by EC law. In essence, national courts cannot apply national law in those areas covered by EU law when there are directly applicable provisions of EU law extant.

Turning to the sources of EU law, the Treaties themselves are of primary importance. However, in terms of direct use, the most important type of Community legislation is secondary legislation, of which three types are intended to have legal force; **Regulations**, **Decisions**, and **Directives**.

Article 189 provides that **Regulations** shall have 'general application' and '...shall be binding in their entirety and directly applicable in all Member States'. Hence, they require no further measures of incorporation or implementation on the part of those Member States. Indeed, national legislatures are prevented from legislating in their stead. Therefore the provisions of a Regulation would seem to produce direct effect. However this is not automatic and problems arise in situations where for example a provision in a given Regulation is insufficiently precise or, indeed, *does* need further implementation[4]. But, in Steiner's words, ' since a Regulation is of "general application", where the criteria for direct effect are satisfied, it may be invoked vertically or horizontally'[5]. This means that directly effective provisions of a Regulation may be enforced by a private party against another private party (horizontal), or against the State or State authority (vertical direct effect).

A **Decision** is 'binding in its entirety upon those to whom it is addressed' (Article 189). Decisions differ from Regulations in that they are not of general application. Although a Decision may be addressed to one or more Member States, most frequently they are addressed to individuals (as in competition law of the EU). A Decision may be directly effective, as was established in the case of *Grad*[6], provided the criteria for direct effect are satisfied. The direct application of Decisions does not present the same theoretical problems as with Directives, since they will only be invoked against the addressee of the Decision.

It is the status of **Directives** that raises the greatest problems, and which is at the heart of this chapter. The ECJ first held a Directive on its own to be directly effective in *Van Duyn*[7]. Here a Dutch woman was refused leave to enter the UK. Her action against the Home Office was based on Community law (Article 48 of the Treaty of Rome 1957, and Article 3(1) of Directive 64/221) guaranteeing free movement of workers throughout the Community. The UK sought to exclude Van Duyn on the basis of public policy, claiming her potential employment (with the Church of Scientology) to be socially undesirable. The ECJ had to decide as a matter of principle whether or not a Directive could have direct effect. The UK Government, basing its argument upon Article 189 of the EC Treaty believed that it could not. The ECJ held that it could. It was found that Article 3(1) of Council Directive No 64/221 confers upon individuals rights which can be enforced by them in the courts of a Member State, and which the national courts must protect. The Government of the United Kingdom

4 Eg Case 128/78: *EC Commission v UK, Re Tachographs* [1979] ECR 419.
5 J Steiner *Textbook on EEC Law* (4th edn) p 30.
6 Case 9/70: *Grad* [1970] ECR 825.
7 Case 41/74: *Van Duyn v Home Office* [1974] ECR 1337.

had failed to implement Article 3(1) which would have allowed Miss van Duyn to rely on the resulting UK law. The UK government was denying Miss van Duyn her right by its failure to implement the Directive. That failure was a breach of EC law. Legally the ECJ presumed that the government was benefitting from such failure, and that such a failure could not be condoned. The sanction was to allow the applicant party to sue on the provisions of the Directive in the national courts.

Member States are notoriously poor at implementing Directives within the given time parameters, and it would seem that it was for this reason in particular that the ECJ chose to act. As national courts now have the necessary authority to ensure compliance, this avoids Directives having to be enforced through the European Court itself (with a huge demand in terms of cost, time and manpower, which would obviously lead to commensurate delays, and more significantly to the ineffectiveness of EU law at national level).

Article 189(3) of the Treaty provides that a 'directive shall be binding, as to the result to be achieved, upon each Member State to which it is addressed, but shall leave to the national authorities the choices of form and methods'. The ECJ, faced with the possibility of individuals being denied their Community law rights on account of the failure of Member States to transpose directives into national law, allows individuals in certain circumstances to rely directly on the directive in question, but such rights are only enforceable as against the state. This is v*ertical* direct effect.

When Directives are enacted by the Community they are not intended to be law in that form at national level. Nor are they designed directly to affect the individual. However, in V*an Duyn* the ECJ held that a Directive might be relied on by an individual before a national court, and thereby making that measure more effective (*effet utile*). One of the strongest arguments advanced in favour of a Directive having direct effect was advanced in *Ratti*[8], in which the ECJ explained the circumstances in which a Directive can produce direct effects at national level. It was found that under Directive 73/173–

> '[24] ...after the expiration of the period fixed for the implementation of a directive a Member State may not apply its internal law ...to a person who has complied with the requirements of the directive.'

But,

> '[46] ...since a directive by its nature imposes obligations only on Member States, it is not possible for an individual to plead the principle of 'legitimate expectation' before the expiry of the period prescribed for its implementation.'

Thus in *Ratti* the Court held that a Directive may have direct effect, if at all, only after the expiration of the deadline for the transposition into national law.

These cases (V*an Duyn* and *Ratti*) involved claims by individuals against governments (which are taken to include emanations of the State concerned). The question of whether a Directive could be invoked by one individual against another was settled in the *Marshall* case[9], where the ECJ held that a directive could not be so invoked (in other words there is no horizontal direct effect). It

8 Case 148/78: *Pubblico Ministero v Ratti* [1979] ECR 1629. This case established the principle that a state in default cannot take advantage of its own failure to comply with Community law.

9 Case 152/84: *Marshall v Southampton and South West Hampshire AHA (Teaching)* [1986] ECR 723.

considered that according to Article 189 a Directive is binding only on Member States. Consequently, 'a directive may not of itself impose obligations on an individual'[10]. The facts were that Ms Marshall was effectively forced into early retirement at the age of 62, as she was older than the normal expected retirement age for women. She was able to rely on EEC Directive 76/207, requiring equal treatment between the sexes, because she was employed by the State, as the Health Authority for which she was working was considered to be an emanation of the State. However, had she been employed by a private firm she would have been unable to rely on the direct effect of the Directive (see *Duke v GEC Reliance* [1988] AC 618. Similarly, in *Foster v British Gas plc*[11] the ECJ held that British Gas plc had been made responsible by the State for providing a public service, and therefore Mrs Foster was able to rely on the direct effect of Community legislation. The anomaly in respect of individual rights created by the public/private distinction left a serious gap in the direct enforcement of Directives. The UK finally remedied its failure to implement the rules in question in *Marshall* (and *Duke*) in the Sex Discrimination Act 1986, and thus the issue of direct effect of Directives will not recur in this context. However, the general problem is bound to persist whilst other Directives remain unimplemented or inaccurately implemented after their deadlines. This question will be addressed specifically with regard to Directives concerning consumer protection[12] below.

The Court attempted to bridge the public/private distinction in the case of *von Colson*[13] by a principle of indirect effect, whereby national courts, as agents of the State, are obliged under Article 5 to 'take all appropriate measures, whether general or particular, to ensure fulfilment of the obligations arising out of this Treaty or resulting from actions taken by institutions of the Community'. The Court laid down certain rules of construction which were to be used by national courts for interpreting national legislation designed to implement Community Directives. A national court is now required to interpret its national law in light of the wording and purpose of the Directive, even if the Directive did not have direct effect. The case of *von Colson* involved a defendant who was held by a German court to have breached the Equal Treatment Directive (Directive 76/207) by refusing to offer employment on the ground of the sex of the applicant. The ECJ, in effect, held that Article 5 of the EEC Treaty imposed an obligation on the part of national courts to ensure the effectiveness of EEC law, and in particular by interpreting national law in light of the wording and purpose of the Directives concerned.

The *von Colson* rule of interpretation highlights the central role which the ECJ has allocated to national courts in the enforcement of Community law and the fulfilment of State obligations. However, the UK courts have been reluctant to apply the presumption that Parliament intended to comply with EC law with regard to domestic measures which were not specifically designed to implement EC law, and have limited the *von Colson* principle accordingly. This restriction on the part of the UK courts is rooted in the doctrine of

10 Ibid at 749.

11 Case C-188/89: [1990] ECR I-3313.

12 Directive of the Council of the European Communities, dated 25 July 1985 (85/374/EEC), which was implemented into UK legislation by the Consumer Protection Act 1987, the Council Directive on General Product Safety 92/59/EEC implemented by the General Product Safety Regulations 1994, and EEC Council Directive 93/13 on unfair terms in consumer contracts, implemented into UK legislation through the Unfair Terms in Consumer Contracts Regulations 1994 (SI 1994/3159).

13 Case 14/83: *Von Colson v Land Nordrhein-Westfalen* [1984] ECR 1891.

parliamentary sovereignty, and there are basically two reasons for such a restriction. First, an extension beyond this point might be deemed to breach the traditionally important constitutional separation of function between the courts and the legislature. Second, it would raise questions regarding the extent of any transfer of national sovereignty within the European Union.

In November 1990 the ECJ gave its ruling in *Marleasing*[14], which expanded and clarified the scope of its guidelines for interpretation of national legislation in light of Community Directives. The case arose out of a conflict between the Spanish Civil Code and an EEC Company Directive (68/151) which was unimplemented in Spain. The litigation was between private parties, which, following *Marshall*, ruled out the direct effect of the Directive. The importance of the decision in *Marleasing* was to extend the application of 'indirect effect' to all national legislation, regardless of when enacted (before and after the Directive in question) and whether enacted to implement the Directive or not. The ECJ went on to refine the *von Colson* principle by ruling that national courts are obliged to interpret national legislation to conform to the provisions of the Directive only when possible. That was held by the UK Court of Appeal in *Webb v EMO*[15] to open the door to a strict rule of construction. The doctrine of 'indirect effect' has therefore been the subject of severe restriction.

If a Member State fails to transpose a Directive into national law (thereby depriving individuals of otherwise enforceable Community rights), and no national legislation exists to be construed in accordance with *Marleasing*, the dilemma cannot be resolved by judicial interpretation. An opportunity to formulate a solution to this problem presented itself with the case of *Francovich*[16]. This case arose as a result of the Italian Government's failure to implement Directive 80/987, which concerned the protection of employees in the event of their employers' insolvency. The Directive was to have been implemented by 23 October 1983, but by 1991 when the case went to trial it still languished outside Italian national law. There were no provisions of Italian law which could be construed to conform to the Directive under *Marleasing*. Mr Francovich sued his former company and sued the State. He failed against his employer, a 'private party'. However, the State (Italy) was found liable for not implementing or taking steps to implement the Directive. A remedy had to be provided by the national courts on the basis of the principle of State liability for damage to individuals caused by a breach of Community law for which it is responsible (the ECJ held this to be 'inherent in the scheme of the Treaty'). Steiner has commented[17] that '...given the dual purpose of *Francovich*, that of protecting individuals Community rights and ensuring the full effect of Community law, there seems no reason in principle why *Francovich* should not apply to a failure by a Member State to fulfil *any* binding obligation of Community law'.

The Court's finding in *Francovich* that relevant provisions of the Directive were not directly effective was based on a technicality, that the 'guaranteeing institutions'[18] were not established by the Directive, but by the Member States.

14 Case C-106/89: *Marleasing SA v La Comercial Internacional de Alimentacion SA* [1990] ECR 1-4135.

15 Case C-32/93: *Webb v EMO Air Cargo (UK) Ltd* [1994] QB 718.

16 Case C-6/90: *Francovich v Italy* [1992] IRLR 84.

17 *From direct effects to Francovich : shifting the means of enforcement of Community law* [1993] 18 ELR 3.

18 These had to be financed by employers, but independent of them, and were established so as to provide the payment of wages arrears to employees in the event of the employing company becoming insolvent.

It established a principle of State liability that is not encumbered by the problems of direct effect. However, although the case was laid down in the context of a Community provision which was not directly effective, the Advocate General Mischo suggested that the principle of State liability applied 'whether (the EC provisions in question) have direct effect or not'[19].

The success of the new legal order of the Community has depended from the outset on full compliance by all Member States with Community law. Both the Treaty of Rome and secondary legislation have imposed extensive obligations on Member States to act, or refrain from acting, in a manner so as to achieve defined Community goals, but methods of enforcement have been limited.

The development of the principles of direct effect and that of the supremacy of Community law, together with its role under Article 177 EC Treaty, represent the ECJ's major contributions to maximising the effective enforcement of Community law by judicial means. The need to ensure 'effet utile' of Community law has been appreciated and largely accepted by the courts of the various Member States, despite the presence of some delicate and difficult constitutional issues. One major case of constitutional significance was *Factortame*[20], in which the ECJ ruled that national rules excluding a remedy which was otherwise available in the national legal order infringed EC law and were invalid. In that case an interlocutory injunction was ruled available against the Crown, a remedy hitherto unheard of. From then on any national court has been able to issue an injunction effectively against the provisions of an Act of Parliament which infringes European law. This, it has to be said, was a revolutionary step.

Despite these developments however, as long as there remains a discrepancy between national and Community law individuals will remain in a state of uncertainty. Direct effect is a positive concept as far as individuals are concerned, because EC obligations are intended to promote justice and parity throughout the European Union. The main drawback of the doctrine in the case of Directives, the most permanent form of European legislation, remains the fact that it is limited and inadequate as a means of enforcement, which is deleterious when considering the advantages of harmonising Community law in the social and economic spheres.

4.1 RELEVANT DIRECTIVES

As has been stated above, Part 1 of the Consumer Protection Act 1987 seeks to implement the EC Directive on Product Liability; 85/374/EEC. Further the General Product Safety Regulations 1994 seek to implement the council's Directive upon General Product Safety; 92/59/EEC. However in each case there are both obvious examples of significant departures from the content of the Directives and also areas causing some difficulty in interpretation due to a failure to adopt the wording within the Directive. However as yet the Courts (both domestic and ECJ) have not had cause to grapple with the discrepancies between the Directives and the 1987 Act or the 1994 Regulations. Nevertheless it is very important to note the areas of the domestic legislation which may come under attack, and also the areas which when interpreted will require reference to the Directive.

19 At para 85.
20 *Factortame v Secretary of State for Transport* [1989] 2 All ER 692, HL.

4.1.1 Product Liability Directive

Whilst Part 1 of the 1987 Act seeks to implement the Product Liability Directive it does so without strict adherence to the form or words contained within the Directive. Indeed even within the Act it is necessary to cross-reference within sections to gain the full effect. Where an area of doubt as to true construction and interpretation remains, regard may be had to the wording of the Directive under the refined *von Colson* principle of 'indirect effect'. An example of this can be seen in relation to the exclusion of primary agricultural products, which are defined within Article 2 of the Directive as products that have not undergone 'initial processing'. The Act seeks to exclude such products by the combination of section 1(2)(c) and section 2(4) in which products are to be caught only after they have undergone an 'industrial process' or where essential characteristics are attributable to an industrial or other process having been carried out. When considering the difficulties raised by the definitions within the Act[1] regard may be had to the reference within the preamble of the Directive to 'processing of an industrial nature which could lead to a defect'.

Further examples of divergence between the definitions in the Directive and in the Act can be seen in section 5 in relation to actionable damage.[2] However, the most startling departure in the terms of the Directive is contained within section 4(1)(e) of the Act, the much-discussed 'development risks defence'. Whereas Article 7 of the Directive states that it should be a defence if 'the state of scientific and technical knowledge at the time when he put the product into circulation was not such as to enable the existence of the defect to be discovered' section 4(1)(e) states that there is a defence if it can be shown 'that the state of scientific and technical knowledge at the relevant time was not such that a producer of products of the same description as the products in question might be expected to have discovered the defect if it then existed in his products while they were under his control'. The intention of the Act is to allow a number of factors to be brought into consideration when considering the ability to detect the defect at the relevant time. Further, although in the strict wording of the section the word 'reasonably' does not appear, it can easily be argued that it should be incorporated within the clearly objective test under the section. In any event the section considerably waters down the stricter test contained within Article 7 which clearly excludes consideration of such factors as the cost of testing and investigation and the impact on the financial viability of the project. Under the refined *von Colson* principle it is difficult to see how the clear wording within section 4(1)(e) could be interpreted so as to lie with the definition within Article 7. Therefore in the absence of the ability to rely directly upon the Directive ie 'vertical direct effect' it may be that the only step open to an individual whose claim potentially fails by virtue of the expanded interpretation of this defence is a *Francovich* type claim.

4.1.2 Directive on General Product Safety

The General Product Safety Regulations 1994 contain two very significant departures from the content of the Directive. The effect in each case is to produce an exemption from liability which would not otherwise have existed. They are:

1 See s 1.
2 See s 5(1) and (2).

(i) The exclusion of a product which is exclusively used in the context of a commercial activity as set out in Regulation 2. This exemption is not set out within Article 2 of the Directive;

(ii) The defence of due diligence provided by Regulation 14.

Naturally the latter is of very considerable significance as it is likely to be relied upon in many cases.

As both exemptions are clear and unequivocal there is no opportunity to rely upon the *von Colson* principle. Further the doctrine of direct effect is likely to be of no assistance. It is interesting to note the party which is most often adversely affected by these exemptions is in fact an emanation of the State, the local authority. There is no example within European law of one form or type of emanation of the state bringing domestic or European proceedings against the 'government' or another emanation of the state arising out of the failure to properly implement a Directive. It would certainly require an extension or liberal interpretation of the phrase 'an individual' for a *Francovich* type claim to lie in favour of a local authority arguing that the prosecution had failed solely by virtue of the due diligence defence which should not be present within the Regulations. It does however remain open to the Commission to bring its own action in relation to the default of United Kingdom Government and also since the treaty of Maastricht the Court has an ability to fine if a true default is found.

4.1.3 Unfair Terms in Consumer Contracts Directive[3]

The Council of Ministers' express intention in enacting Directive 93/13/EEC, was to protect the citizen qua consumer when purchasing goods and services. The Directive openly states that 'it is the responsibility of the Member States to ensure that contracts concluded with consumers do not contain unfair terms'. 'Unfair term' is taken to mean 'any term which contrary to the requirement of good faith, causes a significant imbalance in the parties' rights and obligations arising under the contract, to the detriment of the consumer'.

Article 10 of the Directive required Member States to adopt the provisions into national law, through regulations and administrative provisions by 31 December 1994, and that those provisions be applicable to all contracts concluded after that date. The UK implementing Regulations[4] came into force on 1 July 1995, and adopt the wording of the Directive *almost* verbatim.

The Directive itself is founded on Article 100a of the EC Treaty enabling the Council to adopt measures aimed at 'the establishment and functioning of the internal market'. Thus, by the approximation of the national laws of Member States the Directive intends to eliminate the many disparities in those various national laws relating to consumer protection, thereby eradicating difficulties thrown up by lack of awareness and misunderstanding within transactions by consumers for the purchase of commodities or services in another Member State. The intention, therefore, is to provide a 'more effective protection of the consumer' by 'adopting uniform rules of law'.

There are some areas of divergence between Directive and domestic Regulations. One purpose of the Directive is to prevent and prohibit the use of unfair terms in consumer contracts (which includes oral contracts), which have

3 Directive 93/13/EEC of 5 April 1993 (OJ 1993 L 95/29).
4 Unfair Terms in Consumer Contracts Regulations 1994, S I 1994/3159.

not been individually negotiated. If one particular term or an aspect of a term has been individually negotiated Article 3 is still capable of applying to the rest of the contract should an 'overall assessment of the contract indicate that it is nevertheless a pre-formulated standard contract'. Regulation 3(4) of the 1994 Regulations is similar except that it omits the word 'nevertheless'.

Further, Article 7(2) of the Directive is not accomodated by the Regulations. It requires Member States to make provision for 'persons or organisations' to take action with regard to unfair terms, but the UK government did not implement it on the grounds that this type of provision is not available under national law. Such representative bodies do not, in the eyes of UK law, have 'a legitimate interest under national law in protecting consumers'.

Chapter 5

CRIMINAL LIABILITY

The Consumer Protection Act 1987 has radically altered the law with regard to civil liability for defective products. At the same time the Act has consolidated and enhanced the criminal law in respect of product safety. Whilst the latter will be considered in greater detail in Part II (under criminal liability), it is important at this stage to note the interaction between the two Sections of the Act.

Section 41(1) of the Act states:

> 'An obligation imposed by safety regulations shall be a duty owed to any person who may be affected by a contravention of the obligation and, subject to any provision to the contrary in the regulations and to the defences and other incidents applying to actions for breach of statutory duty, a contravention of any such obligation shall be actionable accordingly'.

However, it is to be noted that 'safety regulations' is defined by section 45 as regulations under section 11 of the Act. This would therefore exclude the General Product Safety Regulations 1994 (as it also excludes a contravention of Section 10 of the Act). The rationale for this is unclear.

Naturally, a successful prosecution in respect of an allegation of a breach of the relevant Regulations has a huge impact on any civil proceedings in respect of the same product and any personal injury or damage caused thereby. The effect of section 11 and section 12 of the Civil Evidence Act 1968 is to put upon the party against whom such a conviction is proved the burden of disproving the offence to which the conviction relates, albeit on a balance of probabilities[1].

The failure of a prosecution under the Regulations will not, however, place the same level of difficulties upon the Plaintiff in a subsequent civil action. Two major reasons are:

(a) the standard of proof in a civil action is lower (being upon balance of probabilities as opposed to beyond reasonable doubt);

(b) the defence pursuant to section 39 of the Act will not assist with regard to a civil claim because sections 1 to 9 set out a regime of strict liability for defective products.

As with many civil claims such as those arising out of road traffic accidents, it is prudent for those with the conduct of any civil action relating to a defective

1 Conviction has to be expressly pleaded to be adduced in evidence; See Ord 18, rule 7a of the Rules of the Supreme Court.

product to closely monitor the conduct of the criminal proceedings[2]. If a Trading Standards Department takes up a prosecution this may save considerable time and expense in compiling the necessary evidence for a civil action.

2 In the majority of the prosecutions by Trading Standards Officers in respect of alleged breaches of the Regulations the end-user or consumer will not be required to give 'live' evidence. Usually such evidence is given by virtue of a s 9 statement. In the majority of defended actions an allegation that the item was defective will be contested upon expert evidence and/or upon the basis of a s 39 defence. This is very different to the normal trial of an allegation of driving without due care and attention contrary to s 3 of the Road Traffic Act 1988 where the driver or passenger in a vehicle will ordinarily have to give evidence. It is therefore vital that there is full liaison with the Trading Standards Department and full notes taken at trial.

Chapter 6

RUNNING THE ACTION

It is necessary to look at how cases using the provisions of the Act are likely to proceed. Through the use of four case examples of an alleged defect[1] the practice and procedure for establishing liability, together with possible pitfalls can be analysed. Thereafter guidance will be given as to possible sources of evidence.

6.1 CASE EXAMPLES

6.1.1 Construction defect

(a) Case history

A buys a jar of pickle from the local general store known as Ws, which is owned and operated by W as a sole trader. After the jar has spent some days upon a shelf A attempts to open it but finds it to be stiff. Eventually the jar top fractures at the neck and, by virtue of the position of A's arms at the time, a laceration results to the wrist causing severe personal injury. A's solicitor approaches W who states that six jars were purchased from X PLC, the manufacturer, and supplied by its delivery van in a crate. The jars were then put on the shelves in a normal fashion, and one was subsequently sold to A. When contacted, X PLC state that liability for A's injury is denied and that there is complete confidence that the jar was not inherently defective at the time of supply to W.

(b) Discussion

The first point to note is that W would have faced potential liability under section 2(3) if there had been a failure to respond to A's solicitor's request concerning the identify of the manufacturer of the product. This would be the case provided that the request was made within a reasonable period of time and that it was not reasonably practicable for A's solicitor to identify the producer directly from the information supplied on or with the product. In fact with the majority of goods the producer will be easily identifiable provided the packaging is retained. A's solicitor's first step to take is to have an expert analysis of the jar. The expert should be required to say whether the fracture within the

1 There are said to be four generic types of defect; see chapter 1, para 1.2.3 above.

neck was caused by a form of design defect, or a defect within the ordinary production process of the item, (such as a failure to properly anneal the glass), or by another form of defect such as a crack which could have been produced at any time by virtue of the jar being dropped or struck. Clearly, if it is the expert's view that the fracture in the jar was due to the design or to a defect that could only have been caused during the production process, then A's solicitor should first look to X PLC to satisfy the claim. Certainly, if the failure is one within the normal production process (such as the failure to anneal), it is unlikely that X PLC will have a realistically sustainable defence. This is because the company would have to accept that at the time it was supplied it was defective even on X PLC's own standards. The position with regard to the allegation that the jar was inadequately designed (see example 2 below) is far more difficult. X PLC may contend that the design was not defective and state that they will produce their own expert evidence in due course to support this assertion and thereby gainsay the expert employed by A's solicitor. (There may possibly be reliance upon a defence under section 4(1)(e). However, as the manufacture of glass for containers has been carried on for many hundreds of years, it is unlikely that this defence would have a reasonable prospect of success, save in peculiar circumstances. If however such a defence were put forward then A's solicitor would be advised to look to W by virtue of a claim under the contract for the sale of the jar of pickle. The usual implied terms would be present within the contract and these impose, in effect, strict liability).

If A's expert arrives at the conclusion that the eventual break was due to a crack the position is more complicated. The first step is to establish closely and in detail that nothing that A did with the jar could have caused a crack. This could in due course be the subject of detailed cross-examination. Provided that this can be proved the next step is to raise a claim in contract against W upon the basis of the implied terms within the contract. A claim could be intimated against X PLC but it would be highly likely that the defence under section 4(1)(d) would be raised. Clearly A does not know what happened to the jar in the period of its life between coming off the production line and finding its position upon the shelf at W's. It would be a dangerous exercise to accept W's assertion that the jar must have been cracked during packaging or delivery to W's premises. This may well be a matter for W to raise when seeking to join X PLC as third party to the action on the basis of a contractual claim (providing there is no relevant exemption clause). W's only defences upon liability are either that the jar was in no way defective at the time of opening (unlikely), or that it was in some way damaged after it left W's premises and whilst in the possession of A. If for some reason (such as insolvency on the part of W) it is necessary to proceed against X PLC alone although the eventual break of the jar was caused by a crack it must be noted that the burden under section 4(1)(d) will lie upon X PLC. Therefore W could be called to give evidence upon this point providing X PLC with a difficult hurdle. Further, and by way of discovery (and if necessary interrogatories), extensive knowledge can be gained of X PLC's systems of production, sampling and inspection for defects prior to the trial and the strength of the likely defence assessed. Much will focus upon an analysis of the life history of the product to see when the defect in construction *could* have occurred. (Systems required by BS 5750 and now BSEN ISO 9000 will usually provide an ability to trace back to the rest of the batch and thus allow consideration of the possibility of an isolated defect.) For example, if the six jars of pickle were shrink-wrapped together then the expert evidence may be that the crack occurred either prior to shrink wrapping (at the end of PLC's production line) or upon the shrink wrapping being broken (at W's). Hence a significant part of the jar's life can be excluded. Clearly the longer and more complicated the life history between the relevant time for the purposes of section 4(1)(d) (ie the date at which it was supplied by the producer) and the eventual accident the more difficult it may be to pinpoint the time that the certain defects occurred. Sadly for W, if X PLC can still allege that the defect arose post-production (and therefore cannot safely be proceeded against by A), but there was a clear defect within the product as supplied, then W will still face liability for breach of the implied contractual terms.

6.1.2 Design

(a) Case history

C took her child into a motorway service station owned by M Limited in order to eat. For this purpose she was given a highchair with a table. She placed her child in the chair but as she was in the process of collecting cutlery for the meal the child (who was aged 34 months) bounced up and down causing the chair to topple over in the course of which the child sustained serious personal injury. The chair, which was not obviously defective, appeared stable when C put her child into it and the child was fastened in correctly. The chair had no maker's name or other means of identifying the producer. Although in a state of distress C asked the staff for the name of the producer of the chair but they could not assist.

(b) Discussion

The definition of supply under section 46 of the Act includes 'hiring out or *lending*' the goods. The first step for C's solicitor is to make a request pursuant to section 2(3) of the Act[2] within a reasonable time after the accident. It should be stated within the request that it is not possible (reasonably practicable) for C to identify the producer of the item and therefore if M Limited wishes to avoid liability under section 2(3) then the information must be supplied. As M Limited will not face any liability under contract for the supply of the chair and therefore would ordinarily only face a potential liability under section 2(1) of the Occupiers Liability Act 1957 or in negligence, it would be strange if the company had the name and yet did not meet the request and provide the details of the producer. Whilst there would be both a statutory duty and a duty of care at common law such duty would be unlikely to extend to M Limited carrying out complicated tests upon the stability of the chair. However if it transpires that the chair was produced by a company T Limited with the express warning and instruction to M Limited that it should not be used for children over the age of 18 months and M Limited chose not to pass on the warning or instruction to potential users, then a claim in negligence against M Limited may well have a reasonable prospect of success. However by virtue of the provisions of section 2(3) M Limited cannot realistically refuse to name the producer in the hope of avoiding liability.

Once T Limited is identified it should be asked by C's solicitor to provide the item 'in the state that it was supplied to M Limited' for an appropriate test.

2 The request can be made by the agent of the person who suffered the damage.

M Limited should already have been asked to retain the original chair for inspection. A relevant expert should then be instructed to examine and test both chairs as against the relevant standard: (the British Standard for Highchairs). Alternatively C's solicitor could recommend to C that she inform the relevant Trading Standards Authority for the area and give full details of the incident. A Trading Standards Officer will, ordinarily, vigorously follow up any consumer complaint resulting in injury or near injury. This would have the advantage of short-cutting the process set out above and would also mean that the Trading Standards Department would be likely to obtain relevant expert evidence at its own expense. Further, the Trading Standards Department might lay charges by way of Summons on the basis of breaches of the General Product Safety Regulations 1994, or any other appropriate Regulations. This would have the benefit of effectively fighting much of the battle on C's behalf. Alternatively C's own expert may discover a defect such as a failure to warn end-users that a suitably robust child of over two years could cause the chair to overbalance and that therefore its use should be restricted to children of no more than 18 months. This would effectively be a 'warning' case of a similar type referred to below. Alternatively there might be the allegation that the chair allowed the child to lean to one side with the risk of overbalancing and that this was due to the design of the seat. Once this expert evidence was obtained T Limited would be put on notice that if such a defect were to be proved to the Court's satisfaction it would be unlikely that any defence under section 4 would be successful. As the defect would be one of design it is unlikely that any subsequent operation by way of alteration or assembly would cause the defect and hence section 4(1)(d) would not avail. Further, it is unlikely that the state of scientific and technical knowledge at the time was such that producers or products of the same description could not be expected to discover the defect (or reliance could be placed upon the stricter test under Article 7(e) of the Directive). The question is therefore one as to whether there was a 'defect' within the meaning of section 3. That would be essentially a matter of expert evidence specifically considering the matter set out at section 3(2)(a)–(c). T Limited would be faced with the difficult situation that if the defect were proved, all chairs supplied of this design could be deemed defective. Certainly T Limited would have to consider very closely its duties under Regulation 8 of the General Product Safety Regulations 1994. Discovery of documents relating to the design and testing of the item and all other technical data will be of considerable importance. If necessary an order for specific discovery (or Interrogatories) could be aimed at eliciting any information retained by T pursuant to its duties under Regulation 8(1)(b) and (2)(ii) and (iii) of the 1994 Regulations. Whereas previously it may have been alleged that the requesting of such information was a 'fishing exercise', reliance could be placed on a specific allegation of negligence, 'in that T Limited failed to continuously assess or monitor the "safety of its product in the field"'.

Many solicitors faced with this type of action put notices in relevant legal journals seeking the assistance of others who may have information concerning this type of defect. Expert assistance may also be sought from ergonomic specialists. The consequences of T Limited losing such an action are potentially so serious as to warrant consideration of an early settlement of the matter. Nevertheless the continuing duties now imposed by Regulation 8 of the General Product Safety Regulations 1994 mean that consideration has to be given *in any event* as to whether the product should remain on the market. It would also be important for C's solicitor to advise with regard to parental responsibility in relation to children. The parent who is in charge of a child of tender years owes a duty of care to such a child, the breach of which will give rise to an action in negligence if the child is injured as a result of such breach[3].

6.1.3 Warning

(a) Case history

B buys his first microwave oven from Y Limited, an electrical retailer. The box shows that the microwave oven was manufactured by TX PLC. B reads the instruction booklet. The booklet makes no reference to piercing the shell of an egg or other items with a skin such as a sausage. B decides to cook an egg and places a whole egg within its shell in the oven and cooks it for five minutes. When he takes the egg out and attempts to break it, it explodes causing a very nasty burn to the right dominant hand. Supplied with the microwave is a cook book. Within that book is a reference to breaking eggs before cooking them within the oven.

(b) Discussion

B is likely to have little by way of cause of action against Y Limited, save possibly under the implied terms of the contract. As the box in which the oven is contained clearly identifies the manufacturer it is reasonably practicable for B to identify such a person within the terms of section 2(3)(b) and hence the potential liability under section 2(3) against Y Limited is unlikely to 'bite'. Further it is unlikely that there is an action against Y Limited in negligence as the shop is a general electrical retail outlet selling items manufactured by large companies. Y Limited does not have its own quality assurance programme as it is only a small retailer. It relies upon the expertise of the large manufacturers whose products it stocks. It has never had any complaint or problem concerning the sale of a microwave. (Hence it is unlikely that there has been any breach of Regulation 9 of the General Product Safety Regulations 1994.) Further, B's potential action in contract against Y Limited may be difficult to establish and relies upon proof of a defect in the item. Y Limited will however be unlikely to have any specialist knowledge of the area and will usually seek to join Third Party TX PLC in any action based on breach of contract.

As the item was sold in the fashion intended by the manufacturer it is unlikely that TX PLC will readily concede a defect. B's solicitor must refer to the meaning of defect and in particular to the content of section 3(2)(a) and specifically 'any instructions or warnings with respect to, doing or refraining from doing anything with or in relation to the product'. In response to an initial letter before action the response of TX PLC to B's claim may be that:

(a) it is common knowledge that eggs may explode in a microwave and there is no need to warn an adult of this (relying on cases such as *Heil v Hedges* [1951] 1 TLR 512);
(b) there is a clear instruction in the cook book as to how to cook an egg and B did not read this, and hence is the author of his own misfortune; and

3 See for example *McCallion v Dodd* [1966] NZLR 710 at 715; *Jauffur v Akhbar* (1984) Times, 10 February; *Eastham v Eastham* [1982] CLY 2141 (Caulfield J); *Carmarthenshire County Council v Lewis* [1955] AC 549; also see an article by Peter J Rowe, 'Child v Parent', (1974) NLJ 117.

(c) there is a duty to give reasonable warnings and TX PLC cannot provide instructions to cater for every possible scenario of food being placed into the microwave oven.

TX PLC is therefore not relying on any of the statutory defences and is simply saying the item is not defective.

B's solicitors should consider the following courses of action:

(a) using the Trading Standards Department to investigate the matter;
(b) seeking expert ergonomic advice upon the adequacy of the label;
(c) comparing TX PLC's product with other products upon the market. The definition of defect within section 3 only states that nothing shall be inferred from the fact that a product supplied *after* the time of the supply of the relevant product is of greater safety than the product in question. This has to be seen as against the definition of a 'safe product' within the General Product Safety Regulations 1994 which states that 'the fact that higher levels of safety may be obtained or other products presenting a lesser degree of risk may be available shall not of itself cause the product to be considered other than a safe product'. A detailed consideration of the market may show:
    (i) that all other leading microwave manufacturers contain a specific warning within the instructions that eggs should be pierced before being cooked in the oven; and/or
    (ii) that all leading manufacturers of microwaves contain a specific instruction that when contemplating cooking any type of food the 'cook book' which accompanies the instruction book should first be consulted. This book (whether repeating the instruction book or not) makes reference to the need to pierce an egg before cooking.

    Within section 10 of the Consumer Protection Act 1987 (at sub-section 10(2)(c)) there is specific reference to the existence of any means by which it would have been reasonable (taking into account the cost, likelihood and extent of any improvement) for the goods to have been made safer. This has often led in cases to a comparison with other similar items on the market, often with no regard to the obvious difference in cost (or quality). The courts have shown an alarming habit of unfavourably comparing items in question with the equivalent 'top of the range' examples. It is for this reason that the reference to the level of safety of other items is set out within the new General Product Safety Regulations 1994. Clearly there is frequently much to be gained by comparison and it is to be noted that it is not expressly excluded by section 3 of the Act. Here it may be a very powerful weapon for B's solicitors. Further the strength will be increased by the fact that the addition of an instruction relating to eggs would add little or nothing to the cost of the production of the instruction book. The argument can, in essence, be put forward that TX PLC chose to *exclude* this warning, unlike all of the other major producers. In practice it is an evidential shortcut (relieving the burden of proving that a warning was in fact necessary). Further (and not surprisingly) B's solicitors may gain considerable help from TX PLC's competitors bearing in mind that any Court case may bring adverse publicity to TX PLC's product and thereby enhance the sales of its competitors.
(d) It is likely that TX PLC will have within its possession:
    (i) documents relating to the pre-distribution testing of the product and to the evaluation of its instruction booklet;

(ii) an ongoing system (probably part of a BS 5750 or BSEN ISO 9000 system) to enable the company to be informed of risks which the product may produce (by virtue of the General Product Safety Regulations 1994, Regulation 8(b)).

As B's claim relates to personal injuries, consideration may be given to an application under section 33 of the Supreme Court Act 1981 using the provisions of Order 24, rule 7A of the Rules of the Supreme Court, in order to obtain sight of these documents[4].

(e) If there is no application for pre-action discovery then once an action is started Interrogatories or specific discovery may be used to probe the extent of pre-launch testing of the matter with regard to warnings and instructions for the cooking of certain items;

(f) B's solicitor could consider a 'market-research' test upon a small basis to show that a range of adults are not familiar with the hazard of cooking whole eggs in microwaves. TX PLC will then be faced with the difficult position of showing why such a warning or instruction was not necessary. Further, the Company should have already carried out such testing as was reasonably necessary and will be bound by the existence and content of its own documentation. If such documentation either expressly or impliedly alludes to such a problem then the Company will face considerable difficulty and should consider settling the action at an early stage or at least conceding the issue of liability. However, its duties under the General Product Safety Regulations 1994, Regulation 8(1)(a) and (b) will continue and it must not be forgotten that the existence of B's case and the documentation created thereby could be the subject of investigation by the Trading Standards Department, or discovery in a subsequent action. TX PLC could consider seeking a deduction for contributory negligence under section 6(4) of the Act. The basis of this would be that B failed to take reasonable care for his own safety in that he failed to read the 'cook book'.

Finally it should be noted that the £275 threshold under section 5(4) of the Act only relates to loss or damage to property and *not* to personal injury. So B can claim, notwithstanding that his general damages may be less than this figure.

Cases of inadequate warnings also frequently overlap into cases concerning a degree of 'misuse'. It must not be forgotten that a reasonable degree of misuse is to be expected and is catered for within the definition of 'defect' within section 3(2)(b).

6.1.4 Express warranty

(a) Case history

P who has a 'problem scalp' asks his local chemist, S, what type of shampoo might be suitable for his use. The chemist recommends a 'hypo-allergenic shampoo' produced by Q Limited. On the bottle it states 'This shampoo is hypo-

4 However it must be noted that the person against whom an Order is sought under this Rule is generally entitled to the cost of the Application and of complying with any Order made thereon unless the Court otherwise directs. It is therefore important to make an appropriate request in correspondence beforehand. See *Hall v Wandsworth Health Authority* (1985) 129 Sol Jo 188.

allergenic and is so mild it is suitable for all scalp types'. P uses the shampoo but in fact it possesses an active ingredient which aggravates his scalp condition which is subsequently diagnosed as psoriasis. His scalp worsens considerably as a result of the application of the shampoo and P seeks damages for the pain, suffering and loss of amenity caused as a result of months of severely increased problems.

(b) Discussion

P has a potential claim in contract and negligence against S, the chemist, and also a potential claim under the Act against Q Limited. As Q Limited is clearly identified on the bottle as the manufacturer there is not likely to be any potential claim against S Limited under section 2(3). S faces difficulty with a claim in contract based on a lack of fitness for purpose and also the specific defect of a positively misleading assertion or instruction. As this is a claim without the requirement to prove negligence it may well be P's simplest course of action. At the same time a parallel claim in negligence can be alleged against S for a failure to ascertain the exact type of skin condition and to assess whether Q Limited's product would be truly suitable. However in reality S Limited would probably be best off to accept a breach of contract and then seek an indemnity from Q Limited on the basis of its supply of a product which was negligently labelled and therefore in breach of contract (exclusion clauses permitting). P would also have a relatively straightforward claim against Q Limited under the 1987 Act. Further, it may be quicker and easier to obtain settlement from Q Limited bearing in mind the seriousness of the company's position having regard to the product's distribution on the market. Certainly the involvement of the Trading Standards Department will bring with it considerable pressure and Q Limited could well face a prosecution. Q Limited would have to consider the immediate withdrawal of the item nationwide pursuant to its obligations under Regulation 8 of the General Product Safety Regulations 1994. The failure to appropriately test before making a positively misleading statement would be viewed very seriously by the Courts in any criminal matter. This could not be construed as a simple oversight as the express statement is made solely to increase sales. If there was a specific warning or instruction provided to the chemist then different considerations may apply[5].

It would be unlikely that any allegation of contributory negligence would have a realistic likelihood of success and advice may be given to both S and Q Limited to concede liability for P's claim as quickly as possible so as to avoid damaging publicity.

It is also very important to note that where there has been a failure to comply with an express claim or statement that a prosecution may lie under the Trade Descriptions Act 1968. A prosecution under this Act, which is triable either way[6], is usually seen to be a potentially more serious offence than one under the Consumer Protection Act 1987 and the specific Regulations thereunder.

5 See the cases of *Holmes v Ashford* [1950] 2 All ER 76; *Hurley v Dyke* [1979] RTR 265; *Kubach v Hollands* [1937] 3 All ER 907; and *Watson v Buckley Osborne Garrett & Co Ltd* [1940] 1 All ER 174.

6 Ie either summarily or indictment whereas prosecutions under the Consumer Protection Act are triable only summarily. See chapter 11, *Residual Criminal Liability* below.

6.2 EVIDENTIAL SOURCES

The most difficult aspect of a potential civil claim under the Consumer Protection Act 1987 from a practitioner's perspective is usually the requirement of establishing the defective nature of the product. The requirement for the combination of the analysis of the individual facts of the case and an objective assessment of the product means that many practitioners, although they realise the impact of the relevant sections of the Act, face enormous difficulties with the compilation of relevant and beneficial evidence. The problem is often compounded by the fact that the producer has immediate access to a considerable body of evidence both in-house (with records of production, development, marketing and testing) and external (from trade associations, the continuing analysis of the market and the use of external testing such as by public analysts). The following therefore are merely some of the sources which may prove fruitful when considering the question of whether the item was in fact defective.

(a) **Trading Standards Department**
A simple solution when pursuing a civil claim is to 'piggy back' on a Trading Standards prosecution. A Trading Standards Department may have easier access (in terms of the ability to pay for an expert's report and a greater degree of cooperation from particular types of experts such as paediatricians) to expert advice. If a potential plaintiff has been injured by an allegedly defective product it is invariably the case that a Trading Standards Department will undertake a comprehensive evaluation of the circumstances. It is also the case that such Trading Standards Departments will frequently cooperate with an injured person's solicitor. By virtue of the statutory powers of investigation there may be an easier and faster route to the information that the company possesses in relation to the development, testing and history of the product, and any conviction will be of considerable evidential benefit in reversing the burden of proof.

(b) **British Standards**
British Standards cover the design, construction, and testing of a wide range of consumer products. Further, the foreword to a British Standard will usually possess the names of bodies that were represented upon the relevant committees that considered the content of the standard. The various bodies may well provide a ready source of information for standards used within 'the trade'[7]. The British Standards Institute can

7 As an example the explanatory supplement to British Standard 5665 on the 'Safety of Toys' refers to the fact that the document was compiled by the Textiles and Clothing Standards Policy Committee upon which the following bodies were represented: the Association of Consulting Scientists, the Association of Public Analysts, the British Colourmakers' Association, the British Importers' Confederation, the British Paediatric Association, the British Paper and Board Industry Federation, the British Plastics Federation, the British Retailers' Association, the British Textile Confederation, the British Toy & Hobby Association, the British Toymakers' Guild, the Child Accident Prevention Trust, the Consumer Policy Committee of BSI, the Consumer Association, the Department of Education and Science, the Department of Health, the Department of Trade & Industry (Laboratory of Government Chemists), the Department of Trade & Industry (Consumer Safety Unit, CA Division), the Institute of Trading Standards and Administration, the Mail Order Traders' Association, the National Fillings Trades Association, the Paintmakers' Association of Great Britain Limited, the Pressed Felt Manufacturers' Association, the Royal Society for the Prevention of Accidents, the Society of British Printing Ink Manufacturers and the Toy & Giftware Importers Association.

indicate if there is a relevant standard in operation. It must be noted that Regulation 6(2) of the General Product Safety Regulations 1994 has revoked the Approval of Safety Standards Regulations 1987.

(c) **Expert Testers**
Public Analysts in particular test a wide range of consumer products and frequently have a very detailed and extensive knowledge of the area of product safety. Further, they can frequently gain access to other sources of primary information concerning the product, and are usually able to liaise with Trading Standards Departments. Alternatively consulting engineers may also prove to be of assistance with personal injury cases relating to certain types of products.

(d) **Professional Associations**
If there is not a relevant British Standard consideration should still be given as to whether there is a professional association covering the type of product in issue (such as the Council for Registered Gas Installers (CORGI)). Such Associations seek to maintain standards and are only too happy to identify and assist with any rogue product.

(e) **The Royal Society for the Prevention of Accidents**
This Society can give a great deal of background information concerning the nature and extent of consumer accidents.

(f) **The Health and Safety Executive**

(g) **The Child Accident Prevention Trust**

(h) **The Law Society/Specialist Associations**
The Law Society and associations such as APIL keep a register of relevant experts

(i) **Other Competing Producers**

(j) **Foreign Sources**
It should not be forgotten that the intention of the Consumer Protection Directive is to produce a consistent level of safety of products throughout the Community. However, it is quite clear that different countries focus upon differing safety aspects of similar items which can mean that whilst there is a dearth of information upon a particular hazard in the United Kingdom that other Member States may have a wealth of information upon the subject. This is best accessed by the equivalent of the Trading Standards Department ie the enforcement body in the relevant country.

(k) **Advertisement**
Many solicitors faced with the evidential difficulties of running a product liability claim resort to notices, for example in the Law Society Gazette, seeking help from solicitors with claims concerning similar products. A marriage between two cases can frequently provide enormous strength when dealing with a producer in defeating the 'isolated or one-off accident or hazard argument'.

(l) **Pre-Action Discovery**
See paragraph 6.1.3 above.

(m) **Market Research**
There are a number of Consultants who are happy to undertake market-research which can show the attitude or knowledge of a cross-section of the public with regard to any certain product.

(n) **Ergonomic Experts**
Ergonomics is usually defined as the application of human sciences; psychology, physiology, anatomy and sociology to help solve the problems of the interaction of people and technology. It uses physical sciences such as physics and mathematics in order to explain and predict the interaction of people with environments and products. Involvement of such an expert is frequently of assistance when dealing with the 'perversity of human nature' ie an individual who has behaved in a way other than that usually anticipated by a designer or manufacturer.

(o) **Paediatricians and Psychologists**
Such experts can help to explain and predict the abilities and actions of children of certain ages. This is particularly important when considering cases involving consumer items that may be given to, used on or by a child.

Chapter 7

DRAFT PLEADINGS

7.1 PARTICULARS OF CLAIM

Case No. ...

IN THE ST. HELENS COUNTY COURT
BETWEEN:

A *Plaintiff*

and

(1) **W (Trading as "W's")**
(2) **X plc** *Defendants*

PARTICULARS OF CLAIM

1. The First Defendant is and was at all material times the owner and/or operator of the business known as "W's" and engaged inter alia in the sale of food and associated consumer products.
2. The Second Defendant is and was at all material times the manufacturer and/or distributor of a product known as "Country Pickle" consisting of a food preparation contained within a glass jar.
3. On 1 February 1995 the Plaintiff purchased a jar of the said "Country Pickle" from the First Defendant.
4. The following were, inter alia, implied terms of the said contract:
   (i) That the said goods would be of satisfactory quality in that the jar of pickle would be safe, fit for its purpose and/or durable;
   (ii) The said jar of pickle was not damaged and/or defective.
5. On 10 February 1995 as the Plaintiff attempted to open the said jar of pickle the glass jar fractured whilst in her hand causing a laceration to the left wrist.
6. The Plaintiff's said injury was caused and/or contributed to by the breach of contract and/or negligence of the First Defendant.

PARTICULARS OF BREACH OF CONTRACT

The said jar of pickle was not of satisfactory quality, safe, fit for its purpose or durable, in that the glass in which the pickle was contained was damaged and/or of inadequate strength and/or of unsuitable design and/or otherwise defective in that the same was liable to and did cause personal injury as aforesaid.

PARTICULARS OF NEGLIGENCE

(i) Causing, permitting or requiring the said jar to be and/or remain damaged and/or defective such that it was liable to and did cause personal injury as aforesaid;
(ii) Failed to institute or operate any or any effective or adequate system of quality control, inspection, checking or testing of the goods before sale;
(iii) Failed to warn the Plaintiff of the dangerous and/or defective nature of the said jar.

7. Further and/or in the alternative the Plaintiff's injury was caused and/or contributed to by the breach of statutory duty and/or negligence of the Second Defendant, its servants or agents acting in the course of their employment.

PARTICULARS OF BREACH OF STATUTORY DUTY AND/OR NEGLIGENCE

(i) Negligently and/or in breach of section 2 and/or section 3 of the Consumer Protection Act 1987 supplied goods which were defective in that the glass from which the jar was made was damaged and/or of inadequate strength and/or of unsuitable design and/or otherwise defective in that it was liable to and did cause the personal injury aforesaid;
(ii) Failed to institute or operate any or any effective system of the testing and/or inspection of glass jars;
(iii) Failed to take any or any adequate care in the design and/or construction of the said glass jar;
(iv) Caused, permitted or required the said jar to be and/or remain of adequate strength;
(v) Failed to properly anneal the glass;
(vi) Damaged the glass during the course of production in such a fashion that the Plaintiff is currently unable to further particularise.

Further, the Plaintiff will refer to and rely upon the maxim res ipsa loquitur at the trial of this action.

8. By reason of the matters aforesaid the Plaintiff, who is aged 32 years, having been born on 30th July 1963, suffered pain and injury, and sustained loss and damage.

PARTICULARS OF PERSONAL INJURY

Severe laceration of the right dominant wrist. The Plaintiff has suffered considerable pain, discomfort and restriction of movement and has a permanent handicap and scarring. She is handicapped on the open labour market.

The Plaintiff refers to and relies upon the attached medical report.

PARTICULARS OF SPECIAL DAMAGE

See attached schedule.

AND the Plaintiff claims damages which exceed £5,000 and interest thereon (in the case of special damage the full rate from the date of the said accident) pursuant to section 69 of the County Courts Act 1984.

Case No. ...

IN THE SONNING COUNTY COURT
BETWEEN:

A B (a minor, proceeding by her mother and next friend C) *Plaintiff*

and

T Ltd *Defendant*

PARTICULARS OF CLAIM

1. The Plaintiff, who is a minor being born on 1 March 1992, brings this action by way of her mother and next friend C.
2. The Defendant is and was at all material times the manufacturer and distributor of a high chair known as "Babies Hi-Life". Under and by reason of the distribution and thereafter retail sale of the said chair to the public the Defendant owed a duty under the Consumer Protection Act 1987 and/or a duty of care to any person likely to use the same.
3. On 1 January 1995 the Plaintiff was taken by her mother to the "Good Break" service station, Hurst, Berkshire, which was owned and and/or operated by N Ltd.
4. A servant or agent of N Ltd provided C with one of the Defendant's said chairs for the Plaintiff's use. As the Plaintiff's mother was in the process of collecting cutlery the said chair toppled over by virtue of the Plaintiff's movement in the course of which and by reason of which she sustained injury.
5. The accident was caused or contributed to by the breach of statutory duty and/or negligence of the Defendant, its servants or agents acting in the course of their employment/agency.

PARTICULARS OF BREACH OF STATUTORY DUTY AND/OR NEGLIGENCE

(i) Negligently and/or in breach of section 2 and/or section 3 of the Consumer Protection Act 1987:

- (a) Manufacturing the said chair to an unsafe design in that it failed to provide sufficient stability;
- (b) Failed to provide adequate and/or suitable warnings and/or instructions with respect to the use of the said chair;
- (c) Failed in relation to design and/or warning instructions supplied with the chair to have regard to its likely use by children of over 2 years of age;
- (d) Failed to take any or any adequate or proper care in the development, design and/or construction of the said chair;
- (e) Failed to adequately test the said chair;
- (f) Failed to heed and/or act upon the likely nature and/or extent of movement a child aged between 2 and 3 years;
- (h) Failed to adequately investigate the nature and/or extent of a likely and/or reasonable foreseeable use of the said chair;
- (i) Exposed the Plaintiff to a trap and/or serious risk of injury;
- (j) Failed by signs, notice, warnings or other means howsoever to inform the Plaintiff and/or the Plaintiff's mother of the dangers of using the said chair.

Further, the Plaintiff will rely upon the maxim res ipsa loquitur at the trial of this action.

6. By reason of the matters aforesaid the Plaintiff suffered pain, injury loss and damage.

PARTICULARS OF LOSS AND INJURY

The Plaintiff suffered multiple injuries including fractures to the left wrist and right femur.

The Plaintiff refers to and relies upon the attached medical report.

PARTICULARS OF SPECIAL DAMAGE

See attached schedule.

AND the Plaintiff claims damages which exceed £5,000 and interest thereon (in the case of special damage the full rate from the date of the accident) pursuant to section 69 of the County Courts Act 1984.

Case No. ...

IN THE CAMDEN COUNTY COURT
BETWEEN:

B *Plaintiff*
and
TX plc *Defendant*

PARTICULARS OF CLAIM

1. The Defendant is and was at all material times the manufacturer and distributor of a microwave oven known as the "Kwix'n'Easi Oven".
2. The Plaintiff purchased one of the Defendant's said ovens on 1 January 1995 from Y Ltd at its premises at 35 The Mall, High Street, Camden.
3. On 7 January 1995 the Plaintiff used the Defendant's said oven for the purpose of cooking an egg. He placed the egg in the said oven and set the timer for 5 minutes. On taking the egg out of the said oven it burst/exploded causing a burn to the Plaintiff's right dominant hand.
4. The said accident was caused and contributed to by the breach of statutory duty and/or negligence of the Defendant, its servants or agents acting in the course of their employment or agency.

PARTICULARS OF BREACH OF STATUTORY DUTY AND/OR NEGLIGENCE

(i) Negligently and/or in breach of sections 2 and 3 of the Consumer Protection Act 1987
   (a) failed to provide adequate instructions or warnings to accompany the said oven in order to inform users that they should refrain from placing whole eggs in the oven and/or failed to have regard to what

might reasonably be expected to be done with the product;
(b) failed to provide consumers with relevant information to enable them to assess the risks inherent in the product throughout normal or foreseeable periods of use where such risks are not immediately obvious without adequate warnings and/or to take precautions against those risks;

(ii) Failed to adequately test the product and/or research the nature and extent of likely use of the same by consumers;

(iii) Failed to heed and/or act upon the production by other manufacturers of microwave ovens including, inter alia, P plc, Y plc and S plc of specific warnings either on the said machine or in the instruction booklet to the effect that whole eggs should not be placed in the oven.

(iv) Failed to design and/or manufacture the product as a whole so to be safe and to remain safe in ordinary use.

(v) Exposed the Plaintiff to a trap and/or a foreseeable risk of injury.

Further, the Plaintiff relies on the maxim res ipsa loquitur at the trial of this action.

5. By reason of the matters aforesaid the Plaintiff who is aged 32 years, having been born on 30 July 1963, suffered pain and injury and sustained loss and damage.

PARTICULARS OF PERSONAL INJURY

The Plaintiff sustained a severe burn to his right dominant hand which has resulted in permanent scarring.

The Plaintiff refers to and relies upon the attached medical report.

PARTICULARS OF SPECIAL DAMAGE

See attached schedule.

AND the Plaintiff claims damages limited to £5,000 and interest thereon (in the case of special damages at the full rate from the date of the accident) in pursuant of section 69 of the County Courts Act 1984.

Case No. ...

IN THE RILLA MILL COUNTY COURT
BETWEEN:

P *Plaintiff*

and

(1) **S "The Chemist" Ltd**
(2) **Q Ltd.** *Defendants*

PARTICULARS OF CLAIM

1. The First Defendant is and was at all material times a company engaged in the provision of the services of a pharmacy and/or the sale of pharmaceutical products from premises at 4 The High Street, Bodmin.
2. The Second Defendant is and was at all material times the manufacturer and distributor for onward retail sale of a product known as "Fresher" hair shampoo.
3. On 1 March 1995 P attended at the First Defendant's said premises and

asked the First Defendant's servant behind the counter for assistance in the selection of a suitable shampoo. He informed the said assistant that he had a problem scalp, which was red, sore and flaking. The said assistant selected the said shampoo produced by the Second Defendant upon which was a label stating "this shampoo is hypo-allergenic and it is so mild it is suitable for all scalp types".

4. In reliance upon the skill and judgment of the said assistant and/or the content of the label the Plaintiff purchased a bottle of the said shampoo.
5. The following were, inter alia, express and/or implied terms of the said contract:

(i) The said product would be of "satisfactory quality" in that it would be fit for the purpose for which it was commonly supplied and/or would be safe;
(ii) The said shampoo would be safe/suitable for P's scalp condition.
(iii) The shampoo was so mild it was suitable for all scalp types.

6. On 5 March 1995 he used the shampoo to wash his hair and thereafter suffered a severe skin reaction and exacerbation/aggravation of his scalp condition.
7. The development, aggravation and/or exacerbation of the Plaintiff's scalp condition was caused by the breach of contract and/or negligence of the First Defendant, its servants or agents acting in the course of their employment.

PARTICULARS OF BREACH OF CONTRACT

(i) The said shampoo was not of satisfactory quality and/or fit for its purpose and/or safe in that it caused the said skin condition;
(ii) The said shampoo was not safe for P's scalp condition (subsequently diagnosed as psoriasis) in that it caused severe reaction and/or aggravation and/or exacerbation of the condition.

PARTICULARS OF NEGLIGENCE

(i) The Plaintiff repeats the allegations of breach of contract above;
(ii) Selected the said shampoo when it was not safe so to do;
(iii) Failed to advise the Plaintiff to seek expert medical advice as to his scalp condition;
(iv) Failed to warn the Plaintiff of the dangers of using the said shampoo;
(vi) Failed to adequately inspect and/or assess the Plaintiff's scalp condition;
(vii) In the premises failed to take any or any adequate care of the safety of the Plaintiff.

8. Further and/or in the alternative the development, aggravation and/or exacerbation of the scalp condition was caused by the breach of statutory duty under sections 2 and 3 of the Consumer Protection Act 1987 and/or negligence of the Second Defendant, its servants or agents in the course of their employment/agency.

PARTICULARS OF BREACH OF STATUTORY DUTY AND/OR NEGLIGENCE

(i) Negligently and/or in breach of sections 2 and 3 of the Consumer Protection Act 1987 manufactured a product which was defective in that:
    (a) It contained excessive quantities of X, an active ingredient;

(b) Asserted by label that it was suitable for all scalp types when it was not suitable for a scalp with psoriasis;

(c) Encouraged people with psoriasis to use this shampoo when it was unsafe so to do;

(ii) Failed to take any or any adequate care in the development, formulation, testing, design, development or manufacture of the said shampoo;

(iii) Used the said chemical composition when it was unsafe so to do;

(iv) Failed to institute or operate any or any effective testing of the shampoo including, specifically, to evaluate the safety of the use of the shampoo upon a scalp with psoriasis;

(v) Encouraged people with all scalp types to use the shampoo when it was unsafe so to do;

(vi) Failed to inform/warn consumers that they should seek medical advice before using the shampoo upon their scalp and/or to seek advice as to the nature and extent of any medical condition of their scalp from which they might be suffering;

(vii) Failed to warn the Plaintiff of the risk of an adverse reaction to the said shampoo;

(viii) Exposed the Plaintiff to a foreseeable risk of injury.

The Plaintiff refers to and relies upon the maxim res ipsa loquitur at the trial of this action.

9. By reason of the matters aforesaid the Plaintiff who is aged 32 years, having been born on 30 July 1963, suffered pain and injury and sustained loss and damage.

PARTICULARS OF INJURY

The Plaintiff suffered a severe reaction to the shampoo. He suffered continuing pain and discomfort in the scalp.

The Plaintiff refers to and relies upon the attached medical report.

PARTICULARS OF SPECIAL DAMAGE

See attached schedule.

AND The Plaintiff claims damages limited to £3,000 and interest thereon (in the case of special damage at the full rate from the date of the said accident) pursuant to section 69 of the County Courts Act 1984.

7.2 DEFENCES

1. Naturally the nature and extent of the pleaded defence depends upon what is admitted, not admitted or denied[1]. Clearly if it is denied that the defendant was the supplier or producer then the defence will be straightforward. In other cases the following matters should be noted as they must be specifically pleaded if relevant:

1 There is a difference between a non-admission of fact and denial. A non-admission merely puts the plaintiff to proof, whereas a denial reserves the right to produce positive evidence in rebuttal of the plaintiff's assertion.

(a) Limitation, ie the relevant limitation period has expired[2];
(b) That the product was not defective;
(c) That the supply of the product was otherwise than in the course of the business (section 4(1)(c));
(d) That the defect did not exist in the product at the relevant time (section 4(1) (d));
(e) That the state of scientific and technical knowledge at the relevant time was not such that a producer of products of the same description as the products in question might have been expected to discover the defect if it had existed in his products (section 4(1)(e));
(f) There was no defect in the product save as wholly attributable to the design of a subsequent product in which the first mentioned product had been comprised (section 4(1)(f));
(g) That the loss or damage was to the product itself or was the loss of or damage to the whole or any part of the product which was supplied with the product in question comprised in it (section 5(2);
(h) That the claim is for loss or damage to property which is of the description of property not ordinarily intended for private use, occupation and consumption and was not intended by the person suffering the loss or damage mainly for his private use, occupation or consumption (section 5(3)(c)).

2. It is to be remembered that any positive averment must be adequately pleaded otherwise Further and Better Particulars will be sought. Further, consideration should always be given as to whether third party proceedings are necessary (for example by a relevant supplier against a manufacturer).

2 See chapter 3, para. 3.3.

Part 2

CRIMINAL LIABILITY

Chapter 8

CRIMINAL LIABILITY

8.1 INTRODUCTION

The sections of the Consumer Protection Act 1987 dealing with Criminal Liability and Consumer Safety consolidate the Consumer Protection Act 1961, the Consumer Safety Act 1978 and the Consumer Safety (Amendment) Act 1986. Further, the Act introduced the new feature of the general safety requirement contained in section 10 and ensured that the majority of safety regulations then in existence continued in force. Regulations therefore continued to cover a large range of items but to the extent that there were no specific regulations the general safety requirement under section 10 came into operation. The section set out certain criteria for the determination as to whether the safety requirements had been satisfied and set out certain guarantees that would enable those who supplied goods to be assured that they were complying with the relevant requirements. Principally this meant compliance with safety regulations or any standards of safety which were approved pursuant to the approval of the Safety Standards Regulations 1987 (SI 1987/1911).

The Act provides several methods for acting upon a potential breach of its provisions, for example section 14 concerns 'Suspension Notices' reenacting the power contained within the Consumer Safety (Amendment) Act 1986. Sections 27 to 35 contain provisions for enforcement including test purchases, powers of search, seizure and detention. Sections 36 to 50 contain supplemental provisions. Section 39 provides a defence of due diligence to an allegation of offences under certain sections, most importantly sections 10 and 12. Section 40 allows for liability of persons other than the principal offender. Sections 45 and 46 define certain terms within the Act.

The Consumer Protection Act 1987 (Commencement No 1), Order 1987 brought a number of the provisions into force on 1 October 1987 including those relating to Consumer Safety and Enforcement.

The most important change was the introduction of the new General Safety Requirement, nicely timed to match the implementation of the 1985 Directive within Part 1 of the Act. It meant that the UK was going further than the 1985 Directive required and further than many of the Member States in providing a criminal sanction for breach of a general safety duty in relation to consumer goods. It produced a safety net covering products not the subject of specific Safety Regulations and also catered for the circumstance where specific Regulations or standards did not cover a particular new 'genus' of product.

However it is important to note that it is a defence to an allegation of a breach of section 10 to show that the goods were not to be used or consumed in the United Kingdom. Hence the Act did not seek to ensure safety for any citizen of another EC country who might be importing relevant goods.

8.1.1 Directive

The disparity of levels of protection under domestic safety laws throughout the Community to avoid the supply of 'unsafe products' caused considerable concern and led to the creation of internal trade barriers and perhaps more significantly the effective 'dumping' of products by companies from one country into another. In response the Council Directive 92/59/EEC on General Product Safety was adopted by the Council of Ministers on 29 June 1992 and sought to ensure an equivalent right to and protection for all EC citizens in relation to the safety of consumer goods ie to provide a minimum standard of protection. The Directive imposed a requirement on producers to place only safe goods on the market and it applied to all products intended for use, or likely to be used by consumers. Although the new requirement was similar to the pre-existing General Safety Requirements under section 10 of the Consumer Protection Act 1987 it produced a significantly wider protection and in so doing imposed new obligations on both producers, distributors and relevant national authorities. Where Community Law by comprehensive Directive governed a specific aspect of a product's safety then the Directive did not seek to trespass upon that territory. It produced a new definition for 'a safe product' as any product which, under normal or reasonably foreseeable conditions of use, including duration, does not present any risk or only the minimum risks compatible with a product's use, considered as acceptable and consistent with a high level of protection for the safety and health of persons, taking into account certain specific points. Further the Directive required Member States to impose a positive duty on producers to take appropriate measures to acquaint themselves with the risks which their products might present or produce and to enable appropriate action where necessary to withdraw the product in question from the market to avoid these risks coming to fruition. Specific measures, such as marking products so that they can be subsequently identified when in the market place, sample testing of marketed products, and investigating complaints are expressly set out. In addition distributors are specifically required to act with due care in order to ensure compliance with the General Safety Requirement by not supplying products which it was known or should have been known would not comply with the Requirement. Importantly, distributors had a new specific duty to participate in the monitoring of the safety products placed on the market.

The Directive also specifies that where there are no specific community provisions governing the safety of the products in question that they shall be deemed safe when they conform to the specific rules of national law for Member States in whose territory the product is in circulation. In the absence of such specific rules of national law conformity may be assessed in the light of relevant voluntary European or national standards. This was a significant departure from the content of section 10(3) which stated that consumer goods were not to be regarded as failing to comply with the General Safety Requirements under that Section by reason of a failure to do more than was required by either any Safety Regulation or any standards of safety approved for the subsection imposing requirements in respect of that matter. Hence British National standards of safety faced an immediate 'demotion'. Further, the Directive established a community-wide information exchange scheme on dangerous goods (in light of the then existing RAPX Scheme) and retained powers for the Commission to act directly in certain circumstances.

Member States had until June 1994 to implement the Directive.

8.1.2 Regulations

The General Product Safety Regulations 1994 (SI 1994/2328) came into force on 3 October 1994. They were made under section 2(2) of the European Communities Act 1972 and *not* pursuant to a power in the Consumer Protection Act 1987. The department of Trade and Industry had already announced that from 2 August 1994 all standards given approved status under the Consumer Protection Act 1987, section 10(3) were cancelled. (The General Product Safety Regulations went on to revoke the approval of Safety Standards Regulations 1987 and repealed section 10(3)(2) of the Act.)

Clearly the Regulations were intended to implement the provisions of the Council Directive on General Product Safety although as with the implementation of the 1985 Directive by the 1987 Act there are areas of clear disparity. The Regulations specifically disapply section 10 in so far as it imposes a general safety requirement on those engaged in the normal course of the vast majority of types of and activities with supply. Indeed section 10 is only realistically going to continue to have practical effect upon the supply of products which are excluded from the relevant definition of Regulation 2 by virtue of the fact that they are 'used exclusively in the context of a commercial activity even if used for or by a consumer' (provided always and for the avoidance of doubt that this exception shall not extend to the supply of such a product to the consumer[1]) eg a shopping trolley in a supermarket. The Regulations do not define supply but the definition contained within section 46 and therefore relevant to section 10 of the Act includes not only the selling but the hiring out or lending of goods. The Regulations are somewhat complicated and provide some legal concepts and definitions new to the domestic law of product liability. There are likely to be many interesting arguments upon the scope of certain provisions. Further the Regulations specifically implement the defence of due diligence and reasonable precautions to mirror that contained within the 1987 Act by section 39. As no such defence is included within the Directive this is a possible area of considerable conflict[2].

Nearly all of those involved by way of commercial activity in supply (in its various guises) of consumer products will now have to look to the 1994 Regulations for their duties and obligations (and the criminal sanctions that are faced if there is a failure to comply with them). The new emphasis upon systems and information will be unwelcome by many, particularly those now caught by the definition of 'distributors'. Nevertheless they must be faced and embraced.

1 Further, s 10 will continue to apply to distributors (in this sense meaning other than the person who first placed the item on the market) of products which are subject to specific product Directives where the UK implementing Regulations only impose obligations on the person who first places the product on the market (eg the Personal Protective Equipment at Work Regulations 1991 (SI 1992/2966), implementing Directive 89/656).

2 See chapter 4, *European Perspective* above.

8.2 POTENTIAL LIABILITY FOR UNSAFE GOODS OR PRODUCTS

8.2.1 'Goods' or 'products'

Whereas the central theme of the provisions relating to civil liability under the 1987 Act, concerns defective products, criminal liability revolves around the existence of 'unsafe goods'. The existence of such parallel concepts within the two parts of the Act can be seen as a somewhat unnecessary confusion. For potential civil liability under the Act a relevant product as defined by section 1 is required. This states that 'products' means any goods or electricity and, subject to section 1(3) includes a product which is comprised in another product, whether by means of being component part or raw material or otherwise. The word 'goods' is further defined in section 45(1) to include 'substances, growing crops and things comprised in land by virtue of being attached to it and any ship, aircraft or vehicle'. Criminal liability under Part 2 of the Act makes reference to 'goods' and section 10(7) creates a sub-division of 'consumer goods' meaning any goods which are ordinarily intended for private use or consumption not being growing crops or things comprised in land, water, food, feeding stuff or fertilizer, gas, aircraft or motor vehicles. Further, section 11 allows the Secretary of State to make regulations for the purpose of securing that goods, other than those set out in section 11(7) are safe. Section 11(7) provides that growing crops, water, food, feeding stuff and fertilizer, gas, controlled drugs and licensed medicinal products are excluded. Hence criminal liability under the Act was restricted to a range of 'consumer' goods and goods the subject of specific regulations under section 11.

The General Product Safety Regulations 1994 reflecting Article 2 of the Council Directive on General Product Safety[3] has returned to the definition of a 'product'. The definition within Regulation 2 is stated to be any product intended for consumers or likely to be used by consumers, supplied whether for consideration or not in the course of a commercial activity and whether new, used or reconditioned; provided, however, a product which is used exclusively in the context of a commercial activity even if it is used for or by the consumer shall not be regarded as a product for the purposes of the Regulations provided always that this exception shall not extend to the supply of such a product to a consumer. Within the preamble to the Directive it is stated that it is necessary to establish a community level requirement 'for any product placed on the market that is intended for consumers or likely to be used by consumers, whereas certain second-hand goods should nevertheless be excluded by their nature; whereas production equipment, capital goods and other products used exclusively in the context of a trade or business are not to be covered by the Directive'. Regulation 3 seeks to implement this aspect of the Directive and specifically excludes:

(i) second-hand products which are antiques;
(ii) products supplied for repair or reconditioning before use, provided that the supplier clearly informs the person to whom he supplies the product to that effect.

It can therefore be seen that the effect of the Regulations is to catch and cover products previously excluded from the provisions of section 10 as not being

3 92/59/EEC.

'consumer goods'. As the Regulations are not made pursuant to the power under section 11 of the Act they are not caught by the specific exclusions set out under section 11(7). There is now therefore little difference between the definition of a product for the provisions relating to civil liability and those relating to criminal liability. In respect of the criminal liability provisions, if an item is not one of the 'goods' for which there are specific Regulations in force under section 11 of the Act it is likely to be a product falling within the definition of the General Product Safety Regulations 1994. However, there is an exclusion under the General Product Safety Regulations for products used exclusively in the context of a commercial activity, although it is difficult to see how this exclusion can be justified upon the basis of the Directive.

8.2.1 'Unsafe'

Whereas civil liability deals with the concept of a 'defective' product as set out in section 3 of the Act, criminal liability revolves around the concept of a product being 'unsafe'. Section 3 states that a product is defective if its safety is not such as persons generally are entitled to expect and in determining what this objective standard is to be, account should be taken of all the circumstances including:

(a) the manner in which and the purposes for which the product has been marketed, its get-up, the use of any mark in relation to the product and any instructions for, or warnings with respect to, doing or refraining from doing anything with or in relation to the product;

(b) what might reasonably be expected to be done with or in relation to the product; and

(c) the time when the product was supplied by its producers to another (with the further specific statement that nothing in the section shall require a defect to be inferred from the fact alone that the safety of a product which is supplied after that time is greater than the safety of the product in question).

However, Part 2 of the Act chose to impose a different standard. Section 19 carries a definition of 'safe' in relation to any 'goods' meaning that there shall be no risk or no risk apart from one reduced to a minimum that the actions set out in sub-sections (a) to (d) will cause death or personal injury. Section 10 qualifies this duty by requiring under section 10(2) that consumer goods fail to comply with the General Safety Requirements if they are not *reasonably* safe[4]. Not only does the Section dilute the requirement to safety but it also sets out different aspects for consideration, specifically:

(a) the manner in which, and purposes for which, the goods are being or would be marketed, the get-up of the goods, the use of any mark in relation to the goods and any instructions or warnings which are given or would be given with respect to the keeping, use or consumption of the goods;

(b) any standards of safety published by any person either for goods of a description which applies to the goods in question or for matters relating to goods of that description; and

(c) the existence of any means by which it would have been reasonable (taking into account the costs, likelihood and extent of any improvement) for the goods to have been made safer.

4 See *R v Walsall Magistrates, ex p PMS*, (17 March 1994, unreported), DC, per Laws J.

Thereafter in sub-section 3 it is also stated that goods will not be regarded as failing to comply with the General Safety Requirement, inter alia, in respect of any failure to do more than it is required by any standard of safety. Section 11 allows regulations to secure safety by specific provisions in relation to certain goods. Hence there is a considerable difference between the tests for a defective product and unsafe consumer goods under the Act. In disapplying section 10 in relation to the vast majority of goods, the General Product Safety Regulations 1994 have introduced yet further criteria for the determination of the safety of an item. Within Regulation 2 it is stated that a safe product means any product which under normal or reasonably foreseeable conditions of use, including duration, does not present any risk or only the minimum risks compatible with the product's use, considered as acceptable and consistent with a high level of protection for the safety and health of persons, taking into account:

(i) the characteristics of the product, including its composition, packaging, instructions for assembly and maintenance;
(ii) the effect on other products, where it is reasonably foreseeable that it will be used with other products;
(iii) the presentation of the product, the labelling, any instructions for its use and disposal and any other indication or information provided by the producer; and
(iv) the category of consumers at serious risk when using the product, in particular children.

Finally the Regulation states that the fact that higher levels of safety may be obtained or other products presenting a lesser degree of risk may be available shall not of itself cause the product to be considered other than a safe product. Hence it can be seen that the Regulations do not qualify safety and hence the concept of reasonable safety is rejected. (The requirement under Regulation 7 is not to place any product on the market unless the product is safe, as opposed to 'reasonably safe'.) Further it is clear that the Regulations allow a range of products with different relative degrees of safety. Products are therefore not necessarily to be free from risk but free from 'unacceptable' risk. The practical effect of the new Regulations, although retaining a wider and different test, is to reduce the wide divergence that existed between the test for assessing whether a product was 'defective' and the test, as enshrined in section 10, for criminal liability for whether a product was unsafe (when no specific regulations existed). The tests are still separate but are now similar as to nature and extent.

When considering criminal liability it is therefore first necessary to consider whether the item which is the subject of consideration is one within the range of 'goods' which are the subject of specific Regulations under section 11 of the Act, or whether there are specific provisions in rules of Community law governing *all* aspects of the safety of the product[5]. If not, then consideration

5 In keeping with the Directive, the Regulations make no provision for exemptions as such, but they do *not* apply in cases where a product is subject to specific Community legislation. Where a product is subject to specific Community legislation which is comprehensive in terms of safety (ie covers all aspects of the safety of a product) (regulation 3(c)) the Regulations are completely disapplied. However, where specific Community legislation covers only certain safety aspects of a product, the Regulations will apply to the remaining aspects of that product (regulation 4). When assessing whether a Directive is comprehensive in terms of safety both the intent of the particular Directive and its coverage must be considered. An example of a Directive which is comprehensive is the Toy Safety Directive (88/378/EEC). This is clear when Art 2, which states that 'toys may be placed on the market only if they do not jeopardise the safety and/or health of users or third parties when they are used as intended or in a foreseeable way, bearing in mind the normal behaviour of children', is taken with the general principles

must be given to the General Product Safety Regulations 1994 and to whether there is any exemption under Regulation 2 or Regulation 3, for example if a product was supplied for repair or reconditioning before use[6]. If the product is caught by specific Regulations or Community law in relation to aspects of safety then clearly due regard must be had to the nature and content of the governing provisions. If not, safety has to be assessed under the General Product Safety Regulations 1994[7] unless there is a specific exemption. Consideration must then be given to the definition of 'safe'.

The definition of a 'safe product' under the General Product Safety Regulations and the definition of safe within Section 19 of the Act both refer to the concept of risk of death or personal injury[8]. It is important to distinguish between risk and hazard[9] and many cases will in practice turn upon this point. The Consumer Protection Act 1987 does not involve the concept of total safety (ie no risk of a hazard causing injury). When assessing safety the first step is to consider the hazard (the potential source of harm or method of causing injury, such as, for example by lead poisoning). Thereafter it is necessary to consider the risk of the hazard occurring, (using the above example, the amount of soluble lead and the nature of the item may be such that it would be extremely unlikely that it would ever come into contact with a mouth for any length of time, and hence that any lead would in fact be absorbed into the body. Hence, although the hazard exists and indeed would be serious, the risk may be so small as to render the item safe notwithstanding the existence of the hazard). A failure to appreciate this fundamental concept has led to a considerable number of unsuccessful prosecutions.

8.3 THOSE WITH A DUTY

Having considered the nature of relevant goods and also whether the items are covered by the General Product Safety Regulations, or specific Safety Regulations under section 11[10], it is then necessary to consider who is subject to potential liability under the Act and/or the General Products Safety Regulations 1994. The interaction of the Act and the Regulations produces three distinct categories:

(i) the producer;
(ii) the distributor;
(iii) other individuals.

8.3.1 The producer

Prior to the arrival of the General Product Safety Regulations 1994 the principle obligations were not to supply items which failed to comply with the general

of the essential safety requirements (Annex II.I) of the Directive. Thus this Directive covers *all* aspects of the safety of toys – whether or not an aspect of safety is specifically mentioned in the latter parts of Annex II or addressed by a mandated European standard is irrelevant.

6 Provided that the supplier clearly informs the person to whom he supplies the product to that effect. See Reg 3(b).

7 Or in exceptional cases s 10 of the 1987 Act.

8 As does s 3 with regard to the meaning of 'defect'.

9 See General Product Safety Regulations, Reg 2, and ISO/IEC Guide 51.

10 Or specific Community law or s 10 of the Act in certain peculiar circumstances.

safety requirement or the requirement of individual and specific Safety Regulations under section 11. Section 10(4)(b) gave a defence where goods were supplied by way of retail business. It did not benefit wholesalers, importers or any other individual involved in the manufacture or production of the final item. Hence all those above the retailer in the supply chain had similar, although not the same duties[11]. There were some specific requirements in relation to manufacturers and the importers into the Community within some Regulations[12], but generally speaking there was not a great deal to distinguish between manufacturers, importers into the Community, importers into the United Kingdom or large scale wholesalers. By creating two different major species 'the producer' and the 'distributor' the General Product Safety Regulations 1994 have altered the position. A 'producer' as defined by Regulation 2 now means:

(i) the manufacturer of the product, including any person presenting himself as the manufacturer by fixing to the product his name, trade mark or other distinctive mark. (Individuals who recondition products are also caught);
(ii) if the manufacturer does not have a representative established in the Community the importer of the product will be deemed to be the 'producer'. This should mean the first importer of the product into the Community[13].
(iii) if the manufacturer has a representative established within the Community eg an agent, that person;
(iv) any other 'professional in the supply chain' whose activities 'affect the safety properties' of a product placed on the market[14].

These differing classes of individual are then subject to specific duties under Regulation 8 'within the limit of their activities'[15], and also subject to Regulation 13. As the requirements under Regulation 8 are particularly onerous, particularly when seen against the requirements of 'distributor' as set out under Regulation 9, it is now particularly important to know whether an individual is likely to be held to be a 'producer' or not. Companies who usually import from other Community companies, but on occasion import from companies outside the Community who do not have a representative within the Community, and wholesalers or other individuals who occasionally alter the packaging of items such as to materially alter safety aspects, will now fall to be considered as 'producers' for those items as opposed to 'distributors'. However, when the same company imports from within the Community, or deals with a company with a representative or agent within the Community, or in the case of a wholesaler simply sells on without altering the packaging in any way, the same company will fall to be considered as a 'distributor'.

The Safety Provisions of the Consumer Protection Act 1987 do contain some specific references to manufacturers, however, these relate to requirements within Safety Regulations under section 11[16]. Further, there are provisions which will solely be of concern to importers particularly relating to the activities of

11 See the differing duties with regard to due diligence and reasonable precautions under s 39 (chapter 10 below).
12 See for example the Toys (Safety) Regulations 1989.
13 See Reg 2.
14 Any professional in the supply chain whose activity does not affect the safety property of the product is a 'distributor'.
15 This refers to the capacity of a person, given his position in the supply chain, to influence the safety of a product.
16 See s 12(2).

Customs Officers[17]. However, the new general safety Regulations create a 'two tier system', and the primary requirement under Regulation 7 is specifically aimed at the 'producers', and states that no producer shall place a product on the market unless the product is a safe product. It is clear that the effect is to place a principle duty at the door of those who control initial supply onto the market as opposed to those later involved in the supply or distribution.

8.3.2 Distributor

As the General Product Safety Regulations 1994 disapply section 10 in the vast majority of cases the retailer has lost the benefit of the defence under section 10(4)(b). The retailer now falls to be considered with other 'professionals within the supply chain' whose activities do *not* affect the safety properties of a product[18]. Interestingly, many wholesalers who previously did not have the benefit of a defence under section 10(4)(b) now have the benefit of this description. However, Regulation 9 now provides a new specific duty to act with due care in order to help ensure compliance with the requirements of Regulation 7 (ie to ensure that no producer places a product on the market unless the product is a safe product). In particular there are specific duties in that:

(i) a distributor shall not supply products to any person which he knows or should have presumed, on the basis of the information in his possession and as a professional, are dangerous products[19].

(ii) within the limits of his activities, a distributor shall participate in monitoring the safety of products placed on the market, in particular by passing information on the product risks and cooperating in the action taken to avoid those risks.

Whilst these duties are less onerous than those on the producer they are clearly very significant and affect all professionals within the supply chain. It is specifically stated that any distributor who fails to comply with (ii) above will not be able to rely upon the defence of due diligence[20]. It is an offence to contravene (i) above and also to offer or agree to place on the market or to supply any dangerous product or to expose or possess any such product for supply or placing on the market[1]. It is the clear intention of the Regulations that there should be considerable interaction between producers and distributors, and it is now clear that because of the specific duties upon distributor a failure to interact and/or cooperate with producers will mean that it will be difficult to avoid liability if there is an allegation of a contravention of Regulation 9(A) or Regulation 13.

8.3.3 Other individuals

8.3.1.1 Any individual

Some safety regulations made pursuant to section 11 of the Act require information to be given by 'any person' from whom it is requested. Section 12(4)

17 See for example ss 31 and 37.
18 See Reg 2.
19 Regulation 9(A).
20 See Reg 14(5).
1 See Reg 13.

makes it an offence to fail without reasonable cause to comply with the requirement or to give incorrect information. Further, under section 18 of the Act the Secretary of State may serve notices upon any person likely to be able to furnish relevant information or records. It is an offence[2] to fail to comply or give incorrect information. By section 29(2) there is a power given to a duly authorised Officer to inspect any goods and enter any premises other than premises occupied only as a person's residence. By virtue of section 32 any person who intentionally obstructs an Officer of an enforcement authority who is acting in pursuance of any of the relevant criminal provisions within the Act, or obstructs any Customs Officer, or who intentionally fails to comply with the requirement made of him by any Officer of an enforcement authority, or without reasonable cause fails to give any Officers of any enforcement authority such assistance or information as the Officer may reasonably require, shall be guilty of an offence. Hence it can be seen that a wide range of individuals may face potential liability under the Act in the event of a failure to cooperate with a proper request made by a duly authorised person.

On the other hand, if there is a suspension notice or detention of any goods under any provision by an enforcement authority any person having an interest in the goods may apply by way of appeal for the goods to be released[3]. Again this may cover a wide range of individuals.

8.3.3.2 Directors

Where a body corporate is guilty of an offence under the Act in respect of any default which is shown to have been committed with the consent or connivance or to be attributable to any neglect on the part of any director, manager, secretary or other similar officer of the body corporate[4] he, as well as the body corporate, shall be guilty of that offence and therefore can be proceeded against by way of summons[5]. This section is clearly aimed at individuals holding relevant authority within the business entity, (ie some control of the acts or omissions of the company). It is clear that even a failure to perform a duty which an individual knows ought to have been carried out may be sufficient for liability under the Act[6]. However, a summons will usually only be laid where there has been the express approval of an action at management level (for example, if goods were imported into the Community by a company under the direction of an individual manager who, despite knowing that the goods may well be of a dangerously substandard nature, decided to undertake no test or sampling within this country but to supply straight onto the market).

The General Product Safety Regulations 1994 also provide the same potential liability by means of Regulation 15(2) which mirrors the provision with the main Act[7].

If an offence under the Act is caused by the act of an employee of a company it is usually necessary to consider the nature of the act and the employee's status. Under section 40(1), where the commission by any person

2 Section 18(3).
3 See ss 15 and 33.
4 Or any person who is purporting to act in such a capacity.
5 See s 40(2).
6 See *Re Hughes, Rea v Black* [1943] Ch 296; *Crickitt v Kursaal Casino Ltd (No 2)* [1968] 1 All ER 139; *Huckerby v Elliott* [1970] 1 All ER 189.
7 It was necessary to insert a specific provision within the Regulations as they were not made pursuant to s 11 of the Act.

of an offence to which section 39 applies is due to the act or default committed by some other person in the course of any business of his the other person may be guilty of an offence. However, the phrase 'of his' has been held[8] to mean a proprietary or controlling interest and an ordinary employee does not fall into this category[9]. Therefore the effect of the section, (which is closely mirrored by Regulation 15(1) of the General Product Safety Regulations 1994), is that an ordinary employee cannot be prosecuted under the Act for his act or default. Further, an employee who is not part of the directing mind of a company can be 'another person' for the purposes of the statutory defence under section 39 of the Act[10]. Hence, if the company has taken all reasonable steps and exercised all due diligence it will escape liability if this individual can be properly identified and the requisite information given to the prosecuting authority[11]. However whilst a corporation may be able to escape liability by naming an employee as the person whose act or default has led to the commission of the offence safe in the knowledge that the prosecution cannot proceed against that individual, this is not the same case when the employee has some managerial or higher status within the company[12]. A director, manager, secretary or other similar officer holding some relevant authority or any person purporting to act in such capacity, who is named, may face liability under the Act as well as the company. In fact the lifting of the corporate veil to pursue individuals is not frequent practice. However, if a decision can clearly be identified as being taken by an individual and tends to indicate a complete disregard for the safety of consumers at large enforcement authorities will upon occasions act. If an individual is 'singled out' then, as with dishonest breaches of the Consumer Protection legislation by way of the provision of misleading information, sanctions can be severe[13].

8.4 LIABILITY AND CONTRAVENTION

There are two separate areas of potential liability. The first relates to supply and the preparatory acts for supply (including production and supply by contravention of a suspension notice or prohibition notice), and the second relates to a failure to comply with residual duties under the Act or 1994 Regulations.

8.4.1 Supply

Generally speaking a person shall be guilty of an offence if he supplies, offers or agrees to supply, or exposes, or possesses for supply, unsafe goods. These may be goods that fail the safety requirement; see section 10(1) or the specific Safety Regulations made pursuant to section 11; see section 12(1), or the General

8 *R v Warwickshire County Council, ex p Johnson* [1993] AC 583, [1993] 1 All ER 299, HL.

9 See also Wells 'Corporate Liability and Consumer Protection' [1994] 57 MLR 817.

10 See *Tesco Supermarkets Ltd v Nattrass* [1971] 2 All ER 127, HL.

11 See s 39(2).

12 In relation to junior employees see also Cranston 'Consumers and the Law' (Weidenfeld & Nicolson, 2nd edn, 1984) p 271.

13 'UK Courts have said that Defendants who dishonestly breach consumer protection statutes can expect custodial sentence and the need for effective sanctions is particulary great where physical integrity is involved'; see Cartwright [1995] MLR 222; and the case of *R v Hewitt*, [1991] RTR 357, HL.

Product Safety Regulations 1994; see Regulations 12 (Regulation 7) and Regulation 13. Further, as indicated above, if the offence is due to the act or default of another that person may be proceeded against by virtue of the provisions of section 40(1) of the Act or Regulation 15(1) of the General Product Safety Regulations 1994. These are the primary offences under the Act and form the vast majority of criminal cases before the Courts.

Both the Act and the Regulations retain the usual 'preparatory acts' to supply (ie offer, agreement, exposure or possession for supply). All are preparatory in the sense that there has been no execution of an agreement to supply[14]. There is usually little advantage in alleging any one of these categories above another. However, in practical terms it is sometimes easier to allege possession for supply as opposed to offer or exposure. For the final category, a concluded agreement, will be required[15].

8.4.2 Production

Further, there may be liability in the making or production of supply if it is in contravention of specific requirements within the Regulations. Under section 12(2) there is an offence where Safety Regulations (made under section 11) require a person who makes or processes any goods:

(i) to carry out a particular test or to use a particular procedure in connection with the making up processing of the goods with a view to ascertaining whether the goods satisfy any requirement of such Regulations; or

(ii) to deal or not to deal in a particular way with a quantity of the goods of which the whole or part does not satisfy such a test or does not satisfy the standards connected with such a procedure

and there is a failure to comply.

8.4.3 Contravention of a notice

Further, if there has been a suspension notice[16] or a prohibition notice[17], supply or the preparatory acts leading to supply are not ordinarily allowed[18]. Any supply (or preparatory act for supply) in direct contravention of a prohibition notice or a suspension notice will usually attract a severe penalty.

8.4.4 Residual duties

There are two different types of residual duty. Firstly there are the duties of 'cooperation' and the provision of information under the Act, and secondly positive duties under the Safety Regulations and the new General Product Safety Regulations 1994.

14 See the footnotes to Reg 13 of the General Product Safety Regulations below.
15 *Lacis v Cashmarts* [1969] 2 QB 400.
16 Section 14.
17 Section 13.
18 Under s 14(1) acts may be done with the consent of the authority.

8.4.4.1 *Cooperation and information*

Where Safety Regulations require any person to give information to another for the purpose of enabling that other to exercise any function, then if there is no reasonable cause why the information should not be supplied it is an offence not to supply it[19]. Further, if in the giving of any information an individual makes a statement which he knows is false or indeed recklessly makes a statement which is false in material particular then that will be an offence[20]. Further, section 32 of the Act provides an offence of obstruction of an authorised Officer. This includes intentionally failing to comply with any requirement made by an Officer of an enforcement authority under any of the Criminal Liability Provisions of the Act or without reasonable cause failing to give any Officer of the Enforcement Authority such other assistance or information which the Officer may reasonably require for the purpose of the exercise of the Officer's functions under any of the provisions. As with the liability under the specific Regulations a person is also guilty if in giving the information he makes a false statement or recklessly makes a statement which is false in material particular[1]. Clearly the duty under section 32 is a significant one as enforcement authority Officers are given a wide power to seek information or assistance.

In addition, under section 18 of the Act the Secretary of State may require information by service of notice upon any person likely to be able to furnish it. The information is for the purpose of deciding whether to make, vary or revoke the Safety Regulations or prohibition notices or to serve or revoke a notice to warn. The notice may require information or records to be produced. It is an offence to fail without reasonable cause to comply with the notice or to furnish false information or recklessly to furnish information which is false in the material particular[2].

8.4.4.2 *Positive duties*

Certain of the Safety Regulations made under section 11 impose positive duties in respect of the taking of certain steps, or the retention or creation of records to facilitate the provision of information. Reference has already been made to section 12(2) in relation to the requirement within certain Regulations for tests to be carried out or particular procedures used in the making or processing of goods. If particular Safety Regulations apply or potentially apply to a product it is always necessary to have strict regard to their content in order to assess any positive duties[3]. The General Product Safety Regulations 1994 have gone further than other Safety Regulations currently in operation in that specific duties have been imposed upon two categories: 'producers' and 'distributors'[4]. Regulation 8 now requires a producer within the limits of his activity to:

(i) provide consumers with relevant information to enable them to assess the risk inherent in a product throughout the normal or foreseeable period

19 See s 12(4).
20 See s 12(4)(A) and (B).
1 See s 32(2).
2 See s 18(13).
3 For example under the Toys (Safety) Regulations 1989 there is a requirement to keep available and give information about toys which bear the EC mark (a mark of conformity), frequently known as the duty to keep a 'technical file'.
4 See chapter 9 in relation to the distinction between producers and distributors.

of its use, where such risks are not immediately obvious without adequate warnings, and to take precautions against those risks; and

(ii) to adopt measures commensurate with the characteristics of the products which he supplies, to enable him to be informed of the risks which these products might present and to take appropriate action, including, if necessary, withdrawing the product in question from the market to avoid these risks. Sub-section 2 gives specific examples of measures which may be appropriate including the marking of products or product batches, sample testing of marketed products, investigating complaints, and keeping distributors informed of such monitoring.

Regulation 9 sets out parallel duties for distributors. A distributor is to act with due care in order to help ensure that no producer places a product on the market unless it is a safe product. In particular, and expressly without limiting the generality of this duty a distributor:

(i) shall not supply a product to any person which he knows, or should have presumed on the basis of the information in his possession and as a professional was a dangerous product;

(ii) within the limits of his activities, a distributor shall participate in monitoring the safety of products placed on the market, in particular by passing on information on the product risks and cooperating in the action taken to avoid those risks[5].

The duties seek to force cooperation between producer and distributor to monitor the sale and use of the product and further forces each to have systems in operation to cover the 'limits of their activities'.

8.5 METHODS OF ENFORCEMENT

Part 4 of the Consumer Protection Act 1987 covers enforcement of parts 2 and 3. The enforcement provisions give powers to duly authorised individuals within the enforcement authority to obtain information and records, make test purchases, search premises, seize and detain goods or records[6], and any obstruction of an authorised officer when carrying out these tasks is an offence under section 32. The recovery of the expenses of enforcement is specifically catered for within section 35 of the Act. Thereafter there is the power to issue a suspension notice[7] to seek forfeiture of the goods[8], or to commence prosecution. In appropriate circumstances liaison with the Secretary of State may lead to a prohibition notice or a notice to warn pursuant to section 13 of the Act. It can therefore be seen that an enforcement authority through its Officers has very wide powers to seek to ensure that unsafe goods are not placed onto the market. Many of the powers contained within sections 27 to 35 of the Act are rarely used, and there is still a heavy reliance upon test purchases followed by correspondence and/or an interview pursuant to the provisions of the Police and Criminal Evidence Act 1984, possibly leading to a prosecution. Reasons behind the frequent adoption of this somewhat 'traditional' approach are that it is thought to avoid potentially falling foul of technical provisions,

5 If a distributor has contravened this second limb then no reliance can be placed upon the due diligence defence under s 14(1) or s 39(1) of the 1987 Act.
6 There is also a power under s 31 for Customs Officers to detain goods.
7 Section 14.
8 Section 16.

avoids criticism of 'heavy handedness' and also the possibility of compensation for the seizure or detention of goods or the issuing of suspension notice if in due course the fears of the enforcement authority are not 'well founded'[9]. Further, if the prosecution is unsuccessful the Defendant will ordinarily only be entitled to an order of costs from central funds, thus limiting the potential liability of the enforcement authority[10]. Manufacturers' and importers' representatives in several product areas have argued for a more pro-active and structured approach, principally revolving around the 'Home Authority' principle[11].

9 See ss 14(7) and 34.

10 See chapter 10, *Costs*.

11 The 'Home Authority' principle involves the local enforcement authority regularly inspecting a resident company's goods, systems and premises, and hopefully preventing unsafe goods from ever reaching the market. The authority is available for liaison purposes upon questions of safety and by regular monitoring can ensure that the company has at least the basic systems in operation to comply with the requirements under the Act and Regulations. It has been stated that the practice of authorities over the country instituting 'ad-hoc' criminal proceedings in relation to random items means that the roots of the problems (ie the systems that some companies operate) are frequently not tackled. Trade associations have complained that companies who have an 'open door' policy to the enforcement authority and have proper and adequate systems in operation are being 'undercut' by competitors within the marketplace who have no such systems in operation and are prepared to take the chance upon the enforcement authority locating an item by 'test-purchase' within the market or by way of a consumer complaint.

Chapter 9

BUILDING THE PROSECUTION CASE

9.1 IDENTIFICATION OF THE PROBLEM

There are three main ways in which the possibility of the contravention of the relevant safety provision by consumer goods may come to light. In order to comply with the specific statutory duty under section 27 of the Act to enforce the safety provisions, most local authorities regularly undertake inspections and make test purchases[1] of a range of consumer goods and thereafter undertake the relevant testing to ensure compliance. For most local authorities this is still the major method of identification of potential problems. The second major source is consumer complaints arising from injury or concern as to possible injury. Finally, there is an indirect method, that of communication between authorities. If one local authority has identified a problem (whether through test purchase, or consumer complaint) and resulting tests have confirmed a failure to comply with the safety provision, then information will frequently be placed upon relevant communication systems[2] in order to allow other authorities to be aware of the potential supply of these unsafe items within their own areas. Each of these potential sources of information has drawbacks. In relation to the test purchase, it is frequently the case that such testing will not reveal contravention of any safety provisions, and thus will result in wasted time and expenditure. In relation to the consumer complaint, considerable evidential difficulties may arise if a subsequent prosecution is mounted. Whereas evidence can be painstakenly compiled when there is a test purchase so as to avoid any potential problems in relation to intermediate 'treatment' or 'tampering with' the item, the very nature of a consumer complaint is that the item is likely to have been the subject of some use. Therefore unless a subsequent test purchase or some form of investigation can reveal either a design defect or a defect prevalent within other items from the same source of supply, there can be difficulty in establishing the condition of the item at the time of purchase. In relation to the use of information provided by another authority very often the difficulty lies in the obtaining of accurate and comprehensive information as

1 See ss 28 and 29 of the Act. It is very important to note that a routine inspection by a Trading Standards Officer using the powers under s 29 is a search and therefore subject to the provisions of Code B of the Police and Criminal Evidence Act 1984 (s 66): see *Dudley Metropolitan Borough Council v Debenhams plc* (1994) 159 JP 18.

2 Usually a computer system which can be accessed by all authorities.

to the problem (for example if a problem only relates to one batch which was supplied within a defined area then there is little point in another authority some distance away undertaking a number of test purchases and thereafter paying for expensive analysis).

It has long been argued by those who face investigation (ie manufacturers, importers or distributors) that adherence to the 'home authority' principle will frequently prevent the problems referred to above. Further, the local authority coordinating body on Food and Trading Standards (LACOTS) actively promotes and encourages use of the 'home authority' principle which can apply to all food hygiene, food safety and other Trading Standards matters. Under this principle the home or local authority for the individual or company involved (ie the local authority for the decision making place of an enterprise[3]) accepts the primary responsibility for advising, liaising with, and raising other authorities' concerns with the company or individual. The advantage to the company or individual is that it can seek advice and preventative guidance on a systematic and regular basis and thus hope to avoid the contravention of safety provisions. An 'open door' policy is encouraged whereby trust is built up between the company, individual and local authority such that there can be regular expressions of any mutual concerns as to the supply of any item. When a problem or potential problem is identified by another local authority, that authority should then liaise with the relevant home authority on all aspects of the matter. Ordinarily the home authority should be best placed to consider the nature and extent of the problem and the culpability, if any, of the individual or company. As the Department of Trade and Industry has stated[4] 'The home authority principle is aimed at promoting uniformity of approach to Trading Standards matters, reducing the duplication and assisting businesses to comply with the law'. It is therefore important that once a problem is established, consideration be given as soon as possible to identifying any potential home authority for the relevant manufacturer or supplier and establishing liaison and the exchange of information for mutual benefit. It is submitted in relation to the investigation of consumer complaints or action upon secondary information from other authorities that this should be prior to expenditure upon any testing.

Part of the process of investigation for potential problems is the initial testing for compliance with the relevant Safety Regulations or the Act. Frequently this test is carried out by the local authority's Public Analyst. When contemplating such testing it is important to consider the following points:

(i) that in due course it may be necessary to produce evidence as to the stages up to and including presentation of the item for testing. A simple but accurate adage is 'the less hands it passes through the better'. Certainly the less individuals involved in the transfer of an item from its initial receipt to the Public Analyst, the better. This reduces the risk of confusion and also the ability of anyone representing the individual or company to raise the issue of interference with or informal testing of the item prior to submission to the expert;

(ii) that close regard should be given to what tests are required and/or upon what question the opinion of the Analyst is sought. In *Balding v Lew-Ways Ltd* ((1995) 159 JP 541), the problem of testing for compliance with a British Standard (BS5665) as opposed to the Safety Requirements of the Regulations in force was highlighted. The converse is equally the case (ie

3 Usually the registered address or company's headquarters or main place of business.

4 See the General Product Safety Regulations 1994; Guidance for Business, Consumers and Enforcement Authorities.

that it may not be sufficient to establish that an item fails to comply with a relevant Standard as opposed to the relevant Regulations). It is important that any expert examining the item should be asked to consider it against all *relevant* safety legislation ie the Act and any pertinent Regulations as well as any specific tests contained within Standards[5].

It is also important to ensure that any Analyst conducting tests on behalf of the local authority understands the matters set out above and that the testing processes themselves may be the subject of cross-examination in future[6].

Identification of the problem also includes a preliminary analysis of where the problem may lie within the chain of supply. If an item is sold by a retailer in what appears to be the condition in which it would have been supplied by a wholesaler (or indeed manufacturer or importer) then attention should be quickly focused upon those higher up the chain of supply. Indeed it may be possible to quickly give assurances to a small retailer that he/she is unlikely to be the subject of a prosecution in due course. The advantage of this step is that it frequently assists in the speedy compilation of information and evidence. If, however, the retailer is a large concern such that there may be consideration of whether it has complied with its duties as a distributor[7] or that the contravention of the Safety Provision may be due to the act or default of the retailer (for example by damaging the item prior to sale or repackaging the same in any unsafe way) then great caution must be exercised at this stage as the retailer may well be a future Defendant to a prosecution.

9.2 FINDING THE SOURCE

Once a problem is discovered it is necessary to identify the likely 'primary source' as quickly as possible. In the case of the vast majority of items supplied this will involve asking the retailer to give the relevant information and/or to produce the relevant records and, if necessary, tracing back through the wholesaler or other supplier to the manufacturer or importer. In the case of some goods it will be possible to short circuit this procedure as the item itself will show the name and address of the manufacturer or importer[8]. Although it may be possible to issue a suspension notice to a retailer, or even an intermediate distributor at this stage it is often a dangerous exercise to consider taking such step against an importer and manufacturer until the full circumstances of the potential contravention are known. As with the seizure and detention of goods, if an Enforcement Authority serves a suspension notice which is subsequently set aside

5 This requirement has gained further importance by virtue of the revocation of the approval of Safety Standards Regulations 1987 by Reg 6(2) of the General Product Safety Regulations 1994.

6 Many prosecutions have failed because the actual testing was not carried out by a public analyst or under his direction and control although the eventual certificate was assigned by the public analyst. In many cases actual tests will be carried out by technicians as opposed to the public analyst and if the results are to be the subject of analysis at court then it is necessary to obtain evidence from both the analyst and the technician.

7 See the General Product Safety Regulations 1994 below.

8 This is now required under some Regulations. For example the Toy Safety Regulations require a CE mark of compliance accompanied by the name and address of the manufacturer or importer.

there may be a liability to pay compensation to any person having an interest in the goods[9]. It is vitally important when considering the source of items that if the goods do not have the name and address of the manufacturer or importer that the supply chain can be proved beyond doubt[10]. As stated above[11] an Enforcement Authority, through its officers has very wide powers to investigate potential breaches of the Act and to obtain relevant information or evidence. Providing a warrant is obtained it is possible to enter the relevant premises by force (see section 30(2)). It is also worth noting that containers or vending machines may be opened (section 29(7)). There is a power to seize and detain goods (section 29(4)(b)) and to require a person carrying on a business to produce records relating to the business. Further, copies of any entry in any records may be taken (section 29(4), section 29(5) and section 29(6))[12]. The requirement of the production of records and information should ordinarily ensure an ability to trace the chain of supply back to the original source. It is a specific offence under section 32 of the Act to fail without reasonable cause to give officers of the enforcement authority relevant assistance or information or to intentionally obstruct such an Officer. Further, it is to be noted that the expenses of enforcement, including those in connection with any seizure or detention of goods by or on behalf of the authority may in due course be recovered if there is an order for the forfeiture of any goods or a successful prosecution. As distributors are now subject to specific duties under section 9 of the General Product Safety Regulations 1994 information may now be more readily forthcoming than has previously been the case. It is certainly difficult to see how a distributor could properly and adequately participate in the monitoring of the safety of products placed on the market such as to comply with Regulation 9(b) and not be able to immediately identify the relevant source of these products ie the wholesaler or manufacturer/importer from whom the goods have been obtained.

Sometimes evidence must be compiled at this stage without prejudice as to whether anyone other than the manufacturer or importer may be the subject of a prosecution. Through the exercise of relevant powers the information possessed by any retailer or distributor may be obtained in order that there may be identification of the likely supplier of the goods. Such documentation may be put to a manufacturer, importer or distributor higher up the chain within a letter or interview or indeed the same powers may be exercised in order to establish and prove the final link. Many authorities will effectively sacrifice the ability to prosecute a retailer or distributor in order to facilitate the obtaining of evidence of supply. If such a practice continues or is encouraged it may effectively negate the specific duty imposed under Regulation 9 of the 1994 Regulations.

9 See s 14(7).

10 Many prosecutions have failed because of an inability to establish which of one or more importers actually supplied the item to a wholesaler. If a particular type of product or 'line' is popular then wholesalers will frequently receive supplies from one or more companies. Even if a wholesaler is partially uncooperative an analysis of records kept under BS 5750 or BSEN ISO 9000 procedures or an analysis of stock taking or consignment notes should reveal the relevant supplier.

11 See chapter 8, para 8.5, *Methods of Enforcement*.

12 It is important to note that s 34 provides for compensation for seizure and detention of goods if there has been no contravention in relation to the goods of any Safety Provision or of any provision made by or under Part III of the Act providing that the exercise of the power was not attributable to any neglect or default of the person who seeks such compensation.

9.3 EVIDENCE

Once the entire supply chain has been identified and the initial act or omission which caused contravention of the safety provision isolated consideration should be given as to the dual task of the obtaining of further information and evidence. If not already contacted it is always advisable to involve any relevant home authority at this stage in order to gain full background information including as to the history, nature and extent of trading and the existence of any in-house systems and procedures. Thereafter, preliminary information is initially requested by letter. Such a letter ordinarily requests confirmation that the item was in fact supplied by the company in the circumstances already apparent from the investigation into the supply chain. Thereafter an interview, pursuant to and under the provisions of the Police and Criminal Evidence Act, is usually sought. This is often seen as a critical stage in the building of a prosecution case. However it is often the case that companies, usually acting through legal representation, will indicate that whilst assistance will be given in correspondence, an interview will not be granted[13]. At this stage it is necessary to consider the full nature and extent of the powers available under Part IV and whether a visit to the company's premises and/or a demand for the production of records and information and/or a request for 'other assistance', should be made. All too frequently local authorities accept the refusal by an individual or company to assist in the investigation of a matter other than in a very limited fashion. They fail to consider whether the combination of the specific powers granted to the authority and the officer, and the sanction under section 32 of the offence of obstruction of an officer (including, specifically, the intentional failure to comply with a requirement of an officer or a failure without reasonable cause to give officers of an enforcement authority any other assistance or information which the Officer may reasonably require) means (given the circumstances of the alleged contravention) that the initial lack of cooperation should not be accepted. Further, many local authorities choose only to investigate the prima facie commission of the offence and do not consider at this stage the nature and extent of any statutory defence available to a company or individual under section 39. However, a detailed and thorough examination of the facts surrounding the alleged offence, and the compilation of evidence (such as to enable an informed decision as to whether a suspension notice should be issued or a prosecution initiated) should ordinarily involve a full evaluation of whether a company may have a defence that it exercised all reasonable precautions and took due diligence to avoid the commission of an offence[14]. It is to be noted that the procedural requirements of reliance upon the defence are not onerous and this may mean that if a prosecution takes place the company can reveal the nature and extent of its reliance upon a due diligence defence very late within the proceedings[15]. Certainly, the duties under Regulation 8 and Regulation 9 of the General Product Safety Regulations 1994 require systems which would ordinarily produce considerable information about the history of the production and supply of the item and analysis and investigation of such systems should quickly reveal whether this is the first occasion that the problem has arisen with the particular item in question.

13 This practice may change by virtue of the 'new caution'.
14 See s 39 of the Act and Reg 14 of the General Product Safety Regulations 1994.
15 Not less than 7 clear days before the hearing of the proceedings a notice has to be given pursuant to s 39(2) and (3).

9.4 DECISIONS

Once information and evidence has been obtained an informed decision can be taken as to what action, if any, is to be taken against the relevant individuals or companies. The first consideration should be to ensure that unsafe goods do not remain upon the market. Suspension notices can be issued pursuant to section 14 of the Act where an enforcement authority has reasonable grounds for suspecting that any safety provision has been contravened in relation to any goods. The notice will last for an initial six month period unless proceedings in respect of contravention of the safety provision or for forfeiture are pending at the end of that period. It must always be noted with the issue of a suspension notice that the authority shall be liable to pay compensation to any person having any interest in the goods if in due course it is established to the satisfaction of the Court that there has been no contravention in relation to the goods of any safety provision, and the issue of the suspension notice was not attributable to any neglect or default by the relevant person[16]. Great caution therefore has to be exercised before a suspension notice is issued. Suspension notices issued at different stages within the chain of supply will of course have radically different effects. If investigation and evidence has identified that contravention of the safety provision is in respect of only one defined batch, then it may be necessary to issue suspension notices to the relevant wholesalers or retailers but it may not be necessary to issue a suspension notice to the manufacturer or importer in respect of other goods of the same type not within the relevant batch. Even if a suspension notice is not issued consideration should ordinarily be given as to whether a manufacturer, importer or wholesaler should be asked to recall by way of letter, notice, or other means. It is to be noted that by virtue of Regulation 8(b) of the General Product Safety Regulations 1994 a producer has a duty to adopt measures commensurate with the characteristics of the products to enable him to take appropriate action including, if necessary, withdrawing the product in question from the market. There is no such express parallel duty upon a distributor. In appropriate circumstances the authority should seek to have input as to the nature, extent and terms of any recall letter or notice[17]. Whilst a distributor does not have a specific duty under the Regulations to have such a system in operation it should be noted that whilst products which contravene the safety provisions remain on the market the distributor has potential liability for a future prosecution. It will be certainly difficult for such a distributor to claim that it had acted with all due diligence and reasonable precautions to avoid commission of an offence if having been made aware of a problem no immediate steps were taken to recall the item in question.

The next consideration is whether an order for forfeiture pursuant to section 16 of the Act should be sought or a prosecution brought. Certainly if a suspension notice is to be issued this will lapse if a decision to adopt one of these two courses is not taken within a six month period[18]. If either course is adopted and pursued to a successful conclusion there can be recovery of the expenses of enforcement under section 35 of the Act. It is to be noted that applications for forfeiture are frequently made after the conclusion of a

16 Section 14(7).
17 See for example the problems encountered in *Coventry City Council v Ackerman Group plc* [1995] Crim LR 140.
18 See s 14(4).

successful prosecution[19]. Local authorities have differing tests and criteria for the decision to prosecute. It is submitted that the two major criteria that weigh *against* a decision to prosecute are:

(i) that the content of relevant Regulations or of a relevant standard allows differing interpretations and opinions as to whether there has indeed been a relevant contravention;

(ii) where the company or individual has a strongly arguable defence under section 39 of the Act or Regulation 14 of the General Product Safety Regulations 1994.

In each of these cases it is vital to note that the criminal standard ie proof beyond reasonable doubt is required and that this is a high threshold. Frequently, steps taken during the investigation of the matter will have led to the resolution or removal of possible risk of a problem and the prosecution must therefore be seen in the light of its likely overall benefits as opposed to the risk of failure[20].

Finally, consideration must be given as to which companies or individuals are to face prosecution. Under Section 40 of the Act where the commission of an offence by one individual or company is due to an act or default permitted by some other person or company then that other person or company may be proceeded against whether or not proceedings are taken against the first mentioned person. This enables proceedings to be instituted against manufacturers, importers and others, (usually some form of distributor), within the supply chain. Further, where a body corporate is guilty of an offence which is shown to have been committed with the consent or connivance or to be attributable to any neglect on the part of a director, manager, secretary or similar other officer, or a person purporting to act in such a capacity he, as well as the body corporate shall be liable to be proceeded against[1]. The General Product Safety Regulations which provide for offences within Regulations 7, 9(a) and 13 have essentially the same provision with regard to the liability of persons other than the principal offender at Regulation 15. Hence, any person whose act or default has caused the commission of the offence can also be proceeded against as can an individual with the status or duties referred to above[2]. The decision to prosecute should always be referable to the alleged degree of culpability. It has certainly been recognised that in the case of small or 'one-man' companies, prosecution recorded against an individual as opposed to or in addition to the company (which may trade for only a short period of time before being replaced by a new corporate vehicle) is desirable in terms of the long term of enforcement of legislation. Much depends upon the nature and extent of a contravention as to where the exact 'fault' is alleged to lie. It was recognised by the House of Lords in *Tesco Supermarkets Ltd v Nattrass* [1962] AC 153 that when members of senior management of a company set up systems and ensure to the best of their ability that they are carried out it would not be in accordance with the spirit of the Act to seek to hold them personally responsible for the acts or omissions of ordinary employees. However, if the contravention of the safety provision was due to the actions of an individual who is clearly the directing mind and will of the company (which is often merely a vehicle for his actions) then prosecution against that individual may well be justified. It has long been recognised that some Directors take the decision to dispense with what they know to be essential safety systems in order to cut costs

19 See s 16(2)(a).
20 Particularly having regard to the costs implications; see chapter 10 below.
1 Section 40(2).
2 See s 15(2).

and enhance profit[3]. In such circumstances subsequent prosecutions against and fines imposed upon the company may not alter the long-term philosophy of the relevant individuals. Prosecutions against individual directors or others with equal status are therefore powerful weapons in ensuring long-term compliance with the duties under the Act or Regulations[4].

9.5 FORM

Once the nature and extent of the alleged contravention has been identified and the likely Defendant established it is necessary to consider the specific section or Regulation, the relevant time limits and the form and number of offences which will be alleged. Ordinarily this is a straightforward exercise but due regard must be had to what has to be proved to establish the offence. Two examples of how the prosecution can unwittingly create problems by choosing the wrong form of offence are:

(i) *Preparatory Acts*
It may not be possible to prove an agreement to supply. Further, it may be difficult to prove an actual agreement and therefore far easier to allege exposure, or perhaps more straightforwardly, possession for supply. Although with possession for supply it is necessary for the prosecution to prove the Defendant did intend to supply[5] it is not necessary to consider the nature and extent of any additional agreement;

(ii) *Knowledge or Intent*
Under Regulation 9(a) of the General Product Safety Regulations 1994 a distributor shall not supply products to any person which he knows or should have presumed were dangerous products and contravention shall be an offence. However, it is also an offence under Regulation 13(a) for a distributor to offer or agree to place on the market any dangerous product or expose or possess any such product for placing on the market or to offer or agree to supply any dangerous product or expose or possess any such product for supply. Clearly alleging an offence under Regulation 9(a) will require proof and/or examination of state of knowledge which is not necessary when alleging contravention of Regulation 13.

Further, a summons (or indictment) should be comprehensive and give adequate details such as to alert the Defendant to the exact nature of the alleged offence. Duplicity (alleging more than one offence in a summons) must be avoided.

9.6 TIME LIMIT

There is a specific time limit for the bringing of a prosecution in respect of an alleged offence under the General Product Safety Regulations 1994[6] and many

3 Indeed it is sometimes alleged that the possibility of criminal prosecutions and fines levied as a result are built into company economic strategies as 'consequential costs'.
4 See chapter 11 below, and the provisions of the Fair Trading Act 1973.
5 *Birkett v McGlassons Ltd* [1957] 1 All ER 369.
6 See Reg 16.

Regulations made pursuant to the power under section 11[7], of twelve months. The time limit in respect of an alleged offence contrary to section 10 of the Consumer Protection Act 1987 is the ordinary six month time limit. Further, this time will also apply to other offences alleged under the Act for example obstruction of an authorised Officer contrary to section 32.

9.7 EVIDENCE IN REBUTTAL

On occasions it will be necessary during the course of preparation for a prosecution, or an appeal against a suspension notice or the detention of goods, to seek further or rebuttal evidence. It is to be noted that there is no duty upon the Defendant to exchange expert evidence or give details of the nature and content of any evidence save as required by the procedure set out under section 39 of the Act and Regulation 14 of the General Product Safety Regulations 1994 (in relation to the claim of the exercise of all due diligence and reasonable precautions). As stated above this means that it is important to attempt to assess the nature and extent of any potential defence available during the collection of information and/or evidence at the outset of the matter. If or when the nature and extent of the defence comes to light consideration should be given to obtaining evidence in rebuttal. Regard should be given to all available and usual evidential sources (see those set out in relation to civil claims above[8]). However, it must also be recognised that if a well qualified expert (for example, a consultant paediatrician) is willing to put forward an unequivocal view to gainsay that of an expert already retained by the prosecution, that it will not usually suffice to simply get another expert. Unless the opinion of the defendant's expert can be exposed as flawed or entirely misconceived it will ordinarily raise a reasonable doubt such that the prosecution, in seeking to establish criminal liability, should fail[9]. When compiling expert evidence for use during the prosecution it must also be remembered that cases are frequently heard by a lay bench of Magistrates who do not have considerable experience of dealing with technical expert evidence. The benefit of any confusion or lack of understanding will usually be given to a defendant.

7 See specifically s 11(3)(e).
8 Chapter 6, para 6.2, *Evidential Sources*.
9 In an appeal against a suspension notice the view of the defendant's expert may not be sufficient to *establish* to the Court satisfaction that there has not been a contravention of a safety provision such that the notice will be set aside. This reflects the importance of considering whether a prosecution should be embarked upon as opposed to seeking alternative methods of ensuring compliance with the Act.

Chapter 10

DEFENDING THE CASE

10.1 INTRODUCTION

This chapter deals with best practice when dealing with allegations of involvement in the commission of offences under the 1987 Act or the Regulations thereunder, or under the General Product Safety Regulations 1994. Further, responses to alternatives to prosecution such as suspension notices will be considered.

The overriding consideration when contemplating an allegation of contravention of a relevant safety provision is that the enforcement authority has an armoury of wide ranging investigative powers (as discussed within the last chapter). Therefore, if at all possible, the position of the individual or company faced with an investigation by an enforcement authority should be considered *prior* to the provision of any response, the giving of any information or records or the granting of any interview. It is vital that an investigation of the complaint is made as soon as practicable so that the facts and matters that the company can already establish are known to those who have to advise. All relevant records should be obtained together with full information from all those involved in the purchase, production, marketing or supply of the item. A distributor should seek full information from those higher and (if any) lower within the supply chain and an overview of the matter obtained. If any steps are to be taken to recall the item and to acknowledge a problem it is vital that they are taken as soon as possible. Any delay may fatally prejudice reliance in due course upon a defence of due diligence[1] (particularly if the prosecution during the course of investigation allege an offence in relation to a supply after the date of 'effective knowledge' of the problem). An enforcement authority will always be better disposed to an individual or company who has acknowledged a problem and taken immediate steps to remedy the situation. Even if a prosecution follows, such steps will be important when considering mitigation. It is virtually always better to undertake a speedy and comprehensive evaluation as opposed to awaiting the determination of the enforcement authority and seeing what evidence it is able to compile (and serve) before considering the response.

It is also to be noted that the rationale behind the Act and the 1994 Regulations is to ensure compliance by placing emphasis upon in-house systems to avoid commission of the offence. As can be seen from the matters set out

1 Under s 39 of the 1987 Act or Reg 14 of the General Product Safety Regulations 1994.

below in relation to the statutory defence of the exercise of 'due diligence and all reasonable precautions' a comprehensive evaluation of the company's actions and its systems is required to ensure that they have any ability to withstand scrutiny within any criminal proceedings. Those engaged within the manufacture, importation or subsequent supply of consumer products are therefore well advised to seek regular advice as to whether the systems that they operate comply with the requirements of the domestic statutory framework[2].

10.2 SUPPLY

Once a problem is notified by either a dissatisfied consumer or an officer of an enforcement authority[3] it is important to determine at the outset whether the item in question has at any stage been supplied by the individual or company concerned. Modern in-house systems of quality assurance[4] usually mean that items can be identified such that the supplier can be traced. Further, certain Regulations require the name and address of the supplier or importer to be prominently displayed[5]. If there is any doubt over supply then it should be clearly stated to anyone raising a potential complaint or problem that there is doubt as to whether the product was supplied by the company or individual. Any failure to deal with this issue at the outset could cause prejudice at a later stage by virtue of an argument that the company or individual has tacitly accepted that it supplied the item[6].

The second major issue concerning the supply of the item is to ensure that it was purchased and/or tested by the enforcement authority in the same condition in which it was supplied by the company or individual. Under section 28(2) if the enforcement authority has carried out a test purchase there is a specific power to request (if practicable) that the item be made available for subsequent test on behalf of the company or individual concerned. Further, if goods are seized or detained there is a power under section 30(6) to seek a similar inspection or test. (It is also important to note that under section 30 the enforcement authority has a duty to inform the individual or company of the results of its tests but no such duty arises under section 28.) It is therefore important at the outset to have the actual item which is the subject of complaint tested. It is pointless to spend time, effort and money having other items within the same or other batches of production tested if in due course it transpires that the item on which the prosecution is based was a 'rogue' example. Testing of the item will usually reveal how the defect has come about and may then allow for proper analysis of in-house production or testing methods to see how the problem may have arisen or escaped detection.

2 Very often companies only compare in-house systems against legal requirements once an alleged contravention of a safety provision has been identified. Thereafter systems may be found to be flawed (such that they do not meet the requirements of the Act or Regulations) by virtue of simple acts or omissions which could have been dealt with at an earlier stage with little cost in terms of time or effort.

3 Or a customs officer pursuant to s 31 of the Act.

4 BS 5750 or BSEN ISO 9000.

5 See for example the Toys (Safety) Regulations 1989.

6 Although it is to be remembered that the prosecution must always prove its case to the requisite standard and supply is always a vital element within that case. A failure to raise the issue which induces a prosecution may mean that the Defendant may not obtain a costs order if the case is discontinued or dismissed at a later stage; see para 10.7, *Costs*, below.

Only when it is has been conclusively shown that the item in question was in fact supplied by the company or individual and (if possible) it has been the subject of an inspection or test by the company can the prospects of successfully defending any prosecution or seeking to appeal against any suspension notice or detention/seizure of the goods be evaluated. However as stated above once a problem is notified to the company or individual the clock starts to run with regard to the potential duty to recall. If there is a failure to act appropriately or in time, this may have the dual effect of resulting in the issuing of a suspension notice and of damaging a possible defence under section 39 of the Act (or Regulation 14 of the General Product Safety Regulations 1994).

Even if it is to be the defence that the item is not unsafe and the prosecution's fears are unfounded, thought should still be given as to whether the item should be recalled or its supply suspended until conclusive determination of the matter. Certainly the enforcement authority should be informed as quickly as possible that it is the view of the company or individual that the item is not defective so that it can consider its position as to whether it wishes to issue a suspension notice.

10.3 DEALING WITH THE ENFORCEMENT AUTHORITY

As stated within the last chapter the enforcement authority has very wide powers with regard to investigation of the commission of a possible offence under the Act or Regulations. At all times it must be recognised that it is a specific offence under section 32 of the Act to obstruct an authorised Officer by way of intentionally failing to comply with a requirement under Part IV or without reasonable cause to fail to give any relevant assistance or information that has been reasonably requested. Further, if the matter proceeds to a prosecution it is likely that each and every response of the company will be put before the Court[7]. It is therefore of the greatest importance that there is consistency and accuracy in the communication of information to the enforcement authority. A refusal to cooperate with reasonable requests may of itself be the commission of an offence[8] but at the very least it may cast the company or individual in an unfavourable light should the matter proceed to a determination before a Court.

Many practitioners advise individuals or representatives of companies not to take part in interviews with enforcement authorities[9]. The rationale behind this advice is that whilst the company is duty bound to provide information this can be given in writing, and an interview can allow cross-examination of the client in circumstances where the prosecution has not fully disclosed 'its hand', or effectively amount to a generalised 'fishing exercise' for information. However, if a comprehensive evaluation of the individual or company's position and the compilation of relevant documentation and/or evidence has already taken place then there is no reason why such an interview cannot be used to 'turn the tables' upon the enforcement authority, particularly if it is thought

7 Ordinarily the Enforcement Officer in charge of the case will annexe all correspondence with the company to his statement and produce the same to the Court.

8 Under s 32.

9 Such interviews taking place under and pursuant to the Police and Criminal Evidence Act 1994. However, regard must be given to the effect of the 'new' caution.

that an unreasonable stance is being adopted[10]. It is the Author's view (and that of several other practitioners) that if the individual or representative of the company is properly 'armed' to face any criticism during an interview that he/she is far more likely to obtain helpful concessions and assistance from the Enforcement Officer than they are to make comments or provide information which in due course may damage the individual's or company's position. This view is fortified by the fact that the enforcement authority has the power to inspect records and demand information in any event.

10.4 EVIDENCE

Manufacturers or importers of items should ordinarily have easy access to relevant experts[11]. Further, individuals or companies who trade within an area should have access to information from other companies (including competitors) as to the history of supply of the relevant item[12]. Hence an initial evaluation of whether there has been a contravention of a safety provision should be easy to undertake. Thereafter the evidential sources which are of assistance are those set out in relation to civil liability in chapter 6 above. It should not be forgotten that when defending a prosecution success will ordinarily be obtained by establishing reasonable doubt as opposed to conclusively proving the safety of the item[13]. Therefore if a relevant and well-qualified expert is willing to give evidence that in his/her opinion the item does not contravene Safety Regulations, then that may be sufficient to defeat a prosecution. This should be borne in mind when considering whether to disclose expert evidence to the prosecution prior to trial. Whilst it is sometimes thought that the early disclosure of such evidence allows the prosecution to seek evidence in rebuttal it should also be accepted that the disclosure of such evidence allows the prosecution to assess its position in relation to the ability to prove the offence to the criminal standard and thus may avoid the case proceeding to trial[14].

10 Analysis of in-house sampling methods provides a good example. Few Trading Standards Officers will ever give advice (including under the Home Authority principle) as to what is an adequate number of items to test to ensure compliance with statute and regulations, ie to ensure that reasonable precautions have been taken and due diligence has been exercised. If in due course the sampling method fails to prevent a rogue item entering the market place there is thereafter often criticism that the number tested simply was not enough. If however the testing system of a company and documentation is clearly put across within an interview the relevant officer can be asked within the interview as to what he identifies as a flaw or fault in the system, what he says should have been done that was not done, and the rationale for his assertions.

11 It is likely that such experts will have been used when assessing the safety of item both on an initial and ongoing basis.

12 Evidence from the trade is ordinarily admissible in proceedings subject to the normal rules of evidence. See *R v Walsall Magistrates, ex p PMS* (17 March 1994, unreported), DC, per Laws J.

13 As opposed to the requirement to establish that there has been no contravention of any relevant safety provision when pursing an Appeal under s 15 in relation to a suspension notice or under s 33 in relation to the detention of goods.

14 Upon the conclusion of a successful defence of a prosecution the defendant will ordinarily ask for an Order of Costs from central funds pursuant to s 16 of the Prosecution of Offences Act 1985. If the defendant is thought to have been unreasonable, for example in refusing to disclose the nature and extent of any expert evidence then this may result in the refusal by the Magistrates to grant such an Order; see para 10.7, *Costs*, below.

10.5 SECTION 40: LIABILITY OF PERSONS OTHER THAN THE PRINCIPAL OFFENDER

If the prosecution seek to invoke section 40 of the 1987 Act and to state that the commission by an individual or company of an offence was due to the act or default committed by some other person and thereby seek to proceed against the other person, consideration should be given as to whether the necessary causative link can be established. It is necessary for the prosecution to prove each element of section 40 beyond reasonable doubt and the 'act or default' must be 'wrongful'[15]. Therefore if it is possible that the defect or problem which has given rise to the contravention of the safety provision arose after the relevant supply by the individual or company concerned detailed consideration should be given to attacking this element of the prosecution case. If the prosecution seek to rely upon section 40(2) and proceed against any director, manager, secretary or similar officer of a body corporate regard must be had to the nature and extent of the knowledge available to the individual and his exact duties within the company. It should be noted that this section allows commission of an offence if the act was attributable to consent or connivance or to any neglect. Although knowledge is an essential requirement for consent[16] and connivance requires something more than mere negligence[17], neglect means that the offence may be committed where there is only a failure to perform a duty which a person knows or ought to have known should have been carried out[18]. It is therefore often surprising how many senior individuals within a company are caught by the scope of this section.

10.6 DEFENCES – DUE DILIGENCE

If it is likely that the prosecution will make out a prima facie case then consideration has to be given as to whether reliance may be placed upon a statutory defence. By far the most important statutory defence is that provided by section 39 of the 1987 Act or Regulation 14 of the General Product Safety Regulations 1994 ie 'due diligence'[19].

10.6.1 Due diligence

Section 39 of the Consumer Protection Act 1987[20] follows the same basic wording contained within section 25 of the Fair Trading Act 1973, section 24

15 See *Noss Farm Products Ltd v Lilico* [1945] 2 All ER 609. See also the footnotes to s 40.
16 See *Lamb v Wright & Co* [1924] 1 KB 857.
17 See *Huckerby v Elliott* [1970] 1 All ER 189.
18 *Re Hughes, Rea v Black* [1943] Ch 296; *Crickitt v Kursall Casino Ltd (No 2)* [1968] 1 All ER 139, HL.
19 See also the defence of 'reasonable cause' when considering an offence under s 32.
20 Also see Reg 14 of the General Product Safety Regulations 1994 which also sets out a defence of due diligence, and states that in proceedings against any person for an offence under ss 10, 12(1), (2) or (3), 13(4), 14(6) or 20(1) it shall be a defence for that person to show that he took all reasonable steps, and exercised all due diligence to avoid committing the offence. It is important to note that the Directive does not contain a provision allowing such a defence and its presence may be open to challenge. See further chapter 4, *European Perspective*.

of the Trade Descriptions Act 1968 and section 100 of the Food Act 1984. Hence, a considerable body of casework has built up in which the phrase has been considered.

Due diligence is in law the converse of negligence, as negligence concedes a reprehensible state of mind and a lack of care for the consequences of physical acts on the part of the person doing them. Therefore, in essence, to establish a defence under this section the defendant needs to show that he acted without negligence. Although the phrase sets out two cumulative elements it seems clear that the obligation to exercise due diligence is virtually indistinguishable from the obligation to exercise reasonable care[1] and essentially the two requirements overlap. The burden of proof for establishing the defence under section 39[2] lies upon the defendant and it is to establish the defence upon balance of probabilities[3]. The defence is open to any defendant regardless of the position within the supply chain, and each case will turn upon its individual facts. Hence, in a case where both the manufacturer and the retailer are being prosecuted each will have to establish its own due diligence defence, bearing in mind the relevant circumstances. Both could succeed or fail or indeed one could succeed and one fail.

As the Consumer Protection Act 1987 does not produce strict liability it allows for the concept of 'blameworthiness'[4]. The application of the Act and offences under it must therefore be viewed in the light of commercial and practical reality if sense is to be made of the presence of the defence.

The duties of both producers and 'distributors' are to a large extent now enshrined in the General Product Safety Regulations 1994. Under Regulation 8(1)(b) and (2) the **producer** shall 'within the limits of his activity'[5] adopt measures commensurate with the characteristics of the products which he supplies, to enable him to be informed of the risks which these products might present and to take appropriate action, including, if necessary, withdrawing the product in question from the market to avoid these risks. Such steps may include:

(i) the marking of the products or product batches in such a way that they can be identified;
(ii) sample testing of marketed products;
(iii) investigating complaints;
(iv) keeping distributors informed of such monitoring.

By Regulation 9 a **distributor** shall act with due care in order to help ensure that no producer places a product on the market unless it is a safe product and in particular:

(i) shall not supply products to any person which he knows, or should have presumed, on the basis of the information in his possession and as a professional, arc dangerous products; and
(ii) within the limits of his activities[6], a distributor shall participate in monitoring the safety of products placed on the market, in particular by

1 *Riverstone Meat Co Pty Ltd v Lancashire Shipping Co* [1960] 1 All ER 193, CA.
2 And Reg 14 of the General Product Safety Regulations 1994.
3 *R v Carr-Briant* [1943] 2 All ER 156; *Sherratt v Geralds the American Jewellers* (1970) 68 LGR 56.
4 See *Tesco Supermarkets Ltd v Nattrass* [1971] 2 All ER 127 at 131 D, HL.
5 See the footnotes to the General Product Safety Regulations, Reg 8. In relation to distributors this phrase is likely to refer to the capacity of a person (or company) given his position in the supply chain, to influence the safety of a product. However, in relation to a producer who is at the top of a supply chain this phrase is likely to be seen against a primary duty not to manufacture or import unsafe goods.
6 See the footnote above, and the footnotes to Reg 9 below.

passing on information of the product risks and cooperating in the action taken to avoid these risks.

Thus, in order to comply with the Regulations, systems must be in operation and steps taken to comply with the relevant requirements having regard to whether the company is acting as a producer or a distributor. The clear intention is to require in-house systems to be in place, because in the long run these are the only really effective method of avoiding the placing of unsafe products onto the market. It is also interesting to note the specific reference under sections 8(2)(4) and 9(b) to the passing of information between a distributor and producer. It is very clear that the new regime set out in the Regulations requires monitoring *after* the products are supplied onto the market. Whereas in many previous cases the question of whether due diligence and reasonable precautions could be shown focused upon the steps taken up to the time of supply the test is now likely to be much wider and questions asked as to what steps the defendant took to continue to monitor the safety of the goods after supply. This new duty under the Regulations will considerably increase the burden on both producer and distributor and effectively close the door on the defence to those who do not have specific systems in operation to avoid the supplying of unsafe products onto the market.

When considering a defence of due diligence and reasonable precautions it is necessary to look at the information available to and steps taken by the company. Previous cases can only give general guidance, but they clearly show that the defence will in practice be difficult to establish, and indeed it has been argued that it is gradually 'disappearing'[7]. When analysing whether the defence may be available the following principles are of assistance.

10.6.2 External information

10.6.2.1 Contractual requirements

Whilst the contractual requirements of importers or distributors are an important and perhaps necessary component in establishing the defence it is highly unlikely that they will be sufficient without further steps or precautions. In *Riley v Webb*[8] it was held that contractual condition on the order for the goods that they must conform with statutory safety requirements was of itself insufficient to amount to the taking of reasonable precautions in the exercise of all due diligence.

10.6.2.2 Guarantees, general assurances and other certificates

The effect of the authorities concerning guarantees and assurances seems to be that they should be obtained but cannot of themselves establish the defence. In *Sherratt v Geralds the American Jewellers Ltd*[9] the evidence from the defendant was that a watch had been bought from reputable wholesalers with whom they had dealt for some time and with whom they had had no previous trouble. The defendant relied upon the reputation and experience of the wholesalers, and upon the fact that the watch had been supplied as waterproof. The defence failed

7 See Cotter [1992] 142 NLJ 133, 170.
8 (1987) 151 JP 372.
9 (1970) 68 LGR 256, 114 Sol Jo 147.

as not even an elementary test had been made, such as dipping the watch in a bowl of water. In *Hicks v Sullam Ltd*[10] the subject matter of the prosecution was unsafe electric light bulbs. The importer had no sampling procedure for testing safety and obtained no independent test report, but relied upon verbal assurances from agents as to the quality of the bulbs. The agents had proved satisfactory in the past. It was felt that the company did not 'avail itself of the possibility of professional sampling' and that therefore it could not be right that the defence was made out. There was no specific evidence before the Court that the agent felt able to give any assurances about the goods and no evidence that the importer asked the agents whether they carried out random sampling or whether they submitted any design to independent examination. In *Taylor v Lawrence Fraser (Bristol) Ltd*[11] toys were brought from France on the condition that at the time of the supply they complied with the then current Toys (Safety) Regulations 1989. The importers had purchased the toy and others only having been given an assurance that they complied with the Regulations. The importer did not carry out any sampling or checking nor did they employ any independent person to do so on their behalf. Lord Widgery stated:

> 'I draw particular attention to the practice apparently of these Respondents of relying on assurances of some kind from their suppliers to satisfy the Regulations then in force. Although every case depends on its own facts, I should think that there are very few cases of this kind where reliance on certificates by itself is to be treated as sufficient when there is a possibility of professional sampling, and that possibility has been deliberately rejected by the policy of the company.'

In the case of *Rotherham Metropolitan Borough Council v Raysun (UK) Ltd*[12] the Company dealt with manufacturers through agents based in Hong Kong. The duties of the agents included checking the quality of the crayons by visiting the factory and submitting samples for analysis by a government analyst in Hong Kong. The company had provided the manufacturer with the legal requirements for the production of the crayons. Only adverse reports by the Hong Kong analysist were expected to be conveyed, and no such report had been received. Further, the company had a very moderate in-house test in that a single packet of crayons was taken from each batch of up to 10,000 dozen packets. Lord Justice Woolf referred to the fact that there was no material before the Justices to indicate the basis on which the sampling was carried out by the agent, and also stated that the very moderate sampling by the company of the goods did not indicate the taking of the relevant standard of care. However in the case of *Hurley v Martinez & Co Ltd*[13] a retailer sold wine in which the incorrect percentage of alcohol was stated. When considering the defence under section 24(1) of the Trade Descriptions Act 1968 the evidence showed that the defendant did not carry out any tests or analysis of the alcoholic strength whether on a random basis or not and relied solely on the tests carried out by the producers in Germany. It was held that the question to be asked was whether the risk that an event such as happened might occur was sufficiently large to

10 (1983) 147 JP 488.

11 (1977) 121 Sol Jo 757. However, see *Carrick District Council v Taunton Vale Meat Traders* (1994) 158 JP 347, where there was successful reliance on a local authority meat inspector's certificate.

12 (1988) 158 JP 37.

13 (1990) 154 JP 821. See also *Suffolk County Council v Rexmore Wholesale Services Ltd* (1994) 159 JP 390.

demand that a small local dealer carry out sampling, bearing in mind the expense, nature of analysis and the vast number of wines supplied by the defendant. The defendant consisted of two shops and sold many different types of wine. Lord Justice Mustill stated 'I am not in any way creating a charter for retailers, whether on a large scale or otherwise, to sit back and do nothing in every case, leaving it to others to take care that the goods are what they purport to be. The earliest cases to which I have referred show very clearly that this is not so.' In *Hurley* there was no simple or straightforward test which the retailer could carry out upon the items, unlike the case of *Sherratt* where a rudimentary test was both easy and obvious. The Court was much impressed by the fact that the imposition of testing and analysis upon a retailer may in relation to some types of goods pose a commercially impossible burden. However it is also very clear that the Court was influenced by the fact that the producer was German and therefore within the Community. Lord Justice Mustill further stated 'the factual backgrounds to the cases of *Sullam* and *Raysun* are quite different from the present. Reliance was placed in those cases upon precautions supposed to have been taken by agents abroad whose activities were not subject to independent verification or enforcement by external statutory or other bodies. Here, by contrast, the production and sampling of wine was subject to a tight regime enforceable under European Community law, of which independent verification formed an integral part. Any blameworthy act or omission which might take place in the country of origin would expose the producers at least to the risk of sanctions in that country, a situation very different from that which existed, for example, in the case of *Sullam*'. Bearing in mind the requirements of the General Product Safety Regulations 1994 which mean that there are now harmonised duties for producers and distributors, it is likely that the Court will view producers outside the Community in a very different light to those within the Community. This was regularly the case in the past in any event in relation to Far Eastern imports.

10.6.2.3 Specific assurances

One of the criticisms of the system employed by the Defendant in *Taylor v Lawrence Fraser (Bristol) Ltd*[14] was the failure to specifically ascertain that certain old stock complied with new Regulations. In *Riley v Webb* it was held that the Defendant should have obtained a positive assurance from the manufacturer that pencils conformed to specific Regulations as opposed to a contractual condition that goods must conform to the relevant statutory requirement. Lord Justice Watkins stated 'Nothing short of that will suffice to satisfy the burden of proof for this defence'. Hence the Court felt that each retailer or wholesaler must be aware of the relevant Regulations in relation to each item and call for specific assurances of compliance. The duty to communicate with the supplier higher up the chain and to enquire as to the accuracy of records was also set out in *Wandsworth London Borough Council v Bentley*[15]. It is arguable that the less expertise possessed the greater the duty to make a specific enquiry or take other appropriate steps to ensure that all details supplied are correct[16].

14 Above. However, see *Carrick*, op cit.
15 [1980] RTR 429. See also *Bury Metropolitan Borough Council v United Norwest Co-op Ltd* (CO/1589/93, unreported).
16 See also *Sutton London Borough v Perry Sanger & Co Ltd* (1971) 135 JP Jo 239.

10.6.3 Internal systems

There are two major elements to an internal system. Firstly there should be appropriate sampling and testing of goods, and secondly, a system for the appropriate instruction and supervision of all employees.

10.6.3.1 Testing and sampling

In *Garrett v Boots the Chemist Ltd*[17] Lord Lane LCJ stated '[all] reasonable precautions are strong words. It has been suggested on behalf of the appellant that one obvious and reasonable precaution which could have been taken in the present case was to take random samples of the various batches of pencils which arrived at the premises of Messrs Boots the Chemist Limited. Of course I scarcely need say that every case will vary in its facts; what might be reasonable for a large retailer might not be reasonable for the village shop. But here, dealing with a concern the size of Boots, it seems to me that one obvious precaution to be taken was random sample, whether statistically controlled or not. One does not know whether the random sample would have in fact produced detection of the defective pencils. It might have, it might not have. But to say that it was not a precaution which should reasonably have been taken does not seem to me to accord with good sense'. In *Texas Homecare Products Ltd v Stockport Metropolitan Borough Council*[18] it was stated that 'reasonable diligence required the appellants to establish some kind of system, whether by random sampling of the goods or whatever, to ascertain whether the goods conformed to the description. That does not mean that the system had to be fool proof, no system could be. Nor did the Appellants have to examine every article. But they did have to do something'. In *Taylor v Lawrence Fraser (Bristol) Ltd* Lord Widgery when referring to the practice of relying on assurances from suppliers to satisfy statutory obligations stated that 'there are few cases where reliance on a certificate is sufficient, by itself, when it is possible to have samples analysed'[19]. It is quite clear from *Garrett* and *Riley* that the nature and extent of testing required of a 'distributor' will depend upon the scope of the business. Although *Sherratt* stands for the proposition that where a simple test can be carried out there may well be a duty upon a retailer to perform such a test, *Hurley v Martinez* supports the view that if testing would be unduly onerous it may be reasonable to rely upon the tests or assurances of the producers or importers. It is submitted that it is reasonably clear from the authorities and the effect of the General Product Safety Regulations 1994 that:

(i) a producer or importer *has* to test items to ensure that there is compliance with the relevant Regulations[20];

17 (16 July 1980, unreported), DC.

18 (1987) 152 JP 83, DC. See also *Berkshire County Council v Olympic Holidays* (1993) 158 JP 421 where there was an 'unexplained and isolated' incident involving a computer after 'extensive' testing of the software, and the defence was held to be made out.

19 However, in *Suffolk County Council v Rexmore Wholesale Services Ltd* (1994) 159 JP 390, the Defendant successfully relied upon a certificate produced for its supplier by an independent laboratory and passed on to the Defendant. See also *Carrick District Council v Taunton Vale Meat Traders Ltd* (1994) 158 JP 347, where there was successful reliance upon a local authority meat traders' certificate, and *Hurley v Martinez & Co Ltd*, para 10.6.2.2 above.

20 In *Davies Products (Liverpool) v Jones* 90 Journal of Trading Standards Law (9) 159 toys had been imported from Bulgaria. No toys from the batches had been submitted for analysis although the company had submitted a sample toy provided by the manufacturer for testing before agreeing to import. The toy so submitted proved to be satisfactory. The Judge dismissed

(ii) a distributor will have to consider whether random sampling or external testing of the goods is possible or appropriate. The requirement may depend upon the number of items and the size and concern of the business. There will be a higher duty if the test is easy and straightforward and less if it is expensive, requiring external assistance or the destruction of the item[1]

10.6.3.2 Testing procedures

Although Lord Lane in *Garrett* left open the question as to whether random sampling should be statistically controlled or not, the question was considered in detail in *P & M Supplies (Essex) Ltd v Devon County Council*[2]. In that case the Defendant had an in-house testing procedure by means of random sampling. In relation to a large batch of 77,000 toys 0.49% were sampled. However the Divisional Court held that as the burden of proof in establishing the defence was upon the Defendant it should ordinarily produce statistical evidence as to what was an adequate number of tests. Lord Justice Watkins stated 'the Justices here had a difficult task seeing that they were given no assistance upon the kind of standard which either ought to be adopted or is in fact was adopted by traders such as the Defendants. Whether that evidence could come from the trade itself or from British Standards Institution literature, I feel quite unable in the light of what we know to say, but true it is that where the Defendants have to discharge such a burden, as is implicit in the terms of section 39(1) they simply cannot rely upon the prosecution producing evidence in rebuttal to repair omissions in evidence'. Lord Justice Nolan stated that 'this case illustrates the need for benches of Magistrates to be given help about these matters, preferably in the form of independent statistical evidence as to what should be done by a reasonable trader in these circumstances to avoid the sort of danger which the Regulations are intending to prevent'. Trading Standards Officers have frequently referred to the existence of a British Standard on testing and sampling (BS6000/6001) as a bench mark. Although the Standard does not set out a specific test for any given item it sets out the considerations which a company may then apply to the relevant product. A vital issue will be the degree of homogeneity within the batch. In the case of *Rotherham v Raysun*[3] sampling consisted of the taking of one packet from a total importation of 10,000 dozen. Lord Justice Woolf stated that this was a very moderate sample that by itself it did not indicate the taking of a standard of care required by statutory provisions'. However he continued and stated that 'if there had been sampling supported by evidence indicating that the standard throughout the consignment would be the same it was conceivable that to choose in such a large consignment might be sufficient'. Hence, if the item is proved to be ordinarily consistent throughout the batch (eg because the same batch of paint is used) it may be sufficient only to test a very small number (the argument must be supported by evidence that any other test would be likely to produce the same result). Indeed

an appeal by the company on the basis that one precaution which he considered reasonable which could have been taken but was not was the testing of a sample taken from the goods *actually imported*. This case tends to underline the suspicion of many Trading Standards Officers that test certificates produced outside the Community can often provide little reassurance of compliance.

1 See generally Cotter [1992] 142 NLJ 133, 170.
2 (1991) 156 JP 328.
3 (1988) 153 JP 37.

the only British Standard concerning sampling (BS6000/6001) allows this factor to be taken into account and also allows a degree of reliance upon other factors which may indicate that a small sample would be representative of the whole batch.

There should ordinarily be testing of an item from the actual batch as opposed to a pre-production sample[4] and also evidence that the tests were properly carried out. This may require, if necessary, testing by an external analyst as opposed to 'in-house'[5]. It may be necessary to produce relevant documentary evidence to support any in-house sampling or testing method[6]. It is also important to relate any test results to the requirements under the Regulations and the number of items produced or received. It is clear that simply producing laboratory certificates will not, in the absence of any other evidence, be likely to be sufficient[7]. In the case of *Balding v Lew-Ways Ltd*[8] a company did not call at trial specific evidence but produced a test certificate under the relevant British Standard. However there was no evidence that there had been a test to satisfy the Safety Requirements of the Regulations, as opposed to merely the requirement of the standard. Lord Justice Pill stated that:

> 'the Company has submitted that it was entitled to rely on the the certificate showing compliance with the British Standard. The Company has argued that it has shown due diligence by submitting the toy to a competent and reputable analyst and on receipt of the report it had been reasonable to assume that the requirements of the Regulations were the same as those of the British Standard. (The Company believed that it was entitled to conclude that the toy was good and complied with the safety requirements. Its failure to unearth the Regulations did not show that it had failed to show due diligence.) In my judgment, the Company had to show that due diligence was shown in relation to the Regulations, that is, steps towards avoiding falling below the standard required by the Regulations made under Parliamentary authority. It could not be shown that steps had been taken by showing compliance with other standards'.

His Lordship would not give guidance as to what steps should be taken but noted that there was not due diligence without further inquiries of the analyst of whether or not the toy complied with the Regulations. The company was not entitled to assume that goods complying with the British Standards automatically comply with Regulations laid down by Parliament. Whether an analysis was competent and sufficient to discharge the obligation would depend on instructions given by the company. 'The company could not establish a section 39 defence if it had not asked the analyst whether the product complied with the laws of the land'. This decision will be further strengthened by the impact of the Product Safety Regulations 1994 in significantly reducing the importance and weight to be attached to compliance with the Standards[9].

4 See *Davies Products (Liverpool) Ltd v Jones*, above.

5 See *Sutton London Borough v David Halsall plc* (1994) 159 JP 431.

6 See *Ellis v Price* (1968) 66 LGR 404, DC.

7 See *Dudley Metropolitan Council v Robert Firman Ltd* (1992) Independent, 26 October. However, in *Suffolk County Council v Rexmore Wholesale Services Ltd* (1994) 159 JP 390, the Defendant successfully relied upon a certificate produced for its supplier by an independent laboratory and passed on to the defendant.

8 (1995) 159 JP 541.

9 See General Product Safety Regulations, Reg 6. This case highlights the importance of both asking appropriate questions of an external testing agency and ensuring that the answers are adequate to satisfy the company that the product complies with the relevant Regulations.

10.6.3.3 Employee instruction and supervision

The Courts have for a long time considered it vitally important that there are systems in operation to ensure that employees can avoid the commission of offences[10]. In *Tesco Supermarkets Ltd v Nattrass*[11] Lord Diplock stated:

> '...Nowadays most business transactions for the supply of goods or services are not actually conducted by the person who in civil law is regarded as the party to any contracts made in the course of business, but by servants or agents acting on his behalf. Thus, in the majority of cases the physical acts or omissions which constitute or result in an offence under the statute will be those of servants or agents of an employer or principal on whose behalf business is carried on. That employer or principal is likely to be very often a corporate person. Consumer protection, which is the purpose of statutes of this kind, is achieved only if the commissioning of the prohibited acts or omissions is prevented. It is the deterrent effect of penal provisions which protects the consumer from the loss he would sustain if the offence were committed. If it is committed he does not receive the amount of any fine. As a taxpayer he will bear part of the expense of maintaining a convicted offender in Prison. The loss of the consumer is the same whether the acts or omissions which result in his being given inaccurate or inadequate information are intended to mislead him, or are due to carelessness or inadvertence. So is the corresponding gain to the other party to the business transaction with the consumer in the course of which those acts or omissions occur. Where, in the way the business is now conducted, these are likely to be acts or omissions of employees of that party and subject to his orders, the most effective method of deterrence is to place on the employer the responsibility of doing everything which lies within his power to prevent his employees from doing anything which will result in the commission of an offence. This, I apprehend, is the rationale and moral justification for creating in the field of consumer protection, as also in the field of public health and safety, offences of 'strict liability' for which an employer or principal in the course of whose business the offences were committed, is criminally liable, notwithstanding that they are due to the acts or omissions of his servants or agents which were done without his knowledge or consent or even where contrary to his orders. But this rationale and moral justification does not extent to penalising an employer or principal who has done everything that he can reasonable be expected to do by supervision or inspection, by improvement of his business methods or by exhorting those whom he expected to control or influence, to prevent the commission of the offence'[12].

In the *Tesco* case it was held that the defendants had set up an efficient system for the avoidance of offences under the Act and that there was proper operation of the system in that the Defendants had adequately performed that duty and had not delegated to their store managers the function of ensuring that the system was carried out. It was held that the Manager of a store was 'another person' within the meaning of section 24(1) of the Trade Descriptions Act 1968 and that the Act was due to his act or default. However any system will be closely scrutinised and must actually enable the staff to be able to detect

10 See *Baxters (Butchers) Ltd v Manley* (1985) 4 Tr L 219, *Lewin v Rothersthorpe Road Garage* (1983) 148 JP 87, *Camden London Borough Council v Fine Fare Ltd* [1987] BTLC 317; and generally R G Lawson 'The Defence of "Due Diligence"' 151 JP 499. In *Carrick District Council v Taunton Vale Meat Traders Ltd* (1994) 158 JP 347, Smith J held that the system did not have to be wholly dependent on the company and its employees but could include reliance on a local authority meat inspector's certificate.

11 [1971] 2 All ER 127.

12 See also *Lim Chin Aik v R* [1963] 1 All ER 223 at 228, *Sweet v Parsley* [1969] 1 All ER 347 at 362, and *Re Supply of Ready Mixed Concrete (No 2)* [1995] 1 All ER 135.

that the items are unsafe[13]. If an employee is aware of the relevant law and has been provided with written instructions and there has been a subsequent check that they are in fact read, the fact that employees are not supervised or constantly reminded of the instructions may not defeat the defence[14]. It is however clear that there must be both an adequate system set up (ie adequately enabling the employee to detect a problem), and regular test or inspection to ensure that the system is in fact carried out. If a company can establish these features it will not be necessary to actually prove how an offence occurred and the prosecution will not be able to rely upon the maxim 'res ipsa loquitur' in rebuttal[15]. However, it should not be fogotten that an enforcement authority has a wide range of powers under the Act to secure the production of documents and that evidence will be required to prove the existence of a system at trial. Although it is not always necessary to call evidence from the employees who may have been guilty of the mistake which led to an offence and 'breach' of the system, it will be important to note that they are highly unlikely to be the subject of a prosecution relying upon section 40(1) of the Consumer Protection Act 1987. Indeed, in *R v Warwickshire County Council, ex p Johnson*[16] it was held that a mere employee could not be prosecuted under this Section, Lord Roskill stating that 'in the course of any business' must mean any business of which the Defendant is either the owner or in which he has controlling interest'[17]. A Court will often be influenced by the admission of an employee that he or she has made a mistake notwithstanding the existence of a system of prevention.

10.6.4 Section 39 – essential elements

It is therefore clear that individual producers and distributors, must direct attention to establishing systems to avoid the commission of potential offences not only to comply with the provisions of the General Product Safety Regulations 1994, but also if there is ever to be the prospect of relying upon a defence under Section 39 of the 1987 Act or Regulation 14 of the 1994 Regulations if a mistake occurs. Reliance on contractual requirements, assurances, test certificates or regular inspection by Trading Standards Officers[18] are not of themselves likely to be sufficient to establish a defence. A proper system should contain a number of different elements. Certainly consideration should be given to:

(i) inspection of the importer or producer's premises or credentials[19];
(ii) contractual requirements that items satisfy the specific Regulations relevant to the goods;
(iii) the production of the relevant producer's or importer's test certificates;

13 See *Turtington v United Co-operatives Ltd* [1993] Crim LR 376.
14 See *Hereford and Worcester County Council v T and S Stores plc* (1994) Times, 4 November, DC.
15 See *Cow and Gate Nutricia Ltd v Westminster City Council* (1995) Independent, 24 April, DC.
16 [1993] AC 583, [1993] 1 All ER 299, HL.
17 See footnotes to s 40(1), and Wells: Corporate Liability and Consumer Protection; *Tesco v Nattrass* revisited [1994] 57 MLR 817.
18 See *Taylor v Lawrence Fraser (Bristol) Ltd* (1977) 121 Sol Jo 757. In *Bury Metropolitan Borough Council v United Norwest Co-op Ltd* (CO/3252/93, unreported) reliance upon a warranty said to be in letters was not enough to make out the defence. However, in *Carrick District Council v Taunton Vale Meat Traders Ltd* (1994) 158 JP 347, a defence of due diligence was made out after reliance on a meat inspector's certificate.
19 See *P & M Supplies (Essex) Ltd v Devon County Council* (1991) 156 JP 328 at 331H.

(iv) if necessary, in-house testing and random sampling of the goods;
(v) external testing of the items;
(vi) liaison with local enforcement authorities over any areas of doubt or dispute[20];
(vii) the setting up of a system to ensure compliance with the Regulations and/or that unsafe goods are not supplied upon the market including the instruction of employees as to inspection or testing for quality assurance and safety and the content of the relevant Regulations;
(viii) in-house systems so that products can be traced or relevant production batches identified[1];
(ix) sample testing of marketed products ie testing in the field[2];
(x) a proper system for the evaluating of any problems that come to light in relation to safety or quality assurance, including a detailed follow-up of any deviation within the batch from the required standard and the reasons for this[3];
(xi) liaison with the producer, distributor or any other professionals within the supply chain[4];
(xii) a system for recall or withdrawal of the product in question from the market[5]. Also note the importance of the system having a sufficiently mandatory effect upon retailers or distributors[6];
(xiii) statistical analysis of the testing methods to ensure that appropriate numbers are being sample and/or tested.

All this must be seen as additional to pre-and post-production testing of the item by the manufacturer or producer to ensure that it complies with the relevant design and that there have not been any production mistakes.

Finally it should be noted that if a defence of due diligence and reasonable precaution is established before the Magistrates the Divisional Court will only interfere if there was no evidence or no reasonable bench of Magistrates properly directed could have arrived at the conclusion[7].

10.7 PRACTICAL CONSIDERATIONS WHEN DEALING WITH A COMPLAINT/PROSECUTION

10.7.1 The Due Diligence Notice

In order to rely upon the defence of Due Diligence under either section 39 of the Act or Regulation 14 of the General Product Safety Regulations 1994 it is necessary to comply with the procedural requirements[8]. It is stated that where a party wishes to rely upon the defence that he took all reasonable steps and exercised all due diligence to avoid committing the offence, and that reliance involves an allegation that the commission of the offence was due either to:

20 And possibly also a local authority certificate as in *Carrick* op cit.
1 Regulation 8(2)(i) of the General Product Safety Regulations 1994; see also BS5750 and BSEN ISO 9000.
2 Regulation 8(2)(ii).
3 Regulation 8(2)(3).
4 See Reg 8(2)(4) and Reg 8(1)(B).
5 See Reg 8(1)(B).
6 See *Coventry City Council v Ackerman Group plc* [1995] Crim LR 140.
7 See *R C Hammett Ltd v Crabb* (1931) 95 JP 180.
8 Requirements are the same under s 39 or Reg 14.

(i) the act or default of another; or
(ii) reliance on information given by another
that person shall not, without leave of the Court, be entitled to rely upon the defence unless not less than seven clear days before the hearing of the proceedings, he has served a notice upon the person bringing the proceedings. The notice shall give such information identifying or assisting in the identification of the person who committed the act or default or gave the information as is in the possession of the person serving the notice at the time that he serves it[9]. Save as is set out within the section there is no duty upon the Defendant to disclose either the nature and extent of the defence or evidence that is to be called at the trial. The section is supposed to give the prosecution advance notice so that it is not to be 'ambushed' or surprised during the trial. However, in practice seven clear days gives little time for comprehensive investigation or detailed evaluation of information given within a Due Diligence notice. However, if the notice is served and there is thereafter no immediate application for an adjournment it will frequently be difficult for the prosecution to seek such an adjournment on the day of the trial. If the notice is not served then such an adjournment is usually inevitable, frequently with an accompanying order against the Defendant or its legal advisors for costs thrown away. Only in the most unusual circumstances (or most limited of defences), will the court allow the Defendant to rely upon a defence in the absence of a properly served notice. The seven day period is usually thought to be one which affords the prosecution the minimum of time available and any further erosion of the timescale will not be acceptable. The fact that such little time is available highlights the need for the prosecution to investigate the nature and extent of any possible Due Diligence defence at an earlier stage[10]. In the past those defending an action by way of reliance upon a Due Diligence defence often faced a dilemma of either giving an early and comprehensive disclosure of all information to the prosecution with the hope that the likely establishment of the defence would be accepted and the prosecution dropped, or the provision of very limited information within a notice served in compliance with the minimum time requirements in the hope that the short space of time would not allow the prosecution to comprehensively evaluate the strength of the defence, thereby securing a tactical advantage. However, having regard to the matters set out above in relation to the present requirements for establishing the defence, little is likely to be gained from the latter course. A weak defence is unlikely to succeed in any event and few prosecuting authorities are now happy to proceed with a case against a Defendant who has a strong Due Diligence defence[11].

When considering the providing of details of the fact that the commission of the offence was due to the act or default of another regard should be had to the provisions of section 40 of the Act. The section states that where the commission by any person of an offence to which section 39 above applies is due to an act or default committed by some other person in the course of any business of his, the other person may be proceeded against and punished whether or not proceedings are taken against the first mentioned person. Therefore, if

9 Section 39(2) and (3), Reg 14(2) and (3).
10 See further 9.7, *Evidence in Rebuttal*, above.
11 Strong Due Diligence defences are rare and it the prosecution fails to defeat the defence then it will have to pay its own costs. Further it is possible to give an early and comprehensive disclosure of the Due Diligence defence and to request that the prosecution discontinue the case, failing which application for costs will be sought against the authority itself rather than the usual order from central funds: see *Costs*, below.

the prosecuting authority is informed th ission of defence was due to the act or default of a third party then ıtial communication with that party indicating the possiblity of pros vell secure the immediate provision of comprehensive information ıird party[12].

10.7.2 Publicity

Due to the obviously adverse effects of publicity many Defendants will seek advice as to any method of obviating or minimising the risk of the reporting of any proceedings. However, save in exceptional circumstances, court proceedings must take place in public and the press are free to report. Reporting restrictions can be imposed under section 11 of the Contempt of Court Act 1981 but this power to prevent or restrict the publication of court proceedings is a jurisdiction which is only exercised very sparingly, in exceptional circumstances and only where it can be shown to be necessary[13].

10.7.3 Costs

As to be expected an unsuccessful Defendant will be asked by the prosecution to pay the costs of the investigation and trial. Ordinarily a schedule of such costs will be handed up at the conclusion of the hearing and the Court will make an order in such sum as it thinks fit[14]. Likewise a successful Defendant will ordinarily be able to obtain its costs from central funds if the prosecution is unsuccessful, unless there are positive reasons for not doing so[15]. Sometimes

12 Whereas if the prosecution is only alerted as to the identity of the person whose act or default is said to have caused the commission of the offence *after* the expiry of the period for the commencement of proceedings in relation to the offence, then the threat of this sanction may have little effect and the third party may well be less co-operative.

13 See *R v Dover Justices, ex p Dover District Council and Wells* (1991) 156 JP 433, [1992] Crim LR 371. In this case the justices imposed reporting restrictions on the ground that:
(1) Publication of the details of the prosecution was of itself a penalty highly prejudicial to the Defendant's business;
(2) The publicity would bring about the closure of business in any event;
(3) The Defendant had a defence to each of the Summons including the defence that there had been oppressive actions by the local authority by which the proceedings were brought.

In quashing the order Neil LJ stated that 'each case must be looked at on its own facts, but save in exceptional circumstances court proceedings must take place in public and the press are free to report. There are exceptions as the Courts recognise and indeed as the statute itself recognises, but this is not such a case. All that can be said is that economic damage, perhaps very severe economic damage may be done to the defendant if publicity is not withheld'.

See also *Macdougall v Knight* (1889) 14 App Cas 194; *Scott v Scott* [1913] AC 417; *R v Horsham Justices, ex p Farquharson* [1982] QB 762; *R v Evesham Justices, ex p McDonagh* [1988] QB 553.

14 This will ordinarily be the full sum unless the defence can raise a good argument as to why a particular element should be excluded or reduced.

15 See s 16 of the Prosecution of Offences Act 1985 and the *Practice Direction on Costs in Criminal Cases* [1991] 1 WLR 498; cf *Berkshire County Council v Olympic Holidays Ltd* (1993) 158 JP 421, where costs were not given after successful reliance upon a defence under s 39. Positive reasons for not awarding costs include:
(a) the Defendant's own conduct brought suspicion upon himself or has misled the prosecution into thinking that the case against him is stronger than it is;
(b) the Defence consisted of a reliance upon a technicality; and
(c) the Defendant was convicted of some offences but acquitted of others.

the Court will wish to order a specific sum at the conclusion of the hearing but most Courts will allow the bill to be submitted in due course to be taxed by the relevant court officer. In very unusual circumstances a successful Defendant may apply for an order that the prosecuting authority should pay the costs[16]. Such orders are very rarely made. An unsuccessful prosecuting authority normally has to pay its own costs.

10.8 DEALING WITH ALTERNATIVES TO PROSECUTION

As seen above[17] after or indeed during an investigation as to whether there has been a contravention by goods or any safety provision[18], the relevant authority has the power to issue a suspension notice or to seek forfeiture of the goods. Further, in appropriate circumstances liaison with the Secretary of State may lead to a prohibition notice or a notice to warn. In each case if the step is taken there is an opportunity afforded to the person the subject of the notice, order, or application to contest or challenge the matter. Details are as follows:

(a) *Suspension notice*

A suspension notice is issued under section 14 of the Act and has a life of up to six months unless a prosecution or an application for forfeiture is pending[19]. There is a specific method of challenge by way of appeal set out at section 15 of the Act. It is clear that in ordinary cases this procedure must be followed as opposed to seeking judicial review of the issue of the notice[20]. An application under section 15 may be made in the course of any proceedings brought by way of prosecution or for forfeiture of goods under section 16 or, where no such proceedings have been brought, by way of complaint to the Magistrates Court[1]. It is to be noted that once an application by way of complaint is made under section 15 the enforcement authority may in the proceedings apply for a forfeiture order pursuant to section 16. There has been considerable debate upon the onus and standard of proof under section 15[2]. Ordinarily it should be for the Defendant to prove that there has been no contravention of any safety provision upon the balance of probabilities. Any person who has an interest in the goods in respect of which a notice is for the time in force may apply for the order setting aside the notice. It is of particular importance to note that where an enforcement authority serves a suspension notice in respect of goods and it is subsequently shown by a relevant party that there has been no contravention in relation to those goods of any safety provision (and the issue of the suspension notice was not attributable to any neglect or default

16 See Costs in Criminal Cases (General Regulations) 1986, Reg 3; *DPP v Denning* [1991] 2 QB 532 and *Suffolk County Council v Rexmore*, op cit. See also s 19A of Prosecution of Offences Act 1985; 'a wasted costs order'.
17 See chapter 8, *Methods of Enforcement*.
18 See in this respect Reg 11 of the General Product Safety Regulations 1994.
19 See s 14(4).
20 See *R v Birmingham City Council, ex p Ferrero Ltd* [1993] 1 All ER 530, CA.
1 See s 15(2)(b).
2 See footnotes to s 15 below.
3 See s 14(7).

by the party challenging the notice) then that authority is liable to pay compensation to that party[3]. Any dispute as to the amount of compensation payable under the section should be determined by arbitration (sub-section 8);

(b) *Application for forfeiture*
By virtue of section 16 of the Act an enforcement authority may apply for an order for forfeiture of any goods on the grounds that there has been a contravention in relation to the goods of a relevant safety provision. An order may be sought within a prosecution in relation to an alleged offence, where there has been an appeal against a suspension notice or against the detention of goods[4], or otherwise by way of complaint to the Magistrates Court. The Court shall make the order for forfeiture only if it is satisfied that there has been a contravention in relation to the goods of a safety provision. Hence it is for the prosecution to prove contravention beyond reasonable doubt. Even if there has been a contravention of a relevant safety provision the Court does not necessarily have to order forfeiture. When considering what to do with the goods the Court may, if it considers it appropriate to do so, direct that the goods to which the order relates shall, instead of being destroyed, be released to a person such as the Court may specify, on condition that the person does not supply those goods to any person other than:
(i) to a person who carries on the business of buying goods and repairing or reconditioning them;
(ii) to a person who purchases the articles as scrap (ie for the value of the materials included in the articles rather than for the articles themselves)[5].

(c) *Prohibition notices and notices to warn*
The Secretary of State may serve on any person a notice prohibiting that person (except with the consent of the Secretary of State) from supplying or otherwise dealing with any goods that the Secretary of State considers are unsafe and are described within the notice. Further, the Secretary of State may serve on any person a notice ('a Notice to Warn') requiring that person, at his own expense, to publish in a form and manner, specified in the notice, a warning about any relevant goods that the Secretary of State considers are unsafe, which that person supplies or has supplied and which are described in the notice[6]. Schedule 2 to the Act contains the procedure as to the issue of and the challenging of prohibition notices and notices to warn. The issue of either type of notice is a rare event.

4 See s 33.
5 See ss 16(7) and 16(7)(a) and (b).
6 See s 13.

Chapter 11

RESIDUAL CRIMINAL LIABILITY

11.1 TRADE DESCRIPTIONS ACT 1968

As can be seen from the Consumer Protection Act 1987[1] and the General Product Safety Regulations 1994[2] the presentation of the product whether by way of packaging, labelling, or instructions for assembly, maintenance, use or disposal, or indeed any other information provided by the producer in written form may be of vital significance when considering overall safety. If a specific 'description' given on or with the product is false, a relevant person may face not only a prosecution under the 1987 Act or the 1994 Regulations but also prosecution under the Trade Descriptions Act 1968. The workings and interpretation of the Act are covered in a number of texts[3]. The following points are however of general significance:

(i) the Act extends to transactions between traders;
(ii) the main offence is contained within section 1, and thereafter sections 2 to 6 of the Act provide definitions of the words and phrases used within this section. The term 'trade description' is defined in Section 2. Section 3 states that a false trade description is a trade description which is false 'to a material degree'. Section 4 deals with the application of the trade description. Section 5 is primarily concerned with trade descriptions used in advertisements, and section 6 deals with the supply;
(iii) when considering a false trade description[4], there is no need to prove an intention to deceive[5];
(iv) section 23 closely mirrors section 40 of the 1987 Act and Regulation 15 of the General Product Safety Regulations 1994 in dealing with the position where the offence is due to the act or default of another, and enables that other to be the subject of a prosecution;
(v) there is a defence of due diligence and reasonable precautions set out in section 24 of the Act;
(vi) the right to prosecute for an offence is not limited to a local or enforcement authority[6];

1 See s 10(2)(a).
2 See Reg 2 and the definition of a 'safe product'.
3 See particularly O-Keefe 'The Law Relating to Trade Descriptions' (Butterworths).
4 See Trade Description Act 1968, s 31.
5 See *Alec Norman Garages Ltd v Phillips* (1984) 148 JP 741 cf s 14 in which *mens rea* is required.
6 See *Snodgrass v Topping* (1952)116 JP 312.

(vii) no prosecution may be commenced after three years from the commission of the offence, or one year from its discovery[7], whichever is the earlier;
(viii) trial may be summary or upon indictment.

In appropriate circumstances enforcement authorities will lay informations alleging breaches of both the 1987 Act (or Regulations made under section 11 or the 1994 General Product Safety Regulations) and the Trade Descriptions Act 1968. Frequently the combination of alleged offences will not reflect additional culpability[8]. It should however be noted that by virtue of the fact that the offence is triable 'either way' courts will frequently perceive an allegation of a breach of the Trade Descriptions Act 1968 as more serious than an allegation of a breach of the Act or relevant Regulations arising out of the same facts.

11.2 THE FAIR TRADING ACT 1973

Part III of the Fair Trading Act 1973 empowers the Director-General of Fair Trading to obtain undertakings from businessmen persisting in conduct detrimental to the interests of consumers and to take proceedings before the Restrictive Practices Court or other appropriate court if necessary. Relevant detriment may be economic or relating to health, safety or otherwise[9]. The Act is aimed at traders whose conduct is regularly in breach of their civil obligations or who persistently contravene duties, prohibitions or restrictions imposed by the criminal law, whether or not the conduct has resulted in a conviction[10]. The Director-General will take in to account complaints received from consumers as well as other information collected by or furnished to him, usually by enforcement authorities. Ordinarily the first step will be to obtain a satisfactory written assurance that the trader will refrain from continuing the course of conduct which has been the source of complaint[11]. If the Director does not receive a satisfactory assurance or if there is a subsequent breach, the Director may bring proceedings in the Restrictive Practices Court under section 35 or in smaller cases in the County Court in the relevant District[12]. If such proceedings are brought the court may make an order that the trader or any accessory, director, or officer of the company, should refrain from the conduct in question. Alternatively undertakings may be sought. Breach of any undertaking given or order made would put the defendant in contempt of court and in severe risk of imprisonment, or at the very least a substantial fine.

7 See *R v Beaconsfield Justices, ex p Johnson & Sons Ltd* (1985) 149 JP 535.
8 This is perhaps most clearly the case where specific Regulations require a mark of conformity within the regulations eg the Toys (Safety) Regulations 1989. If a toy fails to comply with the Regulations then axiomatically the mark denoting conformity is a false trade description.
9 See s 34.
10 See s 34(2) and (3).
11 See for example *R v Director-General of Fair Trading, ex p FH Taylor & Co Ltd* [1981] ICR 292, in relation to the importation of toys and electrical equipment where there had been thirty convictions under the Consumer Protection Act 1961.
12 See s 41.

Chapter 12

NORTHERN IRELAND AND SCOTLAND

Parts II, IV and V of the Consumer Protection Act 1987 apply to both Northern Ireland and Scotland.[1] However it is to be noted that with regard to procedural aspects of the implementation of the criminal liability sections of the Act there is a division between the jurisdictions for England, Wales and Northern Ireland and that of Scotland. This is reflected by the fact that many sections make specific provision for the Scottish jurisdiction. Whilst this text does not cover procedural workings of the Act in Scotland (and regard must be had to specialist texts) the substantive law falls to be interpreted in the same fashion in all of the jurisdictions within the United Kingdom.

Specific provisions in relation to Northern Ireland and Scotland are:

(i) Northern Ireland

Sections 11(3)(d), 15(5)(b), 27(1)(e) and (2), section 30(10), section 33(4)(e) and section 49.

(ii) Scotland[2]

Section 11(3)(f), 14(8), 15(2)(c), 15(4), 17, 27(4), 30(9), 33(2)(c) and 34(2).

(Further it is to be noted that under the General Product Safety Regulations 1994 the Regulations 11(b), 14(2), 15(4)[3] and 16(2) and (3) apply to Scotland.)

1 Parts I and III of the Act do not apply to Northern Ireland.
2 Note also that Sch 1 applies only to England and Wales.
3 Compare the procedural requirements in s 39 which make no reference to the trial diet.

Chapter 13

CASE STUDIES

13.1 A DEFECTIVE TEDDY BEAR

A complains to her local Trading Standards Officer that having bought a large teddy bear from B Ltd, and given it to her two year old daughter to play with, she discovered the child a couple of hours later with the teddy bear's right eye in her mouth. It had become detached from the toy. A states that she threw away the packaging prior to giving the toy to the child, and also removed a label which had been sewn on to the bear's leg. She recalls that the label had a 'CE sign' upon it with a name and address and also the phrase 'Made in China'.

13.1.1 Discussion

The first step for the local Authority is to gain an expert opinion upon the safety of the teddy bear. Happily the left eye remains upon the toy and can therefore be the subject of a relevant test by a public analyst. When sending the item to the public analyst it is important to:

(i) record the item properly and try to restrict the number of people who have to be involved in the delivery of the item to the public analyst;

(ii) instruct the public analyst correctly.

The analyst (who should be familiar with the requirement to document closely any dealings with or tests upon the item and the results) should be asked to note that the item has been the subject of play by a child and hence possibly a degree of 'abuse'. The analyst should therefore closely examine (and possibly photograph) the state of the toy *prior* to testing to give an expert opinion as to the amount if any of relevant wear and tear prior to the said test. The analyst should be asked to apply the relevant test (in this case under EN 71 as a standard setting out the tests appropriate for the general safety requirements contained within the Toys (Safety) Regulations 1989). The analyst should be asked to carry out all other appropriate tests and to give an expert opinion as to whether the toy complies with the requirements of the *Regulations* (as opposed to the standard).

Having established from the public analyst the remaining eye on the bear would fail the requirements of the relevant legislation the Local Authority Officer should immediately contact *and visit* B Ltd. B Ltd should be asked to confirm that the item in question was sold to A. (This is unlikely to be in dispute). Thereafter (and after reference to the powers contained within section 29 and section 32 of the Act), B Ltd should be asked to provide relevant records and information as to who supplied it with the goods. Further, there should be investigation as to whether any goods of the same or of a similar type remain in the premises. These goods can be seized and/or detained; see section 29, and a suspension notice (if necessary) issued (section 14). B Ltd should be asked to explain its in-house systems, procedures, and other steps taken to comply with the requirements of domestic safety legislation (particularly if subject to Regulation 9 of the General Product Safety Regulations 1994). Bearing in mind the matters set out above[1] in relation to the defence under section 39 once all relevant information from B Ltd has been obtained a view can be taken as to whether there is likely to be a prosecution of this company in due course. If there is to be no prosecution then B Ltd can be asked to provide a statement so as to help prove the chain of supply.

B Ltd refers to documentation showing that the item was supplied by a large scale importer (C Plc). It also produces four other examples of this type of bear retained in B Ltd's stock.

The officer should then contact C Plc as well as sending the other four bears to the analyst for testing. As these items have been effectively seized and detained regard should be given to the duty under section 30(6) to allow scope for C Plc to have one or more of the four bears tested (as the first item was not a test purchase section 28 will not apply to the original bear). Consideration should therefore be given to asking the analyst to test a percentage of the bears or to test one eye on each of the bears.

C Plc should be approached to confirm that the item in question was supplied by the company. Copies of the accompanying documentation (usually enclosing a photograph of the item in question) should be sent. C Plc should be asked either for facilities for an inspection of the relevant records (again relying upon section 29 and section 32), or if appropriate an interview within the provisions of the Police and Criminal Evidence Act 1994. It would probably be premature at this stage to issue a suspension notice under section 14, particularly bearing in mind the compensation provisions if the notice were to be issued and there was subsequently found to be no contravention of the relevant safety provisions.

13.1.2 C Plc

C Plc should consider the following matters:

(i) was the item in question actually supplied by the company and further can the prosecution prove that it was so supplied. As it appears that A cannot assist as to the manufacturer or importer of the item, much will depend upon B Ltd's records. If those records prove that the item was supplied by C Plc then there should be an immediate admission of this fact;

(ii) using any documentation provided by B Ltd, C Plc should immediately try and trace the item back to any batch or consignment and investigate whether any other items from the same generic group are defective. If it is the case that other items are defective then consideration must be given to an immediate recall of the whole batch by contacting relevant distributors. Further consideration should be given as to whether provisional steps should be taken to try and increase the scope of

1 See chapter 9, *Evidence in Rebuttal.*

individuals informed of the requirement to return the item (eg by use of the press/media);

(iii) If no other items in the batch have been reported to be defective then examples from remaining stock should be sent to the public analyst for further testing. These should be cross-referenced against any earlier tests (eg pre-distribution) carried out by analysts to see if there has been any deviation within the batch.

Thereafter, a detailed analysis of all steps taken to avoid commission of any offence should be drawn up so as to evaluate the strength of any section 39 defence. All tests, reports and documentation together with statistical analysis of the number of items tested in-house and externally, should be assembled[2].

The matters set out above should be addressed as soon as possible as it is highly unlikely that the enforcement authority will be prepared to wait any extended length of time for further information. Once the information has been compiled consideration should be given as to C Plc's stance *before* attending any interview with the enforcement authority, or entering into detailed correspondence. C Plc should consider:

(i) an admission that the company did supply the item;

(ii) whether it is believed that the item as supplied was safe or not (for example, if no other tests have produced a defective item consideration may be given as to whether the item was damaged by someone within the employ of B Ltd, or indeed by A or some other person in the household before giving the toy to the child). C Plc should in any event request that the prosecution submit details of any test reports so that they can be cross-referenced against C Plc's own analyst's results and possibly request examples of the bears seized by the Authority, so that they can be inspected. It may be that the method of testing can be challenged (although in the instant example this would be unlikely). It is also possible that the labelling on the box or on the item itself (as discarded by A) would materially alter the safety of the item. Again consideration should be given as to whether the item as a whole would pass the requirements of the relevant legislation (in the present example by virtue of the content of European Standard EN 71 any warning that a soft toy should not be given to a child under the age of three years would be deemed to be of no effect. The item should be tested as if it were to be given to a child under three years of age);

(iii) what steps have been taken to remedy the problem. If only one or more of the items within the *batch* are likely to have been defective a restrictive recall may be sufficient;

(iv) the strength of a section 39 defence. This requires detailed examination of all the information, and the relevant law[3].

13.1.3 Suspension notice

At any interview or once the information has been provided the enforcement authority will consider its next step which could involve the issue of a suspension notice, the seeking of a forfeiture order, or a prosecution. Close consideration should be given to the fact that if a suspension notice is issued and it is subsequently found that there has been no breach of a safety provision then C

2 See chapter 10, *Due Diligence Defence* above.
3 See chapter 10, *Due Diligence*.

Plc may seek compensation. Further, any prosecution may be met by a section 39 defence. The authority should seek to fully evaluate the nature and extent of any argument that the item was in fact safe, and further the strength of any section 39 defence. If it is likely that the company will succeed in a section 39 defence then an order for the forfeiture of the goods may be sought as a useful alternative to prosecution. As with a suspension notice, the issue of which C Plc can appeal against (section 15), if a forfeiture order is sought (section 16) this can be contested. Indeed even if the magistrates are satisfied that there has been a contravention of a relevant safety provision then an order under section 16(7) can be sought that the items are not destroyed but released on condition that they are only supplied to a third party for the purposes of repair, reconditioning (removal of the eyes and replacement with safety eyes), or for scrap.

It is also to be noted that as the item was supplied with a CE mark denoting conformity with the Regulations if the item was in fact in breach then it can be argued that a false trade description had been applied thus constituting an offence under the Trade Descriptions Act 1968. If summons was brought under this Act then section 24 allows a due diligence defence.

13.2 A CRAFT KIT

F Ltd produces a range of craft products, and amongst those products is a kit for the assembly of a Welsh folk doll. A prosecuting authority notices the item in a craft shop and undertakes a test purchase. The officer of the authority is concerned that the kit contains a needle. Apart from a reference under list of contents there is no other warning that it contains the needle and the kit is for the construction of a doll and hence may be attractive to children of an age at which adults would not wish them to use a needle without supervision. The officer issues and serves a suspension notice under section 14 of the Consumer Protection Act 1987 and Regulation 11(b) of the General Product Safety Regulations 1994. The officer does not believe that the craft kit falls within the definition of a toy and hence the General Product Safety Regulations apply to it. The notice prohibits the supply of the specific kit in question by F Ltd.

13.2.1 Discussion

F Ltd is a producer within the definition contained within the General Product Safety Regulations 1994, and hence has duties under sections 7 and 8. Ordinarily the enforcement officer will have requested sight of the information retained for the purposes of complying with Regulation 8, (particularly 8(b) and 8(c)). This may well contain expert opinion as to the effect of the labelling and packaging, and specifically whether the warning is sufficient to ensure that the item is safe having regard to the definition of a 'safe product' under Regulation 2.

The first step for F Ltd is to consider the details set out in the notice and to compile evidence concerning the safety of the item. The more supportive evidence that can be compiled the better, bearing in mind the damage to F Ltd's business caused by the item being under a suspension notice (and also the fact that ordinarily that such a notice has only a six month life span and that the enforcement authority will seek to take further action usually either by way of a prosecution or an application for forfeiture within this primary period). There should be investigation of all useful evidential sources[4]. If F Ltd is able to produce sufficient evidence to support a strong case that there has been no contravention of a safety provision[5] then F Ltd should consider an immediate appeal (section 15). As there have been no proceedings brought by the enforcement authority a summons should be laid by way of complaint in a convenient Magistrates Court (section 15(2)(b)). It is often helpful to approach a number of Magistrates Courts to see which could offer the quickest listing of a substantive trial of the action.

The enforcement authority should have close regard to section 14(7) and to the potential liability to pay compensation to any person having an interest in the goods (obviously F Ltd has such an interest) in respect of any loss or damage caused by the service of the notice if it is subsequently found that there has been no contravention in relation to the goods of any safety provision. It is difficult to see how F Ltd could be accused of any neglect or default so as to bring about the service of the notice and thus to disentitle the company to an award of compensation under section 14(7)(b). The enforcement authority should therefore liaise with F Ltd and/or its legal advisors and seek voluntary disclosure of all information upon the subject with the understanding that the suspension notice may be withdrawn if the enforcement authority is in real doubt as to a possible contravention of a safety provision. However, F Ltd may be best served by 'keeping its powder dry' and compiling a substantial body of evidence with the dual aim of successfully appealing and also gaining an award of compensation. If an appeal is lodged then the prosecuting authority should also consider applying for forfeiture of the goods by virtue of section 16(2)(b).

There is no specific duty upon F Ltd to disclose the nature and extent of its evidence prior to the hearing of the appeal on the suspension notice although any failure to do so may incur a penalty as to costs[6]. Further, it could be argued that in resect of liability to pay compensation the failure to produce relevant information prior to the trial of the issue was due to the fault or neglect of F Ltd and that any loss or damage caused by reason of failure to revoke the suspension notice as a result should not be the subject of compensation. This argument involves interpretation of the phrase 'the service of the notice' within section 14(7) such as to include 'and the failure to revoke or alter the same'.

At the appeal the burden would be upon F Ltd to prove that there had been no contravention of a safety provision, and the standard would be the balance of probabilities. There has been some debate upon the onus and standard of proof under the section such that the order of presentation of evidence is still considered somewhat of a 'grey area'[7]. In the present case, as the notice clearly sets out the concerns of the enforcement authority, there is

4 See chapter 6, *Evidential Sources*.

5 For example by reference to the fact that the needle is a functional element, or that the kit would only be suitable for sale to a late teenager or adult, or that the item is only supplied to craft shops and never toy shops, or that the finished item would be a folk doll and not a doll for play, such folk dolls being excluded under the provisions of the Toys (Safety) Regulations 1989 in any event, or that the needle is referred to in the list of contents, and that in any event there has never been any complaint or incident involving the kit despite the supply of many thousands of the item.

6 Ordinarily F Ltd should seek its costs from the local authority as this is a complaint. However, if relevant information has been withheld which would have resulted in a concession that the suspension notice should not have been issued then there could well be argument as to whether an award of costs should be made; see *Costs*, chapter 10.

7 See Miller, 'Product Liability and Safety Encyclopedia'(IV) 165.

no reason why F Ltd cannot open the case and produce its evidence first. If the prosecuting authority produced any 'surprise evidence' not envisaged within the notice then F Ltd could seek the right to call rebuttal evidence.

F Ltd should also consider a response to any accompanying application for a forfeiture order in the event that there is found to have been a contravention of a safety provision. Particular regard should be had to section 16(7) as to whether an order that the items be destroyed can be avoided by possible repair, reconditioning, or sale as 'scrap'.

If the court finds that there has been no contravention in relation to the goods of any safety provision and that the service of the notice (and of any failure to revoke or alter the same) has not been attributable to the neglect or default of F Ltd then the authority should be liable to pay compensation. Any disputed question as to the amount of compensation shall be determined by arbitration[8].

8 See Halsbury's Laws Vol 2; Arbitration and the Arbitration Acts 1950 and 1979.

Part 3

CONSUMER PROTECTION ACT 1987

Chapter 14

PART 1 PRODUCT LIABILITY

1. Purpose and construction of Part I

(1) This Part shall have effect for the purpose of making such provision as is necessary in order to comply with the product liability Directive and shall be construed accordingly[1].

(2) In this Part[2], except in so far as the context otherwise requires –

'agricultural produce' means any produce of the soil, of stockfarming or of fisheries[3];

'dependant' and 'relative' have the same meaning as they have in, respectively the Fatal Accidents Act 1976 and the Damages (Scotland) Act 1976;

'producer[4]', in relation to a product, means –

(a) the person[5] who manufactured it[6];
(b) in the case of a substance which has not been manufactured but has been won or abstracted[7], the person who won or abstracted it;
(c) in the case of a product which has not been manufactured, won or abstracted but essential characteristics of which are attributable to an industrial or other process having been carried out (for example in relation to agricultural produce), the person who carried out that process[8];

'product[9]' means any goods[10] or electricity and (subject to subsection (3) below) includes a product which is comprised in another product, whether by virtue of being a component part or raw material or otherwise[11]; and

'the product liability Directive' means the Directive of the Council of the European Communities, dated 25th July 1985, (No 85/374/EEC) on the approximation of the laws, regulations and administrative provision of the member States concerning liability for defective products.

(3) For the purposes of this Part a person who supplies any product in which products are comprised, whether by virtue of being component parts or raw materials or otherwise, shall not be treated by reason only of his supply of that product as supplying any of the products so comprised[12].

NOTES

1 The full text of the Directive is set out at Part 4. It is important to note that the Act does not always follow the exact wording contained within the Directive (see for example s 4(1)(c)), and that due regard will be given to the paramount status of the Directive. See chapter 4, *European Perspective*.

2 Sections 1-9 of the Act.

3 See Art 2 of the Directive, the footnotes below and the footnotes to s 2(4). Concern has been raised by the possible limitations of the reference to 'of the soil'. It is submitted that the phrase is likely to be interpreted as including 'soil substitutes' and methods such as hydroponics.

4 See Art 3 of the Directive and the liability imposed by s 2(2)(a). See also the defence set out at s 4(1)(c).

5 See Interpretation Act 1978, s 5. The definition includes a body of persons corporate or unincorporate.

6 It is submitted that this is likely to mean the construction or production of articles by physical labour or machinery or the adaption or alteration of materials such that the end form is fit for use.This definition (as taken with the definition of a product as set out later in the section) may indeed be wider than anticipated or intended so as to include:
(a) those who package or label items(See ss 2(2)b, 2(5) and 4(1)f);
(b) printers (a contrary argument may be raised relying upon parliamentary debate upon the subject, see HOCOR Vol 116);
(c) those who recondition, re-fit or renovate goods (as opposed to those who merely service or repair).The distinction can be a fine one and is a matter of fact in each case. Much will depend upon the nature and extent of 'new parts or additions' or any express description; and
(d) those who assemble parts or items (as opposed to those who merely affix or install). Again the distinction may on occasions be a fine one.

7 Likely to mean removal or separation from source or site of natural origin.Whilst this will obviously cover such substances as water or fossil fuels, there seems to be no logical reason why it could not also be construed so as to include produce of the soil, but see note 8 below.

8 A reference to those who change by processing 'natural' or 'raw' products which have not been manufactured, won or abstracted, (eg agricultural produce). Analysis of the interaction of this section with s 2(4) provides potential difficulties (partially due to a failure to adopt the wording and structure of the Directive and partially due to a lack of fine definition within the Directive) in relation to the exemption for agricultural products. Article 2 of the Directive gives an exemption to 'primary' agricultural products that have not undergone 'initial processing'.There is no definiton of this phrase but reference within the preamble to'processing of an industrial nature which could lead to a defect'. It is interesting to note that within this part of s 1 there is reference to essential characteristics being attributable to an industrial process or to any 'other process', (ie a process other than an industrial one), whereas the reference at s 2(4) is solely to an industrial process (the phrase not being further defined). Hence, (and, it is submitted, unfortunately), this definition is likely to cover a wider range than those 'caught' by s 2(4). In practice this could mean an argument that although a product had been the subject of a form of 'initial processing' which led to a defect (eg application by a farmer of a chemical to a crop at harvest time), and although he fell within the definition of a producer, reliance could be placed upon the fact that an industrial process has not taken place and hence, neither s 2(2) or (3) will apply.
A possible further argument is that the processing envisaged by this section must be such that thereafter it can be said that essential characteristics are attributable to such processes (as opposed to merely being 'initial'). If the harvesting or collection of agricultural produce cannot be considered as abstraction (See note 7 above. The specific reference to agricultural produce within this sub-paragraph produces considerable difficulty for that argument), the farmer who applied chemicals to his crop could argue that whilst there may well have been a minor effect, there was no change in the essential characteristics, and hence he did not fall within the definition of a 'producer'.

9 The definition within the Directive is set out at Art 2; 'all movables, even though incorporated into another movable or into an immovable'. The preamble also refers to 'movables which are used in the construction of immovables or are installed in immovables'.This definition would cover the majority of building materials and such things as heating and air conditioning systems, but not a building itself.

10 See the definition at s 45(1). Unlike s 10(7), which formerly dealt with criminal liability for the majority of consumer goods (cf the new General Product Safety Regulations at Reg 2), there are no specific exemptions within this section.

11 See also s 2(5). If a defective component or piece of raw material is used within the production of a product, both the producer of the defective 'ingredient' and of the 'end product' may be jointly and severally liable.

12 The critical words are 'treated...as supplying any of the component parts'.This sub-section negates the effect of s 2(3) with respect to component parts or raw materials.

2. Liability for defective products

(1) Subject to the following provisions of this Part[1], where any damage is caused wholly or partly by a defect[2] in a product[3], every person[4] to whom subsection (2) below applies shall be liable[5] for the damage[6].

(2) This subsection[7] applies to –

(a) the producer[8] of the product;
(b) any person who, by putting his name on the product or using a trade mark or other distinguishing mark in relation to the product, has held himself out to be the producer of the product[9];
(c) any person who has imported the product into a Member State from a place outside the member States in order, in the course of any business[10] of his, to supply it to another[11].

(3) Subject as aforesaid, where any damage is caused wholly or partly by a defect in a product, any person who supplied[12] the product (whether to the person who suffered the damage, to the producer of any product in which the product in question is comprised or to any other person[13]) shall be liable for the damage if –

(a) the person who suffered the damage[14] requests the supplier to identify one or more of the persons (whether still in existence or not) to whom subsection (2) above applies in relation to the product.
(b) that request is made within a reasonable period[15] after the damage occurs and at a time when it is not reasonably practicable[16] for the person making the request to identify all those persons; and
(c) the supplier fails, within a reasonable period after receiving the request, either to comply with the request or to identify the person who supplied the product to him[17].

(4) Neither subsection (2) nor subsection(3) above shall apply to a person in respect of any defect in any game or agricultural produce if the only supply of the game or produce by that person to another was at a time when it had not undergone an industrial process[18].

(5) Where two or more persons are liable by virtue of this Part for the same damage, their liability shall be joint and several[19].

(6) This section shall be without prejudice to any liability arising otherwise than by virtue of this Part[20].

NOTES

1 Sections 1-9.
2 See s 3.
3 See notes to s 1 above.
4 See s 1, note 5 above.
5 See Defences at s 4 below.
6 See s 5 below.
7 See Arts 1-3 of the Directive.
8 See s 1 above and notes 4-8.
9 See Art 3(1). The question as to whether a person has 'held himself out' or 'presented himself' as the producer will be a question of fact. Clearly those who produce 'own brand' products such as large supermarkets will fall within the section whereas individuals, such as celebrities, who merely endorse a product will not. However, as with many other definitions within the Act there will be large grey areas of potential liability. One area, the position of Pharmacists, has already caused concern (HOLOR Vol 483, see also s 1 and note 6 above).
10 For the definition of business see s 45(1); 'includes a trade or profession and the activities of a professional or trade association or of a local authority or other public authority'. In relation to activities or normal practice within a business, see *Havering London Borough v Stevenson*

[1970] 3 All ER 609 at 611. See also Section 1(1) Trade Descriptions Act 1968, *Davies v Sumner* [1984] 3 All ER 831; *R & B Customs Brokers Co Ltd v United Dominions Trust Ltd* 1988] 1 All ER 847; *Southwark London Borough v Charlesworth* (1983) 147 JP 470; *Devlin v Hall* [1990] RTR 320.

11 See Art 3(2) which makes reference to a person who imports 'into the Community'. A person is only caught by this section if the importation is from a place outside the Community and means that any movement within the Community will not create additional liability.

12 See s 46 for the meaning of supply, which includes selling, hiring out, giving away or lending the goods.

13 No immediate link with the relevant supply is needed.When taken together with the definition of supply this means that the section has far reaching effect.

14 Or presumably his agent or other person acting upon his behalf (solicitor or parent). Section 6(2) post makes provision in the event of death of the relevant person.

15 This is a matter of fact. Reference may well be made to delay having regard to the normal life of the product, periods during which it is reasonable to expect records to be retained and relevant limitation periods.

16 The phrase should be compared with the stricter requirements of 'practicable', see *Marshall v Gotham Co Ltd* [1954] AC 360, HL.

17 See Art (3). The section is wide-ranging in effect and is particularly important when goods are 'anonymous' or unmarked. It highlights for businesses, particularly retailers (however small) the vital importance of keeping full records concerning the supply of any item.

18 See s 1 and note 8 above. It is submitted that whilst freezing of items will fall within the definition of an industrial process (certainly this would appear to be initial processing), washing, drying, cooking, and other forms of preparation may not.There are likely to be difficult borderline areas.

19 See Art 5. Thus the Plaintiff may look to more than one person (providing liability is established) to satisfy the full extent of a claim. See also, as between those liable, the Civil Liability (Contribution) Act 1978.

20 Principally a reference to claims in respect of negligence and breach of contract. See chapter 3, *Residual Liability* for circumstances of when such claims may be an important or only form of redress.

3. Meaning of 'defect'[1]

(1) Subject to the following provisions of this section, there is a defect in a product for the purposes of this Part[2] if the safety of the product is not such as persons generally are entitled to expect[3]; and for those purposes 'safety', in relation to a product, shall include safety with respect to products comprised in that product and safety in the context of risks[4] of damage to property[5], as well as in the context of risks of death or personal injury.

(2) In determining for the purposes of subsection (1) above what persons generally are entitled to expect in relation to a product all the circumstances shall be taken into account[6], including –

(a) the manner in which, and purposes for which, the product has been marketed, its get-up, the use of any mark in relation to the product and any instructions for, or warnings with respect to, doing or refraining from doing anything with or in relation to the product[7];

(b) what might reasonably be expected to be done with or in relation to the product[8], and

(c) the time when the product was supplied by its producer to another[9];

and nothing in this section shall require a defect to be inferred from the fact alone that the safety of a product which is supplied after that time is greater than the safety of the product in question[10].

NOTES

1 See Art 6.

2 Sections 1-9. It is important to note that there are very significant differences between the scope and extent of provisions within this section and those within The General Product Safety Regulations 1994.

3 See the preamble to the Directive and the phrase,'the safety which the public at large is entitled to expect'. Clearly the intent is to cover a population which possesses a great inherent diversity of physical and mental attributes. Whilst it is not intended to produce an entitlement to protection for each and every possible use, regard must be had to likely use by a representative cross-section of the target population. The test applied will be objective.

4 Risk as opposed to hazard. A hazard is a method of injury, the risk is the likelihood of the hazard occurring.

5 See s 5 below.

6 All relevant circumstances should be considered. A comparison may be made with the matters set out within s 10 and the General Product Safety Regulations 1994, Reg 2; 'safe product'. The similar phrase within s 10 was considered by Laws J; 'This legislation is not to be construed so that (the Court when considering the item) must only receive evidence which treats (the item) entirely in isolation from surrounding circumstances, such as may relate to a comparable (item) or the views and experience of a body such as the British Standards Committee. Materials of that kind are well within the circumstances which (a Court) will need to assess.'; *R v Walsall Magistrates, ex p PMS* (17 March 1994, unreported), DC. Relevant circumstances may be:

(a) Regulations and National Standards; See Reg 10, The General Product Safety Regulations 1994. If there are none which are specifically aimed at the product (non-compliance with Regulations is likely to constitute an offence under s 12 post), regard may be had to those for products with similar characteristics or components or produced using similar methods. Whilst the effect of Reg 5 in disapplying s 10(2)(b),is to significantly reduce the effect of non-compliance with safety standards (cf Reg 10(2)(i)), the Courts are likely to still hold such standards in very high regard; 'Such Standards represented the consensus of professional opinion and practical experience as to sensible safety precautions. Whilst they were not legally binding, they were guides which provided strong evidence of the competence at the date when they were issued'; *Ward v Ritz Hotel (London) Ltd* [1992] PIQR P315, CA, cf Lloyd LJ dissenting;

(b) The nature and extent of categories of consumers 'at serious risk' when using the product; see Reg 2 of The General Product Safety Regulations 1994;

(c) Other items on the market at the time; Reg 2 of The General Product Safety Regulations 1994 states; 'the fact that higher levels of safety may be obtained or other products presenting a lesser degree of risk may be available shall not of itself cause the product to be considered other than a safe product'. This is to be compared with s 10(2)(c) which in practice encouraged such direct comparisons. The issue is frequently one of cost and manufacturers and importers have long complained that it is unrealistic to compare items which are obviously inexpensive and not of a high quality with items of the same type at the top of the price range. Whilst it is possible at a cost to improve the safety or durability of certain items, the market proves that this is not what the consumer requires. As one judge has stated 'A consumer does not expect to get a hammer which can be handed down through generations at a cost of £1.25. Such an item will obviously deteriorate quicker than its counterparts retailing at well over ten times that price'. Comparisons are, however, frequently useful (and were expressly approved by Laws J; see above), and there will be cases when the public at large is entitled to expect that a product possess a certain feature notwithstanding the cost.

(d) Expert opinion at the time; (see Laws J above. The case concerned the exclusion of evidence by the Chairman of the relevant British Standards Committee to the effect that the Committee had received advice from a number of experts and as a result decided *not* to incorporate a particular requirement within a British Standard);

(e) The history of supply of the particular product (and other products with the same or a similar relevant feature).

(f) The extent to which the relevant danger is obvious and known or unavoidable if the item is to retain its utility or serve its purpose.

(g) The likely effect on other products (see *Whirlpool (UK) Ltd and Magnet v Gloucestershire County Council* (1993) 159 JP 123.

7 See Art 6(1)(a) which simply refers to 'the presentation of the product', s 10(2)(b) and Reg 2 of the General Product Safety Regulations 1994, specifically sub-paragraphs (a) and (c) under 'safe product'. Reference to this section will frequently be in relation to a failure to provide adequate or accurate information, instructions or warnings. This is often an area of dispute and merges into consideration of the proper assessment of the likely end-user, likely use and also misuse. Do persons generally expect that account should be taken of ignorance or stupidity? The answer, whilst not as firm and resounding as that across the Atlantic, (a recent American court decision held that safety pin manufacturers must print a warning on

products pointing to the dangers if the pins are swallowed whilst open) should be taken to be in the affirmative. The reference to a mark is usually important when considering claims of conformity with a standard or a voluntary code of practice, such as the 'kite' mark or the mark of a manufacturers or importers association. However, it may be compulsory as with the CE mark for Toys (see Toys (Safety) Regulations 1989).

8 See Article 6(1)(b). This sub-section is likely to be interpreted to include reasonably forseeable degrees of misuse. See also Regulation 2 of The General Product Safety Regulations 1994 which refers to 'any product which, under normal or reasonably foreseeable conditions of use, including duration, does not present any risk or only the minimum risks compatible with the product's use...' In practice this is one of the most difficult of areas for producers. Whilst certain assumptions have to be made, for example that ordinarily adequate warnings will be heeded and that there will be a reasonable level of parental supervision in the home, arguments are frequently put forward that under normal conditions of use packaging is often quickly discarded and that regard must be had to the item as it is to found someway into its use. Another area of potential difficulty is with exposure. Although some parental supervision may be assumed and age or other warnings may be clearly placed upon items such as toys, (or novelties) they are under normal conditions of use frequently within the reach of or given to children younger than the intended range. It is therefore argued that items intended and marketed for 'younger' children should in fact be safe for use by the very young child (the 'toy-box' argument). It will be a question of fact and degree in each case and the weight and quality of evidence from experts in favour of a producer predicting the most extreme misuse may often be surprising. Adequate and well documented market testing will often assist in this regard. The ability to reduce an award for contributory negligence set out at s 6(4) should always be borne in mind (cf young children).

9 This section assesses a potential defect at the time of supply. This is of particular importance when subsequent information comes to light or standards improve (consider also s 4(1)(e) post). However, producers should note Reg 8(1)(b) of The General Product Safety Regulations 1994 and the duties that sub-section now imposes.

10 This refers to a subsequently produced and safer item. However, the section does not mean that the existence of such an item is not relevant,merely that the court considering the matter does not have to take an inference from it. (See *Lambert v Lewis* [1978] 1 Lloyd's Rep 610).

4. Defences[1]

(1) In any civil proceedings by virtue of this Part[2] against any person ('the person proceeded against') in respect of a defect[3] in a product[4] it shall be a defence for him to show[5]–

(a) that the defect is attributable to compliance with any requirement imposed by or under any enactment or with any Community obligation[6]; or

(b) that the person proceeded against did not at any time supply[7] the product to another[8]; or

(c) that the following conditions are satisfied, that its to say –

(i) that the only supply of the product to another by the person proceeded against was otherwise than in the course of a business[9] of that person's; and

(ii) that section 2(2) above does not apply to that person or applies to him by virtue only of things done otherwise than with a view to profit[10]; or

(d) that the defect did not exist in the product at the relevant time[11]; or

(e) that the state of scientific and technical knowledge at the relevant time was not such that a producer of products of the same description as the product in question might be expected to have discovered the defect if it had existed in his products while they were under his control[12]; or

(f) that the defect –

(i) constituted a defect in a product ('the subsequent product') in which the product in question had been comprised; and

(ii) was wholly attributable to the design of the subsequent product or to compliance by the producer of the product in question with instructions given by the producer of the subsequent product[13].

(2) In this section 'the relevant time', in relation to electricity, means the time at which it was generated, being a time before it was transmitted or distributed, and in relation to any other product, means –

(a) if the person proceeded against is a person to whom subsection (2) of section 2 above applies in relation to the product, the time when he supplied[14] the product to another;

(b) if that subsection does not apply[15] to that person in relation to the product, the time when the product was last supplied by a person to whom that subsection does apply in relation to the product.

NOTES

1 See Art 7.

2 Sections 1-9.

3 See s 3.

4 See s 1.

5 The burden of proof rests upon the defendant, and the standard is the balance of probabilities; *R v Carr-Briant* [1943] KB 607. (This can be important in practice as if, for example, a container fractures and the injured party wishes to bring a claim against the manufacturer, it is not necessary to prove that the relevant retailer did not cause the defect by poor handling or storage as the burden will lie upon the manufacturer to establish a defence under sub-s 1(d).)

6 This sub-section is unlikely to have much practical significance as it refers only to a requirement imposed under an enactment or compliance with a Community obligation. It is interesting to compare this sub-section with Reg 10(1) of The General Product Safety Regulations 1994, which lays down a presumption that a product is a safe product when it conforms 'to the specific rules of the law of the United Kingdom laying down the health and safety requirements which the product must satisfy'(see also s 10(3)(a)).

7 See s 46.

8 Article 7(a) refers to proof that 'he did not put the product into circulation'. The principle practical applications will be:

(a) to exclude complaints by employees alleging that injury was caused by their employer's products. As this is adequately covered by the Employers Liability (Defective Equipment) Act 1969, which has the advantage of identifying the employer as the person deemed to be negligent, little is likely to be lost by this exclusion.

(b) injury or damage as a result of 'unauthorised' contact with a product (eg poisoning through pollution). However, it could still be argued that this would constitute the act of 'putting the product into circulation'. In practice the laws of nuisance and negligence are likely to provide more straightforward causes of action for this type of claim.

9 See s 2(2)(c); note 22 above. The sub-section is intended to cover purely private transactions.

10 It is important that the intent is the vital ingredient, and a profit can in fact be made; see *National Deposit Friendly Society Trustees v Skegness UDC* [1959] AC 293.

11 This requires proof of a relevant deterioration (not as a result of inherent qualities present at the time of supply) after the time of supply. The most obvious examples is third party use, alteration or damage.

12 See Art 7; 'the state of scientific and technical knowledge at the time when he put the product into circulation was not such as to *enable the existance of the defect to be discovered*'. (Art 15(1)(b) gave to the member states the power to exclude this defence.) See also s 3 and note 40 above. This is the much-discussed '*development risks defence*.'

During the Parliamentary consideration of the Consumer Protection Bill conflicting views were put forward by those representing 'consumer groups' and those seeking to protect the interests of the 'producers'. On the one hand it was argued that the retention of this defence could leave future victims of any 'Thalidomide' tragedy or other unforseeable product liability disaster without a means of claiming under the Act, on the other hand that exclusion of the defence could raise insurance to crippling levels, jeopardise competition and inhibit innovative research and development of new products. (See further HOLOR Vol 483). Although the end result, ie the incorporation of the defence, is the vital thing, analysis of the debates shows how the intended effect of this sub-section deviates from the strict wording of the Directive. Lord Lucas of Chilworth (speaking against the removal of the defence)stated:

> 'Do noble Lords suggest that this will be an easy defence to prove? It will be of no help to the producer to plead how difficult or how expensive it had or it might have been for him to have found the answers to that defect. If other producers of products of that type had the knowledge available to them, then the defence is of no use to the producer of the product. Neither will it necessarily be of any use to that producer if he shows that he manufactured the products to an accepted national or international safety standard. Neither can the producer point to what other producers of products like his are doing in the manufacture of their products. Only if the producer can prove to the court that he took all the steps that a producer of products of that kind *might reasonably have been expected to take*, and that the state of scientific and technical knowledge would have allowed him to take, will this defence be of any value.'(emphasis added).

Although in the strict wording of the section the word 'reasonably' does not appear, it could easily be argued that it should be incorporated within the clearly objective 'test'. This would considerably water down the test for liability under the Act and bring a number of factors into play (notwithstanding the quotation above) such as cost of innovative testing and investigation and the impact upon financial viability of the project (evidence could be produced from other manufacturers to support, on economic grounds, the stance taken at the relevant time). Article 7 is much stricter and permits no such considerations. (During the passage of the Bill it was amended at one stage to reflect the wording of the Directive, but this was subsequently reversed.)It is therefore submitted that the wording of this section should be treated with considerable caution as it fails to comply with the Directive and reference can be made to the clear intent set out at s 1(1) above and the supremacy of the Directive. (See *Garland v British Rail Engineering Ltd* [1982] 2 All ER 402, and chapter 4, *European Perspective*).

13 See Art 7(f). This defence is aimed at assisting those who produce components (or 'raw materials'). However, the use of the word 'comprised' (with connotations of inclusion within) may cause difficulty, in that it may limit the scope of the defence. (Is the packaging for a dangerous caustic shampoo comprised within the final product?). Unfortunately the wording of the Directive itself also seems to be capable of a stangely restricted interpretation. Note also that the requirements of the two sub-sections are cumulative.

14 See s 46.

15 Eg those liable under s 2(3).

5. Damage giving rise to liability[1]

(1) Subject to the following provisions of this section, in this Part[2] 'damage' means death or personal injury[3] or any loss of or damage to[4] any property[5] (including land[6]).

(2) A person shall not be liable under section 2 above in respect of any defect in a product for the loss of or any damage to the product itself[7] or for the loss of or any damage to the whole or any part of any product which has been supplied with the product in question comprised in it[8].

(3) A person shall not be liable under Section 2 above for any loss of or damage to any property[9] which, at the time it is lost or damaged[10], is not –

(a) of a description of property ordinarily intended for private use, occupation or consumption[11]; and

(b) intended by the person suffering the loss or damage mainly for his own private use, occupation or consumption[12].

(4) No damages shall be awarded to any person by virtue of this Part in respect of any loss of or damage to any property if the amount which would fall to be so awarded to that person, apart from this subsection and any liability for interest, does not exceed £275[13].

(5) In determining for the purposes of this Part who has suffered any loss of or damage to property[14] and when any such loss or damage occurred, the loss or damage shall be regarded as having occurred at the earliest time at which a person with an interest in the property had knowledge of the material facts about the loss or damage[15].

(6) For the purposes of subsection (5) above the material facts about any loss of or damage to any property are such facts about the loss or damage as would lead a reasonable person with an interest in the property to consider the loss or damage sufficiently serious to justify his instituting proceedings for damages against a defendant who did not dispute liability and was able to satisfy a judgment.

(7) For the purposes of subsection (5) above a person's knowledge includes knowledge which he might reasonably have been expected to acquire –

(a) from facts observable or ascertainable by him; or
(b) from facts ascertainable by him with the help of appropriate expert advice which it is reasonable for him to seek;

but a person shall not be taken by virtue of this subsection to have knowledge of a fact ascertainable by him only with the help of expert advice unless he has failed to take all reasonable steps to obtain (and, where appropriate, to act on) that advice.

(8) Subsections (5) to (7) above shall not extend to Scotland.

NOTES

1 See Art 9.

2 Sections 1-9.

3 See s 45(1) for the definition of personal injury; 'Includes any disease and any other impairment of a person's physical or mental condition'. This wide definition obviously covers nervous shock provided that there is indeed an identifiable or positive psychiatric illness or medical condition (See Lord Bridge in *McLoughlin v O'Brian* [1983] 1 AC 410 at 431) such as depression, post-traumatic stress disorder, a type of phobia, paranoia, personality change or anxiety neurosis (Bingham LJ in *Attia v British Gas* [1988] QB 304 referred to the expression 'nervous shock as misleading and inaccurate, preferring to use the title, 'psychiatric damage'). It must be more than mere grief, emotional distress, worry, horror or fear (see *Hicks v Chief Constable of South Yorkshire* [1992] 1 All ER 690).

4 The word 'destruction' as opposed to loss is used in the Directive. The usual definition of damage is sufficiently wide in its meaning to embrace injury, mischief or harm done to property, and in order to consitute 'damage' it is unnecessary to establish such definite or actual damage as renders property useless or prevents it from serving its normal function; per Walters J in *Samuels v Stubbs* [1972] 4 SASR 200; cf *Wormell v RHM Agriculture* [1987] 3 All ER 75, CA, and a failure to confer a benefit.

5 Property is not specifically defined within the Act, but it is submitted that a wide definition will be given so as to encompass most things that are capable of ownership. Section 4(1) Theft Act 1968 defines property as including 'money and all other property, real or personal, including things in action and other intangible property'.

6 Schedule 1 of the Interpretation Act 1978 defines land as including 'buildings and other structures, land covered by water, and any estate, interest, easement, servitude or right in or over land'.

7 See Art 9(b).

8 This is a somewhat peculiar extension to the defence that is set out in the Directive and has received some sharp criticism (See HOLR Vol 482). It is important to note that the defence 'bites' if the item was incorporated at the time of supply. Hence damage caused by subsequently incorporated or replacement parts will not be covered (the example of a car battery has been used. If a defective battery is purchased and fitted into a car and subsequently explodes, a claim may lie for the damage to the car (not the battery). If a car is purchased with a defective battery already in it, which susequently explodes, no claim will lie for the damage to either the battery or the car). If liability is excluded by the effect of this section a claim may still lie in contract or negligence. See chapter 3, *Residual Liability*.

9 See note 5 above.
10 As opposed to the time of supply.
11 It must be noted that the exclusion applies to the damaged property and not the defective product. The test is an objective one.
12 See Art 9(b)(ii). This second section must also be satisfied if liability is to be avoided. Note the word 'mainly'. The question of intention will be one of fact in each case.
13 See Art 9(b); 500 ECU.This only applies to property and not to personal injury. The intention is to prevent a multiplicity of small claims.
14 These ss (5-8) do not cover personal injury.
15 See also Sch 1 below.

6. Application of certain enactments

(1) Any damage for which a person is liable under section 2 above shall be deemed[1] to have been caused –

(a) for the purposes of the Fatal Accidents Act 1976, by that person's wrongful act, neglect or default[2];

(b)-(d) (applies to Scotland only).

(2) Where[3] –

(a) a person's death is caused wholly or partly by a defect in a product, or a person dies after suffering damage which has been so caused;
(b) a request such as mentioned in paragraph (a) of subsection (3) of section 2 above is made to a supplier of the product by that person's personal representatives or, in the case of a person whose death is caused wholly or partly by the defect, by any independent or relative of that person; and
(c) the conditions specified in paragraphs (b) and (c) of that subsection are satisfied in relation to that request,

this part shall have effect for the purposes of the Law Reform (Miscellaneous Provisions) Act 1934, the Fatal Accidents Act 1976 and the Damages (Scotland) Act 1976 as if liability of the supplier to that person under that subsection did not depend on that person having requested the supplier to identify certain persons or on the said conditions having been satisfied in relation to a request made by that person.

(3) Section 1 of the Congenital Disabilities (Civil Liability) Act 1976 shall have effect for the purposes of this Part[4] as if –

(a) a person were answerable to a child in respect of an occurrence caused wholly or partly by a defect in a product if he is or has been liable under section 2 above in respect of any effect of the occurrence on a parent of the child, or would be liable if the occurrence caused a parent of the child to suffer damage;
(b) the provisions of this Part relating to liability under section 2 above applied in relation to liability by virtue of paragraph (a) above under the said section 1; and
(c) subsection (6) of the said section 1 (exclusion of liability) were omitted.

(4) Where any damage is caused partly by a defect in a product and partly by the fault of the person suffering the damage[5], the Law Reform (Contributory Negligence) Act 1945[6] and section 5 of the Fatal Accidents Act 1976[7] (contributory negligence) shall have effect as if the defect were the fault of every person liable by virtue of this Part for the damage caused by the defect[8].

(5) In subsection (4) above 'fault' has the same meaning as in the said Act

of 1945.

(6) Schedule 1[9] to this Act shall have effect for the purpose of amending the Limitation Act 1980 and the Prescription and Limitation (Scotland) Act 1973 in their application in relation to the bringing of actions by virtue of this Part.

(7) It is hereby declared that liability by virtue of this Part is to be treated as liability in tort for the purposes of any enactment conferring jurisdiction[10] on any court with respect to any matter.

(8) Nothing in this Part shall prejudice the operation of section 12 of the Nuclear Installations Act 1965 (rights to compensation for certain breaches of duties confined to rights under that Act)[11].

NOTES

1 This means that this section shall have the effect of widening the scope of this part of the Act. 'The so-called deeming provision is expansive ... if a case falls naturally within a sub-section it is unnecessary to look beyond it', per Viscount Simonds, *IRC v Barclays Bank Ltd* [1961] AC 509, HL.

2 Section 1 of the Fatal Accidents Act 1976 states 'If death is caused by any wrongful act, neglect or default which is such as would (if death had not ensued) have entitled the person injured to maintain an action and recover damages in respect thereof, the person who would have been liable if death had not ensued shall be liable to an action for damages, notwithstanding the death of the person injured'.

3 This section relates to the potential liability of suppliers under s 2(3) and the requirement for a specific request.

4 It is necessary to closely consider this complicated section which concerns derivative liability (to the child) for the birth of a live but disabled child.

5 See Art 8(2).

6 Section 1(1) states that 'damages shall be reduced to such extent as the court thinks just and equitable having regard to the claimant's share in the responsibility for the damage'. Section 4 of the Act states; 'Fault means negligence, breach of statutory duty or other act or omission which gives rise to a liability in tort or would, apart from this Act, give rise to the defence of contributory negligence.'

7 Section 5 states 'Where any person dies as the result partly of his own fault and partly of the fault of any other person or persons,and accordingly if an action were brought for the benefit of the estate under the Law Reform (Miscellaneous Provisions) Act 1934 the damages recoverable would be reduced under s 1(1) of the Law Reform (Contributory Negligence) Act 1945, any damages recoverable in an action brought for the benefit of dependants of that person under this Act shall be reduced to a proportionate extent.'

8 The effect is that contributory negligence applies to claims under Part 1. When considering contributory negligence the standard expected of the Plaintiff to an action is in general the same as that in neglegence itself. It is largely objective and impersonal, although children (see *Yachuk v Oliver Blais Co Ltd* [1949] AC 386) and those under a disability (unlikely to include self-intoxication, see *Owens v Brimmell* [1977] QB 859) are in somewhat of a special category. 'A person is guilty of contributry negligence if he ought reasonably to have forseen that, if he did not act as a reasonable, prudent man, he might hurt himself, and in his reckonings he must take into account the possibility of others being careless'; per Denning LJ in *Jones v Livox Quarries* [1952] 2 QB 608. See also *Stapley v Gypsum Mines* [1953] AC 663.

9 Set out later in this Part.

10 See the Civil Jurisdiction and Judgments Act 1982.

11 See Article 14. Section 12 of the Nuclear Installations Act 1965 is concerned with injury or damage arising from nuclear accidents.

7. Prohibition on exclusions from liability

The liability of a person by virtue of this Part to a person who has suffered damage caused wholly or partly by a defect in a product, or to a dependant or relative of such a person, shall not be limited or excluded by any contract term, by any notice or by any other provision[1].

NOTE

1 See Article 12, and chapter 3 above.

8. Power to modify Part I[1]

(1) Her Majesty may by Order in Council make such modifications of this Part and of any other enactment (including an enactment contained in the following Parts of this Act, or in an Act passed after this Act) as appear to Her Majesty In Council to be necessary or expedient in consequence of any modification of the product liability Directive which is made at any time after the passing of this Act.

(2) An Order in Council under subsection (1) above shall not be submitted to Her Majesty in Council unless a draft of the Order has been laid before, and approved by a resolution of, each House of Parliament.

NOTE

1 The Act may be amended by Order in Council. The power to make such orders may in turn be exerciable by Statutory Instrument; see Statutory Instruments Act 1946.

9. Application of Part I to Crown

(1) Subject to subsection (2) below, this Part shall bind the Crown.

(2) The Crown shall not, as regards the Crown's liability by virtue of this Part, be bound by this Part further than the Crown is made liable in tort or in reparation under the Crown Proceedings Act 1947[1], as that Act has effect from time to time.

NOTE

1 See The Crown Proceedings (Armed Forces) Act 1987.

Chapter 15

PART II CONSUMER SAFETY

10. The general safety requirement[1]

(1) A person[2] shall be guilty of an offence[3] if he –

(a) supplies[4] any consumer goods[5] which fail to comply with the general safety requirement;
(b) offers or agrees to supply any such goods; or
(c) exposes or possesses any such goods for supply[6].

(2) For the purposes of this section consumer goods fail to comply with the general safety requirement if they are not reasonably safe[7] having regard to all the circumstances[8], including –

(a) the manner in which, and purposes for which, the goods are being or would be marketed, the get-up of the goods, the use of any mark in relation to the goods and any instructions or warnings which are given or would be given with respect to the keeping, use or consumption of the goods[9];
(b) any standards of safety published by any person either for goods of a description which applies to the goods in question or for matters relating to goods of that description[10]; and
(c) the existence of any means by which it would have been reasonable (taking into account the cost, likelihood and extent of any improvement) for the goods to have been made safer[11].

(3) For the purposes of this section consumer goods shall not be regarded as failing to comply with the general safety requirement in respect of –

(a) anything which is shown to be attributable to compliance with any requirement imposed by or under any enactment or with any Community obligation[12];
(b) any failure to do more in relation to any matter than is required by–
    (i) any safety regulations imposing requirements with respect to that matter[13];
    (ii) *(Repealed)*[14]
    (iii) any provision of any enactment or subordinate legislation imposing such requirements with respect to that matter as are designated for the purposes of this subsection by any such regulations.

(4) In any proceedings against any person for an offence under this

section in respect of any goods it shall be a defence for that person to show[15] –

(a) that he reasonably believed that the goods would not be used or consumed in the United Kingdom[16]; or

(b) that the following conditions are satisfied that is to say –

(i) that he supplied the goods, offered or agreed to supply them or, as the case may be, exposed or possessed them for supply in the course of carrying on a retail business[17];

(ii) that, at the time he supplied the goods or offered or agreed to supply them or exposed or possessed them for supply, he neither knew or had reasonable grounds for believing[18] that the goods failed to comply with the general safety requirement; or

(c) that the terms on which he supplied the goods or agreed or offered to supply them or, in the case of goods which he exposed or possessed for supply, the terms on which he intended to supply them -

(i) indicated that the goods were not supplied or to be supplied as new goods[19]; and

(ii) provided for, or contemplated, the acquisition of an interest in the goods by the persons supplied or to be supplied.

(5) For the purposes of subsection (4)(b) above goods are supplied in the course of carrying on a retail business if –

(a) whether or not they are themselves acquired for a person's private use or consumption, they are supplied in the course of carrying on a business[20] of making a supply of consumer goods available to persons who general acquire them for private use of consumption; and

(b) the descriptions of goods the supply of which is made available in the course of that business do not, to a significant extent, include manufactured or imported foods which have not previously been supplied in the United Kingdom.

(6) A person guilty of an offence under this section shall be liable on summary conviction to imprisonment for a term not exceeding six months or to a fine not exceeding level 5 on the standard scale or to both[21].

(7) In this section 'consumer goods' means any goods which are ordinarily intended for private use or consumption[22], not being –

(a) growing crops or things comprised in land by virtue of being attached to it;

(b) water, food, feeding stuff or fertiliser;

(c) gas which is, is to be or has been supplied by a person authorised to supply it by or under section 6, 7 or 8 of the Gas Act 1986 (authorization of supply of gas through pipes);

(d) aircraft (other than hang-gliders) or motor vehicles;

(e) controlled drugs or licensed medicinal products;

(f) tobacco.

NOTES

1 Prior to the creation of the General Safety Requirement, safety requirements for individual types of product were governed by specific Regulations. Unfortunately this meant that a whole range of goods were not covered and further that specific Regulations were quickly out of date in respect of many items due to innovation or development of new types of product. In such cases it was residual liability in contract and negligence that afforded a potential

remedy. Section 10 implemented a proposal made in para 47 of the Government White Paper on the Safety of Goods (Cmnd 9302). However this section has now been largely disapplied by the General Product Safety Regulations 1994: see Reg 5, insofar as products are to be:

(i) Placed on the market, offered or agreed to be placed on the market or exposed or possessed to be placed on the market by producers; or

(ii) supplied, offered or agreed to be supplied or exposed or possessed to be supplied by distributors.

However, one area in which potential liability under s 10 of the Act will remain is by virtue of the definition of 'product' within Reg 2 of the Regulations and specifically the exclusion for products which are used exclusively in the context of a commercial activity even if they are used for or by a consumer (provided however that this exception shall not apply to the supply of such products to the consumer). See generally the footnotes to Reg 2 below.

2 This definition includes a company, see s 1, note 5.

3 The burden of proof is on the prosecution in accordance with normal principles (save where there is a specific defence in issue such as under s 39). This means that where there is a qualification to liability it must be disproved by the prosecution; (see *A-G v English* [1983] 1 AC 116). See s 39 with regard to the statutory defence and also s 41 with regard to the ability to base a civil action upon a breach of statutory duty. Section 10 is a Safety Provision for the purposes of s 45(1).

4 See the definition under s 46. See also *United States Tobacco International Inc v Secretary of State for Health* (1990) 155 JP 144 where it was held that 'supply' had to be confined to supply within the United Kingdom.

5 See sub-s (7) and compare with the definition of 'product' within the General Product Safety Regulations 1994.

6 With regard to the definition of offering, agreeing, exposing or possessing for supply see the notes to Reg 13 of the General Product Safety Regulations 1994. It is important to ensure that when any offence is alleged (or indeed particularised in a Summons) that the appropriate wording is used and relevant sub-section quoted. See *Partridge v Crittenden* [1968] 2 All ER 421 and *British Car Auctions Ltd v Wright* [1972] 3 All ER 462. There are advantages in alleging 'agreeing to supply' where it is difficult to prove a concluded supply. It is also to be noted that with exposing or possessing the supply it is necessary for the prosecution to prove that the Defendant did intend to supply. See *Birkett v McGlassons Ltd* [1957] 1 All ER 369.

7 For a definition of 'safe' see s 19(1) and also note the definition of an unsafe product within the General Products Safety Regulations 1994. Note, vitally, the insertion of the word '*reasonably*' within this sub-section.

8 See generally footnotes to Section 3(2). All relevant circumstances should be considered; *R v Walsall Magistrates, ex p PMS* (17 March 1994, unreported), DC, per Laws J.

9 See Section 3(2)(a) and the General Product Safety Regulations, Reg 2.

10 See the General Product Safety Regulations, Reg 10(2) and also Reg 6 which repealed s 3(b)(2) of s 10 and also the approval of Safety Standards Regulations 1987. Hence the weight attached to national standards has been considerably reduced when considering general product safety.

11 See now the General Product Safety Regulations, Reg 2 and the statement that 'The fact that higher levels of safety may be obtained or other products presenting a lesser degree of risk may be available shall not of itself cause the product to be considered other than a safe product'. It is to be noted that this sub-section specifically makes reference to cost.

12 See s 4(1)(a).

13 See the General Products Safety Regulations 1994 and Reg 10 which now produces a presumption of conformity where the United Kingdom lays down specific rules of law with health and safety requirements which a product must satisfy. Further see s 11 in relation to 'Safety Regulations'. This section is meant to apply where the goods are in fact covered by specific Safety Regulations which impose *requirements* with respect to the particular matter. However if the Regulations do not make provision for the matter in question then a prosecution under s 10 may still be permissable.

14 Repealed by Reg 6 of the General Product Safety Regulations 1994.

15 In accordance with the ordinary principles of statutory defences the burden is upon the Defendant and the standard is proof on balance of probabilities; *R v Carr-Briant* [1943] KB 607.

16 The presence of this sub-section shows the difficulties faced by Member States prior to the 1992 Directive which gave rise to the General Product Safety Regulations 1994. Different Member States had different provisions some with no criminal measures at all. This created barriers to trade and distorted competition within the internal market. Further, and

importantly, it led to the 'dumping' of unsafe products upon some Member States within the Community. The solution was to adopt a broad and horizontal legislative framework and this is why s 10 has now been very largely overtaken and disapplied by the 1994 Regulations.

17 Note the new duties upon a 'distributor' contained within the General Product Safety Regulations 1994. Sub-section 5 defines a retail business.

18 A person will 'know' a fact when he suspects that it is the case but takes no steps to follow up his suspicions; see *Taylor's Central Garages (Exeter) Ltd v Roper* (1951) 115 JP 445; *Ross v Moss* [1965] 3 All ER 145, and *Old Barn Nurseries v Oxer* (CO/1764/94, unreported); see also footnotes to Section 32(2).

19 Now see the definition of 'product' within Reg 2 of the General Product Safety Regulations 1994 which includes 'used or reconditioned' goods but excludes second-hand goods which are antiques or are supplied for repair or reconditioning before use (and where the supplier has clearly informed the person to whom he supplies the product to that effect).

20 See s 2; note 22.

21 The time allowed for the laying of any information under this Section is 6 months from the commission of the offence. The period under the General Product Safety Regulations 1994 is 12 months; see Reg 16.

22 See now the definition of 'product' within the General Product Safety Regulations 1994. For further definitions see s 19(1) and s 45(1).

11. Safety Regulations[1]

(1) The Secretary of State may by regulations under this section ('safety regulations') make such provision as he considers appropriate[2] for the purposes of section 10(3) above and for the purpose of securing –

(a) that goods to which this section applies are safe;

(b) that goods to which this section applies which are unsafe, or would be unsafe in the hands of persons of a particular description[3], are not made available to persons generally or, as the case may be, to persons of that description; and

(c) that appropriate information is, and inappropriate information is not, provided in relation to goods in which this section applies.

(2) Without prejudice to the generality of subsection (1) above, safety regulations may contain provision –

(a) with respect to the composition or content, design, construction, finish or packing of goods to which this section applies, with respect to standards for such goods and with respect to other matters relating to such goods;

(b) with respect to the giving, refusal, alteration or cancellation of approvals of such goods, of descriptions of such goods or of standards for such goods;

(c) with respect to the conditions that may be attached to any approval given under the regulations;

(d) for requiring such fees as may be determined by or under the regulations to be paid on the giving or alteration of any approval under the regulations and on the making of an application for such an approval or alteration;

(e) with respect to appeals against refusals, alterations and cancellations of approvals given under the regulations and against the conditions contained in such approvals;

(f) for requiring goods to which this section applies to be approved under the regulations or to conform to the requirements of the regulations or to descriptions or standards specified in or approved by or under the regulations;

(g) with respect to the testing or 1inspection of goods to which this section applies (including provision for determining the standards to be applied in carrying out any test or inspection);
(h) with respect to the ways of dealing with goods of which some or all do not satisfy a test required by or under the regulations or a standard connected with a procedure so required;
(i) for requiring a mark, warning or instruction or any other information relating to goods to be put on or to accompany the goods or to be used or provided in some other manner in relation to the goods, and for securing that inappropriate information is not given in relation to goods either by means of misleading marks or otherwise;
(j) for prohibiting persons from supplying, or from offering to supply, agreeing to supply, exposing for supply or possessing for supply, goods to which this section applies and component parts and raw materials for such goods;
(k) for requiring information to be given to any such person as may be determined by or under the regulations for the purpose of enabling that person to exercise any function conferred on him by the regulations.

(3) Without prejudice as aforesaid, safety regulations may contain provision –

(a) for requiring persons on whom functions are conferred by or under section 27 below to have regard, in exercising their functions so far as relating to any provision of safety regulations, to matters specified in a direction issued by the Secretary of State with respect to that provision;
(b) for securing that a person shall not be guilty of an offence under section 12 below unless it is shown that the goods in question do not conform to a particular standard;
(c) for securing that proceedings for such an offence are not brought in England and Wales except by or with the consent of the Secretary of State or the Director of Public Prosecutions;
(d) for securing that proceedings for such an offence are not brought in Northern Ireland except by or with the consent of the Secretary of State or the Director of Public Prosecutions for Northern Ireland;
(e) for enabling a magistrates' court in England and Wales or Northern Ireland to try an information or, in Northern Ireland, a complaint in respect of such an offence if the information was laid or the complaint made within twelve months from the time when the offence was committed[4];
(f) for enabling summary proceedings for such an offence to be brought in Scotland at any time within twelve months from the time when the offence was committed; and
(g) for determining the persons by whom and the manner in which, anything required to be done by or under the regulations is to be done.

(4) Safety regulations shall not provide for any contravention of the regulations to be an offence[5].

(5) Where the Secretary of State proposes to make safety regulations it shall be his duty[6] before he makes them –

(a) to consult such organisations as appear to him to be representative of interests substantially affected by the proposal;
(b) to consult such other persons as he considers appropriate; and
(c) in the case of proposed regulations relating to goods suitable for use at work, to consult the Health and Safety Commission in relation to the application of the proposed regulations to Great Britain;

but the preceding provisions of this subsection shall not apply in the case of regulations which provide for the regulations to cease to have effect at the end of a period of not more than twelve months beginning with the day on which they come into force and which contain a statement that it appears to the Secretary of State that the need to protect the public requires that the regulations should be made without delay.

(6) The power to make safety regulations shall be exercisable by statutory instrument subject to annulment in pursuance of a resolution of either House of Parliament and shall include power –

(a) to make different provision for different cases; and
(b) to make such supplemental, consequential and transitional provision as the Secretary of State considers appropriate.

(7) This section applies to any goods[7] other than –

(a) growing crops and things comprised in land by virtue of being attached to it;
(b) water, food, feeding stuff and fertiliser;
(c) gas which is, is to be or has been supplied by a person authorised to supply it by or under section 6, 7 or 8 of the Gas Act 1986 (authorization of supply of gas through pipes);
(d) controlled drugs and licensed medicinal products.

NOTES

1 The power to make Regulations is exercisable by statutory instrument. Sub-section 1 sets out general content and by s 5 there is a duty to consult before making such Regulations unless they are of not more than 12 months' duration and there is need to protect the public without delay. Failure to comply with a Safety Regulation will give rise to a civil action for breach of statutory duty: see s 41. Safety Regulations are subject to potential annulment by either House of Parliament as set out under s 6. The Secretary of State means in practice the Secretary of State for Trade and Industry.

2 If the Regulations are objectively justifiable and comply with sub-ss 1(2) and (3) this phrase will have little effect in that it will be extremely difficult to challenge the exercise of a ministerial power. See *Padfield v Minister of Agriculture, Fisheries and Food* [1968] AC 997, HL; *Laker Airways Ltd v Department of Trade* [1977] QB 643, CA.

3 The power to protect a particular class of persons who are peculiarly at risk from a certain hazard.

4 Ordinarily the time limit would be 6 months as it is for an alleged offence contrary to s 10 of the Act. Usually a period of 12 months is stipulated within Regulations and indeed this is the case within the General Products Safety Regulations 1994.

5 This is because s 12 provides for the relevant offences. It is to be noted however that the General Product Safety Regulations 1994 which are not in force by virtue of this section contain within them relevant provisions in relation to offences.

6 This duty in practice involves consultation with the relevant Trade Associations and consumer organisations. Often draft Regulations are sent out for comment. See *Agricultural, Horticultural and Forestry Industry Training Board v Aylesbury Mushrooms Ltd* [1972] 1 All ER 280 and *R v Secretary of State for Health, ex p United States Tobacco International Inc* [1992] QB 353.

7 See also s 10(7).

12. Offences against the safety regulations[1]

(1) Where safety regulations[2] prohibit a person from supplying or offering or agreeing to supply[3] any goods or from exposing or possessing any goods for supply that person shall be guilty of an offence[4] if he contravenes the prohibition.

(2) Where safety regulations require a person who makes or processes any goods in the course of carrying on a business[5] –

(a) to carry out a particular test or use a particular procedure in connection with the making or processing of the goods with a view to ascertaining whether the goods satisfy any requirement of such regulations; or

(b) to deal or not to deal in a particular way with a quantity of the goods of which the whole or part does not satisfy such a test or does not satisfy standards connected with such a procedure,

that person shall be guilty of an offence if he does not comply with the requirement.

(3) If a person contravenes a provision of safety regulations which prohibits or requires the provision, by means of a mark or otherwise, of information of a particular kind in relation to goods, he shall be guilty of an offence.

(4) Where safety regulations require any person to give information to another for the purpose of enabling that other to exercise any function, that person shall be guilty of an offence[6] if –

(a) he fails without reasonable cause[7] to comply with the requirement; or

(b) in giving the information which is required of him –

(i) he makes any statement which he knows[8] is false in a material particular[9];

(ii) he recklessly makes any statement which is false in a material particular[10].

NOTES

1 This section contains the provisions formally within the Consumer Safety Act 1978, s 2(1) to (3). A defence of due diligence is available under s 39 of the Act.

2 See s 11.

3 See s 46 and also the footnotes to Reg 13 of the General Product Safety Regulations 1994 in relation to offering, agreeing, exposing or possessing for supply.

4 Unless the Regulations specifically provide to the contrary (which they usually do) the relevant period for the laying of an information is 6 months. The prosecution has to prove the case on the ordinary principles and any statutory defence has to be established upon the balance of probabilities.

5 This phrase denotes more than an isolated transaction. Further there has to be some degree of management or control: See *Cain v Butler* [1916] 1 KB 759 at 762 cf *Cornelius v Phillips* [1918] AC 199.

6 There is no defence under s 39 to an offence under this section. See s 39(5).

7 See *Nagy v Weston* [1965] 1 All ER 78, *Dixon v Atfield* [1975] 3 All ER 265.

8 See notes to s 10.

9 This is a wide phrase. A particular may be material by virtue of its relevance to another statement, see *R v Tyson* (1867) LR 1 CCR 107 and may be misleading by virtue of the absence of what is said; see *Peek v Gurney* (1873) LR 6 HL 377. It is not necessarily the case that it has to be a statement as to fact providing that it can be proved that the opinion was not genuinely held. However this may be very difficult to prove: see *R v Schlesinger* (1847) 10 QB 670, and also *Curtis v Chemical Cleaning and Dyeing Co Ltd* [1951] 1 KB 805, CA.

10 See *Metropolitan Police Comr v Caldwell* [1982] AC 341, *R v Lawrence* [1982] AC 510, *R v Pigg* [1982] 2 All ER 591, CA; revsd, [1983] 1 All ER 56, HL, and *Goldman v Thai Airways International Ltd* [1983] 3 All ER 693.

13. Prohibition notices and notices to warn[1]

(1) The Secretary of State may –

(a) serve[2] on any person a notice ('a prohibition notice') prohibiting that person, except with the consent of the Secretary of State, from supplying[3] or from offering to supply, agreeing to supply, exposing for supply or possessing for supply, any relevant goods which the Secretary of State considers are unsafe and which are described in the notice.

(b) serve on any person a notice ('a notice to warn') requiring that person at his own expense to publish, in a form and manner and on occasions specified in the notice, a warning about any relevant goods which the Secretary of State considers are unsafe, which that person supplies or has supplied and which are described in the notice[4].

(2) Schedule 2[5] to this Act shall have effect with respect to prohibition notices and notices to warn; and the Secretary of State may by regulations make provision specifying the manner in which information is to be given to any person under that Schedule.

(3) A consent given by the Secretary of State for the purposes of a prohibition notice may impose such conditions on the doing of anything for which the consent is required as the Secretary of State considers appropriate.

(4) A person who contravenes a prohibition notice or a notice to warn shall be guilty of an offence[6] and liable on summary conviction to imprisonment for a term not exceeding six months or to a fine not exceeding level 5 on the standard scale or to both.

(5) The power to make regulations under subsection (2) above shall be exercisable by statutory instrument subject to annulment in pursuance of a resolution of either House of Parliament and shall include power –

(a) to make different provision for different cases; and

(b) to make such supplemental, consequential and transitional provision as the Secretary of State considers appropriate.

(6) In this section 'relevant goods' means –

(a) in relation to a prohibition notice, any goods to which section 11 above applies;

(b) in relation to a notice to warn, any goods to which that section applies or any growing crops or things comprised in land by virtue of being attached to it.

(5) A person guilty of an offence under this section shall be liable on summary conviction to imprisonment for a term not exceeding six months or to a fine not exceeding level 5 on the standard scale or to both.

NOTES

1 See formerly the Consumer Safety Act 1977, s 3(1)(a) to (c). However it is to be noted that s 3(1)(a) contained a provision which is not repeated within this section. This is because Safety Regulations can be made for a period of not more than 12 months where there is a need to protect the public without delay: see s 11(5). A Prohibition Notice is a safety provision within s 45(1) but the Notice to Warn is not.

2 See s 44.

3 See the notes to s 46. Great caution should be exercised to ensure that goods are not supplied (or offered, agreed, exposed or possessed for supply) when caught by the description in the notice. See also *United States Tobacco International Inc v Secretary of State for Health* (1990) 155 JP 144 with regard to supply outside the United Kingdom.

4 See Reg 8 of the General Product Safety Regulations 1994.

5 This Schedule sets out the procedure for Prohibition Notices and Notices to Warn. When considering an appeal against a Prohibition Notice it is important to note that when the person appointed to consider the representations (oral or written) about such a Notice has made his report under s 4(1)(a) it is not ordinarily released to the person making the appeal. Under s 4(2) it is the duty of the Secretary of State to consider any report made to him and to inform the trader of the decision with respect to the Prohibition Notice but again there is no duty to give reasons. As it is highly unlikely that the Prohibition Notice has been issued without the support of cogent evidence it is difficult to challenge a refusal to uphold an appeal upon a Prohibition Notice save upon procedural grounds. As the Schedule sets out the procedure in considerable detail this is also an unlikely occurrence. In the case of the Prohibition Notice concerning 'jelly balls' (and associated products made from memory gel) issued in December 1993 by Baroness Denton considerable dissatisfaction was expressed at the refusal to disclose the report of the appointed person or the reasons behind the subsequent decision that the Prohibition Notice should remain in force. Hearings will generally take place at the DTI and a more detailed written procedure is normally provided to parties wishing to make oral or written representations.

6 There is a defence of due diligence under s 39 of the Act.

14. Suspension notices[1]

(1) Where an enforcement authority has reasonable grounds for suspecting[2] that any safety provision[3] has been contravened in relation to any goods, the authority may serve[4] a notice ('a suspension notice') prohibiting the person on whom it is served, for such period ending not more than six months after the date of the notice as in specified therein, from doing any of the following things without the consent of the authority, that is to say,[5] supplying the goods,offering to supply them, agreeing to supply them or exposing them for supply.

(2) A suspension notice served by an enforcement authority in respect of any goods shall[6] –

(a) describe the goods in a manner sufficient to identify them;
(b) set out the grounds on which the authority suspects that a safety provision has been contravened in relation to the goods; and
(c) state that, and the manner in which, the person on whom the notice is served may appeal against the notice under section 15 below.

(3) A suspension notice served by an enforcement authority for the purpose of prohibiting a person for any period from doing the things mentioned in subsection (1) above in relation to any goods may also require that person to keep the authority informed of the whereabouts throughout that period of any of those goods in which he has an interest.

(4) Where a suspension notice has been served on any person in respect of any goods, no further such notice shall be served on that person in respect of the same goods unless –

(a) proceedings against that person for an offence in respect of a contravention in relation to the goods of a safety provision (not being an offence under this section); or
(b) proceedings for the forfeiture of the goods under section 16 or 17 below[7],

are pending[8] at the end of the period specified in the first-mentioned notice.

(5) A consent given by an enforcement authority for the purposes of

subsection (1) above may impose such conditions on the doing of anything for which the consent is required as the authority considers appropriate[9].

(6) Any person who contravenes a suspension notice shall be guilty of an offence[10] and liable on summary conviction to imprisonment for a term not exceeding six months or to a fine not exceeding level 5 on the standard scale or to both.

(7) Where an enforcement authority serves a suspension notice in respect of any goods, the authority shall be liable to pay compensation to any person having an interest in the goods in respect of any loss or damage caused by reason of the service of the notice if –

(a) there has been no contravention in relation to the goods of any safety provision;and

(b) the exercise of the power is not attributable to any neglect or default by that person[11].

(8) Any disputed question as to the right to or the amount of any compensation payable under this section shall be determined by arbitration[12] or, in Scotland, by a single arbiter appointed, failing agreement between the parties, by the sheriff.

NOTES

1 See formerly s 3 of the Consumer Safety (Amendment) Act 1986 and the proposal regarding the suspension of supplied specified goods contained in the Department of Trade and Industry White Paper ('the Safety of Goods') (Cmnd 9302) para 25. A Suspension Notice is a 'safety provision' within the meanings of s 45(1). This section should also be read together with Section 15 which provides for appeals against Suspension Notices.

2 This is an issue of fact but unlikely in practice to be challenged. By virtue of the appeal procedure and especially the liability to pay compensation under s 14(7) such notices are not likely served by Trading Standards Departments unless there are strong grounds for the suspension. For further discussion of this phrase see *Dumbell v Roberts* [1944] 1 All ER 326; *Hussien v Chong Fook Kam* [1970] AC 942.

3 See s 45(1). It is important to note that the definition of a safety provision means the General Safety Requirement or any provision of Safety Regulations but 'Safety Regulations' means Regulations under s 11 and *not* therefore the General Product Safety Regulations 1994. However this gap is specifically covered by Reg 11 (b).

4 See s 44.

5 See s 46 and also *United States Tobacco International Inc v Secretary of State for Health* (1990) 155 JP 144 in relation to supply outside the United Kingdom.

6 The Notice *must* contain these matters.

7 The effect of this sub-section is to force a Trading Standards Department having served the Notice to follow it through and take such further action as is appropriate failing which the Notice shall expire after 6 months. See also the footnotes to s 15 and chapter 10. If it is the manufacturer's contention that there has not been a contravention of any safety provision then there are tactical considerations when appealing against the Suspension Notice rather than first awaiting any subsequent prosecution or proceedings for forfeiture of the goods.

8 This phrase will ordinarily mean a decision to take action has been made. It is important to note that it is strongly arguable that it does not require a relevant Summons to have been issued and in some cases it may be a period of up to 12 months before any information has to be laid. (Although in others such as under s 10, there is a 6 month limit).

9 It would be difficult in practice to challenge any reasonable and logical requirement. See (with regard to the judicial review of the exercise of such powers) the footnotes to s 11.

10 There is a defence under s 39.

11 See former provisions of the Consumer Safety (Amendment) Act 1986, s 3(6) and Sch 2. See also s 34.

12 See Halsbury's Laws, Vol 2: Arbitration and the Arbitration Acts 1950 and 1979.

15. Appeals against suspension notices[1]

(1) Any person having an interest in any goods in respect of which a suspension notice is for the time being in force may apply for an order setting

aside the notice.

(2) An application under this section may be made[2] –

(a) to any magistrates' court in which proceedings have been brought in England and Wales or Northern Ireland –
  (i) for an offence in respect of a contravention in relation to the goods of any safety provision; or
  (ii) for the forfeiture of the goods under section 16 below;

(b) where no such proceedings have been so brought, by way of complaint to a magistrates' court; or

(c) in Scotland, by summary application to the sheriff.

(3) On an application under this section to a magistrates' court in England and Wales or Northern Ireland the court shall make an order setting aside the suspension notice only if the court is satisfied that there has been no contravention in relation to the goods of any safety provision[3].

(4) On an application under this section to the sheriff he shall make an order setting aside the suspension notice only if he is satisfied that at the date of making the order –

(a) proceedings for an offence in respect of a contravention in relation to the goods of any safety provision; or

(b) proceedings for the forfeiture of the goods under section 17 below,

have not been brought or, having been brought, have been concluded.

(5) Any person aggrieved by an order made under this section by a magistrates' court in England and Wales or Northern Ireland, or by a decision of such a court not to make such an order, may appeal against that order or decision –

(a) in England and Wales, to the Crown Court;

(b) in Northern Ireland, to the county court;

and an order so made may contain such provision as appears to the court to be appropriate for delaying the coming into force of the order pending the making and determination of any appeal (including any application under section 111 of the Magistrates' Courts Act 1980 or Article 146 of the Magistrates' Courts (Northern Ireland) (statement of case)).

NOTES

1 See the former provisions of the Consumer Safety (Amendment) Act 1986. It is clear that in ordinary cases this procedure must be followed as opposed to judicial review if a Suspension Notice is to be challenged; See *R v Birmingham City Council, ex p Ferrero Ltd* [1993] 1 All ER 530, CA.

2 Once an application is made it should be noted that the enforcement authority may apply for a forfeiture order pursuant to s 16.

3 There has been some debate upon the onus and standard of proof under this section: See Miller: Product Liability and Safety Encyclopedia (iv)(165). In practice as the Suspension Notice has to set out the grounds on which the authority suspects that a Safety Provision has been contravened under s 14(2) there is no reason why the burden should not lie upon the party seeking to argue that there has been no contravention in relation to the goods. However this may lead to considerable practical difficulties if the party is unaware of the nature and extent of the full argument of the Trading Standards Department and also its evidence. In practice this has led to Courts allowing rebuttal evidence to be called. However if proceedings have been brought in respect of an offence, as envisaged by sub-s 2(1) it is submitted that the ordinary procedure should be followed. Unfortunately, if this is the case the Magistrates may be left with the difficult task of considering two separate burdens and standards of proof (i.e upon the prosecution to prove the offence upon reasonable doubt

and upon the party upon whom the Notice is served (the defendant) to prove that there has been no contravention of any Safety Provision upon the balance of probabilities).

16. Forfeiture:[1] England and Wales and Northern Ireland

(1) An enforcement authority in England and Wales or Northern Ireland may apply under this section for an order for the forfeiture of any goods on the grounds that there has been a contravention in relation to the goods of a safety provision[2].

(2) An application under this section may be made –

(a) where proceedings have been brought in a magistrates' court for an offence in respect of a contravention in relation to some or all of the goods of any safety provision[3], to that court;
(b) where an application with respect to some or all of the goods has been made to a magistrates' court under section 15[4] above or section 33[5] below, to that court; and
(c) where no application for the forfeiture of the goods has been made under paragraph (a) or (b) above, by way of complaint to a magistrates' court.

(3) On an application under this section the court shall make an order for the forfeiture of any goods only if it is satisfied that there has been a contravention[6] in relation to the goods of a safety provision.

(4) For the avoidance of doubt it is declared that a court may infer for the purposes of this section that there has been a contravention in relation to any goods of a safety provision if it is satisfied that any such provision has been contravened in relation to goods which are representative of those goods (whether by reason of being of the same design or part of the same consignment or batch or otherwise)[7].

(5) Any person aggrieved by an order made under this section by a magistrates' court, or by a decision of such a court not to make such an order, may appeal against that order or decision –

(a) in England and Wales, to the Crown Court;
(b) in Northern Ireland, to the county court;

and an order so made may contain such provision as appears to the court to be appropriate for delaying the coming into force of the order pending the making and determination of any appeal (including any application under section 111 of the Magistrates' Courts Act 1980 or Article 146 of the Magistrates' Court (Northern Ireland) Order 1981 (statement of case).

(6) Subject to subsection (7) below, where any goods are forfeited under this section they shall be destroyed in accordance with such directions as the court may give[8].

(7) On making an order under this section a magistrates' court may, if it considers it appropriate to do so[9], direct that the goods to which the order relates shall (instead of being destroyed) be released, to such person as the court may specify, on condition that that person –

(a) does not supply those goods to any person otherwise than as mentioned in section 46(7)(a) or (b) below[10]; and
(b) complies with any order to pay costs or expenses (including any order under section 35 below) which has been made against that person in the proceedings for the order for forfeiture.

NOTES

1 The power to seek and obtain forfeiture orders was previously contained within the Consumer Safety (Amendment) Act 1986. Applications for forfeiture usually occur at the end of a successful prosecution. There is however a right under this section to apply for forfeiture and by-pass the prosecution process. Under s 29(6) an Officer may seize and detain any goods which he has reasonable grounds for suspecting may be liable to be forfeited. Further, where a suspension notice has been served, a second suspension notice can follow if proceedings for forfeiture under this section are pending. See s 14(4)(b). The combination of these powers means that an Officer can effectively remove goods from the market and seek their destruction notwithstanding that a prosecution is undesirable or not likely to be successful due to a reason other than the fact that the goods do not contravene a safety provision (eg the statutory defence under s 39).

2 See s 45 and also Reg 11(b) of the General Product Safety Regulations 1994 which states that the requirements of those Regulations shall constitute safety provisions for the purposes of ss 14, 15, 16, 17 and 18.

3 See sub-s 4 below.

4 An appeal against a suspension notice.

5 An appeal against detention of goods.

6 It is for the prosecution (or person laying the complaint) to prove contravention and the standard is proof beyond reasonable doubt (see generally *Woolmington v DPP* [1935] AC 462). See also the notes to s 15.

7 The combination of this sub-section and sub-s 2(a) above allows the local authority to seek a forfeiture order of an entire consignment of goods upon the basis of a sample prosecution. However, it is to be noted that this is an inference and it is possible to argue that the specific items which have been the subject of a prosecution or an appeal against a suspension notice or detention or by way of complaint, are not truly representative of the whole batch. Clearly this would not be possible if the question is one of unsafe design but may be possible if it is a question of individual construction and if, for example, by virtue of in-house records and testing it can be proved that defective items relate only to one carton within a batch.

8 Where a Court makes an Order under this section it may in addition order 'any person having an interest in the goods' to reimburse an enforcement authority for any expenditure by the authority in connection with either seizure or detention of the goods or compliance by the authority with directions given by the Court such as under this sub-section; See s 35 post.

9 The Court has a discretion as to whether it is proper to make the Order in the circumstances. For example a Court may consider that the goods if released to a person specified for the purposes of s 46(7)(a) or (b) who is outside the jurisdiction of the Court (eg the Far East) may be re-exported back into the Community through another Member State. Hence the Court may require evidence of the *bona fides* or credentials of the person to whom the goods are to be released. See next note.

10 Sub-section (a) refers to 'supplying goods where the person supplied carries on a business of buying goods of the same description as those and repairing or reconditioning them; and sub-s (b) refers to 'supplying goods by a sale of articles as scrap (that is to say, for the value of material included in the articles rather than for the value of the articles themselves). The value of this section is that it allows a person with an interest in the goods to recoup some value from the goods. Normally the Court will require strong evidence that the specified person will indeed repair or recondition the goods or use their component parts as 'scrap'. It has been held that this section does not cover return of the defective goods by an importer to a *manufacturer* outside the Community; *Yorkshire Trading Standards v PMS* (April 1989, unreported), Crown Court at Wakefield.

18. Power to obtain information[1]

(1) If the Secretary of State considers that, for the purpose of deciding when –

(a) to make, vary or revoke any safety regulations; or
(b) to serve, vary or revoke a prohibition notice;or
(c) to serve or revoke a notice to warn,

he requires information which another person[2] is likely to be able to furnish, the Secretary of State may serve[3] on the other person a notice under this section.

(2) A notice served on any person under this section may require that person –

(a) to furnish to the Secretary of State, within a period specified in the notice, such information as is so specified;

(b) to produce such records as are specified in the notice at a time and place so specified and to permit a person appointed by the Secretary of State for the purpose to take copies of the records at that time and place.

(3) A person shall be guilty of an offence if he –

(a) fails, without reasonable cause[4], to comply with a notice served on him under this section; or

(b) in purporting to comply with a requirement which by virtue of paragraph (a) of subsection (2) above is contained in such a notice –

(i) furnishes information which he knows is false in a material particular[5]; or

(ii) recklessly[6] furnishes information which is false in a material particular.

(4) A person guilty of an offence[7] under subsection (3) above shall -

(a) in the case of an offence under paragraph (a) of that subsection, be liable on summary conviction to a fine not exceeding level 5 on the standard scale; and

(b) in the case of an offence under paragraph (b) of that subsection be liable –

(i) on conviction on indictment, to a fine;

(ii) on summary conviction, to a fine not exceeding the statutory maximum.

NOTES

1 This section is based upon powers contained in the Consumer Safety Act 1978. See also s 38(1)(c) which states that a person shall be guilty of an offence if he discloses any information which was obtained by him in consequence of the exercise by the Secretary of State of a power conferred by s 18 subject to the provisions of s 38(2).

2 Includes a body of persons corporate or incorporate. See Interpretation Act 1978, s 5.

3 See s 44.

4 This will be a matter of fact in each case, but adverse inferences are likely to be drawn from a failure to communicate the 'cause' as soon as possible.

5 See notes to s 12(4)(i).

6 See note to s 12(4)(ii).

7 The difference in seriousness of the potential defences under s 3(a) and 3(b) are reflected in the fact that an allegation as to the former can be tried on a summary basis only whereas the latter can be tried upon indictment with the potential of an unlimited fine.

19. Interpretation of Part II

(1) In this Part –[1]

'controlled drug' means a controlled drug within the meaning of the Misuse of Drugs Act 1971[2];

'feeding stuff' and 'fertiliser' have the same meanings as in Part IV of the Agriculture Act 1970[3];

'food' does not include anything containing tobacco but, subject to that, has the same meaning as in the Food Act 1984[4] or, in relation to Northern Ireland, the same meaning as in the Food and Drugs Act (Northern Ireland) 1958;

'licensed medicinal product' means –

(a) any medicinal product within the meaning of the Medicines Act 1968[5] in respect of which a product licence[6] within the meaning of that Act is for the time being in force; or

(b) any other article or substance in respect of which any such licence is for the time being in force in pursuance of an order under section 104 or 105 of that Act (application of Act to other articles and substances);

'safe'[7] in relation to any goods, means such that there is no risk, or no risk apart from one reduced to a minimum that any of the following will (whether immediately or after a definite or indefinite period) cause the death of, or any personal injury to, any person whatsoever, that is to say –

(a) the goods;
(b) the keeping, use or consumption of the goods[8];
(c) the assembly of any of the goods which are, or are to be, supplied unassembled;
(d) any emission or leakage from the goods or, as a result of the keeping, use or consumption of the goods, from anything else; or
(e) reliance on the accuracy of any measurement, calculation or other reading made by or by means of the goods.

and 'safe' and 'unsafe' shall be construed accordingly;

'tobacco' includes any tobacco product within the meaning of the Tobacco Products Duty Act 1979 and any article or substance containing tobacco and intended for oral or nasal use.

(2) In the definition of 'safe' in subsection (1) above, references to the keeping use or consumption of any goods are references to –

(a) the keeping, use or consumption of the goods by the persons by whom, and in all or any of the ways or circumstances in which, they might reasonably be expected to be kept, used or consumed; and
(b) the keeping, use or consumption of the goods either alone or in conjunction with other goods in conjunction with which they might reasonably be expected to be kept, used or consumed.

NOTES

1 Much of this section derives from definitions contained within the Consumer Safety Act 1978, s 9(4) as amended by the Food Act 1984, s 134.
2 See s 2(1)(a) of the Misuse of Drugs Act 1971.
3 See s 66(1) of the Agriculture Act 1970 which states "'feeding stuff' means feeding stuff for such descriptions of animals as may be prescribed, being animals which, or kinds of which, are commonly kept for the production of food, wool, skins or fur or for the purpose of their use in farming"; "'Fertiliser' means a fertiliser used in the cultivation of crops or plants of any description, including trees".
4 Section 131 but now see s 1 of the Food Safety Act 1990.
5 See s 130 of the Medicines Act 1968.
6 See s 7 of the Medicines Act 1968.
7 The definition of 'safety' relates to the risk of personal injury or death and hence is not concerned with damage to goods. There is a clear distinction between 'risk' and 'hazard' with the risk being the likelihood of a 'hazard' occurring. See also Reg 2 of the General Product Safety Regulations 1994 which provides a definition of a 'safe product'. Section 10 of the Consumer Protection Act 1987 refers to 'reasonable safety'.
8 See sub-s 2 below.

Chapter 16

PART IV ENFORCEMENT OF PARTS I AND II

27. **Enforcement**[1]

(1) Subject to the following provisions of this section –

(a) it shall be the duty of every weights and measures authority[2] in Great Britain to enforce within their area[3] the safety provisions[4] and the provisions made by or under Part III of this Act; and
(b) it shall be the duty of every district council in Northern Ireland to enforce within their area the safety provisions.

(2) The Secretary of State may by regulations[5] –

(a) wholly or partly transfer any duty imposed by subsection (1) above on a weights and measures authority or a district council in Northern Ireland to such other person who has agreed to the transfer as is specified in the regulations;
(b) relieve such an authority or council of any such duty as it is exercisable in relation to such goods as may be described in the regulations.

(3) The power to make regulations under subsection (2) above shall be exercisable by statutory instrument subject to annulment in pursuance of a resolution of either House of Parliament and shall include power –

(a) to make different provision for different cases; and
(b) to make such supplemental, consequential and transitional provision as the Secretary of State considers appropriate.

(4) Nothing in this section shall authorise any weights and measures authority, or any person on whom functions are conferred by regulations under subsection (2) above, to bring proceedings in Scotland for an offence.

NOTES
1 The content of this section was formerly set out in the Consumer Safety Act 1978, s 5(1) as modified by s 11(e).
2 For the definition of 'weights and measures authority' see s 69 of the Weights and Measures Act 1985. The duty is a statutory duty.
3 There is no general duty in relation to enforcement upon a national basis. The result has frequently been that authorities in different parts of the country have conflicting views with regard to the safety or otherwise of various products. Although there is a 'home authority' principle whereby any authority who has a query with regard to a product can contact the

authority with jurisdiction for the area in which the manufacturer or importer is based, there is frequently only minimal contact; see chapter 9, *Building the Prosecution Case*.

4 See s 45(1) and also Reg 11(c)(i) of the General Product Safety Regulations 1994 which sets out a parallel duty upon weights and measures authorities in respect of the content of those Regulations. The duty extends to asking for all relevant information; *Snape v Mulvenna* (1994) Times, 28 December.

5 See formerly s 5(2) of the Consumer Safety Act 1978.

28. Test purchases[1]

(1) An enforcement authority shall have power, for the purpose of ascertaining whether any safety provision or any provision made by or under Part III of this Act has been contravened in relation to any goods, services, accommodation or facilities –

(a) to make, or to authorise an officer of the authority to make, any purchase of any goods; or
(b) to secure, or to authorise an officer of the authority to secure, the provision of any services, accommodation or facilities.

(2) Where –

(a) any goods purchased under this section by or on behalf of an enforcement authority are submitted to a test; and
(b) the test leads to –
  (i) the bringing of proceedings for an offence in respect of a contravention in relation to the goods of any safety provision or of any provision made by or under Part III of this Act or for the forfeiture of the goods under section 16 or 17 above; or
  (ii) the serving of a suspension notice in respect of any goods; and
(c) the authority is requested to do so and it is practicable for the authority to comply with the request[2],

the authority shall allow the person from whom the goods were purchased or any person who is a party to the proceedings or has an interest in any goods to which the notice relates to have the goods tested[3].

(3) The Secretary of State may by regulations provide that any test of goods purchased under this section by or on behalf of an enforcement authority shall–

(a) be carried out at the expense of the authority in a manner and by a person prescribed by or determined under the regulations; or
(b) be carried out either as mentioned in paragraph (a) above or by the authority in a manner prescibed by the regulations.

(4) The power to make regulations under sub–section (3) above shall be exercisable by statutory instrument subject to annulment in pursuance of a resolution of either House of Parliament and shall include power –

(a) to make different provision for different cases; and
(b) to make such supplemental, consequential and transitional provision as the Secretary of State considers appropriate.

(5) Nothing in this section shall authorise the acquisition by or on behalf of an enforcement authority of any interest in land.

NOTES

1 This section contains powers formerly contained within the Consumer Safety Act 1978, Sch 2. See also s 44(4).

2 It will not be practicable for the authority to comply with the request where the goods have been tested to destruction, for example by way of test of flammability. It should be noted that the word 'practicable' produces a strict duty upon the authority and measures may be practicable which are not reasonably practicable; see *Marshall v Gotham Co Ltd* [1954] AC 360, HL.

3 This section does not specifically state that the goods have to be released and it would be possible for an authority to request that any individual who wished to have the goods tested should arrange for the test to take place at the Local Authority's premises. The power is however an important one for the defendant faced with a prosecution or when in receipt of a suspension notice, as it allows an ability not only to test for compliance with the relevant Safety Provision but also to assess whether the item within the possession of the Authority is representative of any consignment or batch as a whole.

29. Powers of search etc[1]

(1) Subject to the following provisions of this Part[2], a duly authorised officer of an enforcement authority may at any reasonable hour[3] and on production[4], if required, of his credentials exercise any of the powers conferred by the following provisions of this section.

(2) The officer may, for the purposes of ascertaining whether there has been any contravention of any safety provision or of any provision made by or under Part III of this Act, inspect any goods and enter any premises other than premises occupied only as a person's residence[5].

(3) The officer may, for the purpose of ascertaining whether there has been any contravention of any safety provision, examine any procedure (including any arrangements for carrying out a test) connected with the production of any goods.

(4) If the officer has reasonable grounds for suspecting[6] that any goods are manufactured or imported goods which have not been supplied in the United Kingdom since they were manufactured or imported he may–

(a) for the purpose of ascertaining whether there has been any contravention of any safety provision in relation to the goods, require any person carrying on a business, or employed in connection with a business, to produce[7] any records relating to the business;

(b) for the purpose of ascertaining (by testing or otherwise) whether there has been any such contravention, seize and detain the goods[8];

(c) take copies of, or of any entry in, any records produced by virtue of paragraph (a) above.

(5) If the officer has reasonable grounds for suspecting[9] that there has been a contravention in relation to any goods of any safety provisions or of any provision made by or under Part III of this Act, he may –

(a) for the purpose of ascertaining whether there has been any such contravention, require any person carrying on a business, or employed in connection with a business, to produce any records relating to the business[10];

(b) for the purpose of ascertaining (by testing or otherwise) whether there has been any such contravention, seize and detain the goods;

(c) take copies of, or of any entry in, any records produced by virtue of paragraph (a) above.

(6) The officer may seize and detain –

(a) any goods or records which he has reasonable grounds for believing may be required as evidence in proceedings for an offence in respect of a contravention of any safety provision or of any provision made by or under Part III of this Act;

(b) any goods which he has reasonable grounds for suspecting may be liable to be forfeited under section 16 or 17 above.

(7) If and to the extent that it is reasonably necessary to do so to prevent a contravention of any safety provision or of any provision made by or under Part III of this Act, the officer may, for the purpose of exercising his power under subsection (4), (5) or (6) above to seize any goods or records –

(a) require any person having authority to do so to open any container or to open any vending machine; and

(b) himself open or break open any such container or machine where a requirement made under paragraph (a) above in relation to the container or machine has not been compiled with.

NOTES

1 This section contains provisions previously within Sch 2 of the Consumer Safety Act 1978. Interestingly, by virtue of the definition of Safety Provision under s 45 of the Act, and as Reg 11 of the General Product Safety Regulations 1994 does not deem the Regulations to constitute safety provisions for the purposes of this section, the powers exercisable under this section will not relate to an alleged contravention of those Regulations. The reasons for this omission are unclear and it may simply be an oversight.

2 Sections 27 to 35 of the Act.

3 This is a question of fact in each individual case. In respect of a request at an unusual time see *Small v Bickley* (1875) 32 LT 726 (Sunday afternoon).

4 This does not mean that the right of entry can only be exercised if a relevant person is present see *Grove v Eastern Gas Board* [1952] 1 KB 77, CA.

5 The premises must be used solely as a residence and not for business purposes. In *Dudley Metropolitan Borough Council v Debenhams plc* (1994) 159 JP 18, it was held that a routine inspection by a Trading Standards Officer was a search within the ordinary meaning of the word, and that the provisions of Code B of the Police and Criminal Evidence Act 1984 (s 66) Codes of Practice relating to search of premises and seizure of property applied.

6 See footnotes to s 14(1) and *Dudley Metropolitan Borough Council v Debenhams plc* (above).

7 There is no power to seize, see sub–s (c). The power therefore is only to inspect the relevant records unless the Officer has reasonable grounds for believing that such records may be required as evidence in proceedings for an offence or relevant to an application for the forfeiture of the goods under ss 16 or 17. See sub–s 6. However, note s 47(1) in relation to legal professional privilege.

8 See s 34 for compensation for seizure and detention where there has been no contravention in relation to the goods of any safety provision.

9 See *Dudley Metropolitan Borough Council v Debenhams plc* (1994) 159 JP 18.

10 See the note to sub–s (4) above; cf s 47(1).

30. Provisions supplemental to s 29[1]

(1) An officer seizing any goods or records under section 29 above shall inform the following person that the goods or records have been so seized, that is to say –

(a) the person from whom they are seized[2]; and

(b) in the case of imported goods seized on any premises under the control of the Commissioners of Customs and Excise, the importer of those goods (within the meaning of the Customs and Excise Management Act 1979).

(2) If a justice of the peace[3] –

(a) is satisfied by any written information on oath that there are reasonable grounds for believing either –

(i) that any goods or records which any officer has power to inspect under section 29 above are on any premises and that their inspection is likely[4] to disclose evidence that there has been a contravention of any safety provision or of any provision made by or under Part III of this Act; or

(ii) that such a contravention has taken place, is taking place or is about to take place on any premises; and

(b) is also satisfied by any such information either –

(i) that admission to the premises has been or is likely to be refused and that notice of intention to apply for a warrant under this subsection has been given to the occupier[5]; or

(ii) that an application for admission, or the giving of such a notice, would defeat the object of the entry or that the premises are unoccupied or that the occupier is temporarily absent and it might defeat the object of the entry to await his return,

the justice may by warrant[6] under this hand, which shall continue in force for a period of one month, authorise any officer of an enforcement authority to enter the premises, if need be by force.

(3) An officer entering any premises by virtue of section 29 above or a warrant under subsection (2) above may take with him such other persons[7] and such equipment as may appear to him necessary.

(4) On leaving any premises which a person is authorised to enter by a warrant under subsection (2) above, that person shall, if the premises are unoccupied or the occupier is temporarily absent, leave the premises as effectively secured against trespassers as he found them.

(5) If any person who is not an officer of an enforcement authority purports to act as such under section 29 above or this section he shall be guilty of an offence and liable on summary conviction to a fine not exceeding level 5 on the standard scale.

(6) Where any goods seized by an officer under section 29 above are submitted to a test, the officer shall inform the persons mentioned in subsection (1) above of the result of the test, if –

(a) proceedings are brought for an offence in respect of a contravention in relation to the goods of any safety provision or of any provision made by or under Part III of this Act or for the forfeiture of the goods under section 16 or 17 above, or a suspension notice is served in respect of any goods; and

(b) the officer is requested to do so and it is practicable[8] to comply with the request,

the officer shall allow any person who is a party to the proceedings or, as the case may be, has an interest in the goods to which the notice relates to have the goods tested.

(7) The Secretary of State may by regulations provide that any test of goods seized under section 29 above by an officer of an enforcement authority shall –

(a) be carried out at the expense of the authority in a manner and by a person prescribed by or determined under the regulations; or

(b) be carried out either as mentioned in paragraph (a) above or by the authority in a manner prescribed by the regulations.

(8) The power to make regulations under subsection (7) above shall be exercisable by statutory instrument subject to annulment in pursuance of a resolution of either House of Parliament and shall include power –

(a) to make different provision for different cases; and

(b) to make such supplemental, consequential and transitional provision as the Secretary of State considers appropriate.

(9) (Applies to Scotland only)

(10) In the application of this section to Northern Ireland, the references in subsection (2) above to any information on oath shall be construed as references to any complaint on oath.

NOTES

1 This section contains provisions formerly contained within the Consumer Safety Act 1978, Sch 2 and s 7.

2 See s 44(4) in relation to vending machines.

3 See the Justices of the Peace Act 1979.

4 'Likely' has been held to mean a 'reasonable prospect'. *Dunning v Board of Governors of the United Liverpool Hospitals* [1973] 2 All ER 454; *McIvor v Southern Health and Social Services Board* [1978] 2 All ER 625, HL and *R v Sheppard* [1981] AC 394 (where it was stated to cover a whole range of possibilities).

5 It is not necessary for the person to have entire control over the premises and it is sufficient for him to share control with others. See *Wheat v E Lacon & Co Ltd* [1966] AC 552 and *Jackson v Hall* [1980] AC 854. Further 'occupier' has been held to include a person who has a licence for possession see *Stevens v Bromley London Borough Council* [1972] Ch 400.

6 See further the Magistrates' Courts Act 1980 in relation to warrants. In relation to one calender month: see the Interpretation Act 1978, s 5.

7 Including persons qualified to undertake tests on any goods.

8 See also s 27(2)(c).

31. Power of customs officer to detain goods[1]

(1) A customs officer may, for the purpose of facilitating the exercise by an enforcement authority or officer of such an authority of any functions conferred on the authority or officer by or under Part II of this Act, or by or under this Part[2] in its application for the purposes of the safety provisions, seize any imported goods and detain them for not more than two working days.

(2) Anything sized and detained under this section shall be dealt with during the period of its detention in such manner as the Commissioners of Customs and Excise may direct.

(3) In subsection (1) above the reference to two working days is a reference to a period of forty–eight hours calculated from the time when the goods in question are seized but disregarding so much of any period as falls on a Saturday or Sunday or on Christmas Day, Good Friday or a day which is a bank holiday under the Banking and Financial Dealings Act 1971 in the part of the United Kingdom where the goods are seized.

(4) In this section and section 32 'customs officer' means any officer within the meaning of the Customs and Excise Management Act 1979.

NOTES

1 This section contains powers formally contained within the Consumer Safety (Amendment) Act 1986, s 2. See also the contents of ss 30, 32, 37 and 38(1)(d) of this Act. Although the period is very limited it must be seen in light of the much wider powers of enforcement authorities set out in the preceding Sections of this Act. It was clearly stated during the committee of the Consumer Protection Bill and the House of Lords that the intention behind this Section was merely to allow preliminary enquiries and also to allow Enforcement Authorities to 'arrive on the scene'.

2 Sections 27 to 35.

32. Obstruction of authorised officer[1]

(1) Any person[2] who –

(a) intentionally obstructs[3] any officer of an enforcement authority who is acting in pursuance of any provision of this Part[4] of any customs officer who is so acting; or

(b) intentionally fails to comply[5] with any requirement made of him by any officer of an enforcement authority under any provision of this Part; or

(c)[6] without reasonable cause[7] fails to give any officer of an enforcement authority who is so acting any other assistance or information which the officer may reasonably require of him for the purposes of the exercise of the officer's functions under any provision of this Part,

shall be guilty of an offence and liable on summary convictions to a fine not exceeding level 5 on the standard scale.

(2) A person shall be guilty of an offence if, giving any information which is required of him by virtue of subsection (1)(c) above –

(a) he makes a statement[8] which he knows[9] is false in a material particular[10]; or

(b) he recklessly makes a statement which is false in a material particular[11].

(3) A person guilty of an offence under subsection (2) above shall be liable –

(a) on conviction on indictment, to a fine;

(b) on summary conviction, to a fine not exceeding the statutory maximum.

NOTES

1 Provisions formally contained within the Consumer Safety Act 1978.

2 See s 1, note 5. A body corporate may commit an offence involving mens rea: see *DPP v Kent and Sussex Contractors Ltd* [1944] KB 146. However it would be necessary for the directing will and mind of the Company to have sufficient involvement; see generally *Tesco Supermarkets Ltd v Nattrass* [1972] AC 153.

3 An action is done intentionally if it is deliberate and wilful as opposed to accidental or inadvertent. This means that the mind of the person who does the act must go with it and hence it is necessary for the prosecution to prove that the act in question was done with the intention of obstructing. However, provided the person did in fact do an act which amounted to obstruction it is not material that he did not appreciate that what he was doing amounted to an offence in law or that his actions were not aimed primarily at the person obstructed. See *Moore v Green* [1983] 1 All ER 663, *Hills v Ellis* [1983] QB 680, *Lewis v Cox* [1984] 3 All ER 672, *Arrowsmith v Jenkins* [1963] 2 QB 561, *Rice v Connolly* [1966] 2 QB 414, *Wershof v Metropolitan Police Comr* [1978] 3 All ER 540, *R v Sheppard* [1981] AC 394. A mere failure to assist is not obstruction unless there is a legal duty to act: see *Swallow v LCC* [1916] 1 KB 224; cf *Baker v Ellison* [1914] 2 KB 762 and *Rice v Connolly* [1966] 2 QB 414; *Bullock v Turnbull* [1952] 2 Lloyd's Rep 303; *R v Williams* [1987] 3 All ER 411. A positive act does not cease to be obstructive merely because it is lawful in itself: *Dibble v Ingleton* [1972] 1 QB 480. Obstruction need not involve any physical violence and may mean no more than making it more difficult for the person to carry out their duty. See *Hinchcliffe v Sheldon* [1955] 3 All ER 406; *Borrow v Howland* (1896) 74 LT 787; *Willmott v Attack* [1977] QB 498.

4 The Officer must be acting within his powers if there is to be an offence: See *R v Waterfield* [1964] 1 QB 164, CCA; *Kenlin v Gardinier* [1967] 2 QB 510.

5 There may be a failure to comply by inaction in the face of a legitimate request under the wide powers given to a enforcement authority under the Act.

6 This sub–section is both wide and vague by reason of both the presence of the phrase 'other assistance or information' and the fact that it must be the subject of a reasonable request or

requirement. Bearing in mind that the prosecution will have the burden of establishing the offence this Section is unlikely to be used save in the most exceptional circumstances.

7 This will be a question of fact in the individual circumstances. Instructions from a superior not to answer do not constitute a defence; see *Snape v Mulvenna* (1994) Times, 28 December.

8 It is to be noted that whilst an offence under sub–s 1 may lead only to summary conviction a positive statement which is false or reckless may lead to conviction upon indictment.

9 See notes to s 10. 'The case of shutting the eyes is actual knowledge in the eyes of the law, ... the legal concept of constructive knowledge has no place in criminal law'; *Roper v Taylor's Central Garages (Exeter) Ltd* [1951] 2 TLR 284 per Devlin J; 'knowledge does not mean merely actual knowledge but covers a case of shutting one's eyes to what is going on'; *Ross v Moss* [1965] 3 All ER 145 per Lord Parker CJ. See also *Warner v Metropolitan Police Comr* [1969] 2 AC 256, HL.

10 See notes to s 12(4).

11 See the note to s 12(4)(b)(ii).

33. Appeals against detention of goods[1]

(1) Any person having an interest in any goods which are for the time being detained under any provision of this Part by an enforcement authority or by an officer of such an authority may apply for an order requiring the goods to be released to him or to another person.

(2) An application under this section may be made –

(a) to any magistrates' court in which proceedings have been brought in England and Wales or Northern Ireland –
   (i) for an offence in respect of a contravention in relation to the goods of any safety provision or of any provision made by or under Part III of this Act; or
   (ii) for the forfeiture of the goods under section 16 above.

(b) where no such proceedings have been so brought, by way of complaint to a magistrates' court; or

(c) (Applies to Scotland only).

(3) On an application under this section to a magistrates' court or to the sheriff, an order requiring goods to be released shall be made only if the court or the sheriff is satisfied –

(a) that proceedings –
   (i) for an offence in respect of a contravention in relation to the goods of any safety provision or of any provision made by or under Part III of this Act; or
   (ii) for the forfeiture of the goods under section 16 or 17 above,

have not been brought or, having been brought, have been concluded without the goods being forfeited; and

(b) where no such proceedings have been brought, that more than six months have elapsed since the goods were seized[2].

(4) Any person aggrieved by an order made under this section by a magistrates' court in England and Wales or Northern Ireland, or by a decision of such a court not to make such an order, may appeal against that order or decision –

(a) in England and Wales, to the Crown Court;

(b) in Northern Ireland, to the county court;

and an order so made may contain such provision as appears to the court to be appropriate for delaying the coming into force of the order pending the making and determination of any appeal (including any application under section 111 of the Magistrates' Courts Act 180 or Article 146 of the Magistrates' Courts (Northern Ireland) Order 1981 (statement of case)).

NOTES

1 Contains provisions formerly within the Consumer Safety (Amendment) Act 1986, s 4 and s 9. Powers of seizure and detention are contained within s 29 above. If an appeal is made the enforcement authority may apply for forfeiture pursuant to s 16(2)(b).

2 This reflects the six month life span of suspension notices under s 14 of the Act.

34. Compensation for seizure and detention[1]

(1) Where an officer of an enforcement authority exercised any power under section 29 above to seize and detain goods, the enforcement authority shall be liable to pay compensation to any person having an interest in the goods in respect of any loss or damage caused by reason of the exercise of the power if –

(a) there has been no contravention in relation to the goods of any safety provision or of any provision made by or under Part III of this Act, and

(b) the exercise of the power is not attributable to any neglect or default by that person.

(2) Any disputed question as to the right to or the amount of any compensation payable under this section shall be determined by arbitration or, in Scotland, by a single arbiter appointed, failing agreement between the parties, by the sheriff.

NOTE

1 This section contains provisions formerly in the Consumer Safety Act 1978, Sch 2. It mirrors the revision in relation to compensation where a suspension notice has been served but there has been no contravention in relation to the goods of any safety provision. See s 14(7) above.

35. Recovery of expenses of enforcement[1]

(1) This section shall apply where a court –

(a) convicts a person of an offence in respect of a contravention in relation to any goods of any safety provision or of any provision made by or under Part III of this Act; or

(b) makes an order under section 16 or 17 above for the forfeiture of any goods.

(2) The court may (in addition to any other order it may make as to costs or expenses) order the person convicted or, as the case may be, any person having an interest in the goods to reimburse an enforcement authority for any expenditure which has been or may be incurred by that authority –

(a) in connection with any seizure or detention of the goods by or on behalf of the authority; or

(b) in connection with any compliance by the authority with directions given by the court for the purposes of any order for the forfeiture of the goods.[2]

NOTES

1 This section contains powers formerly within the Consumer Safety (Amendment) Act 1986, s 13.

2 This includes destruction of the goods pursuant to a forfeiture order.

Chapter 17

PART V MISCELLANEOUS AND SUPPLEMENTAL

36. Amendments of Part I of the Health & Safety at Work Act 1974[1]

Part I of the Health & Safety at Work Act 1974 (which includes provision with respect to the safety of certain articles and substances) shall have effect with the amendments specified in Schedule 3 to this Act; and, accordingly, the general purposes of that part of the Act shall include the purpose of protecting persons from the risks, protection from which would not be afforded by virtue of that part but for these amendments.

NOTE

1 Contained in Sch 3, which is not reproduced in this text.

37. Power of Commissioners of Customs and Excise to disclose information[1]

(1) If they think it appropriate to do so for the purpose of facilitating the exercise by any person to whom subsection (2) below applies of any functions conferred on that person by or under Part II of this Act, or by or under Part I of this Act in its application for the purposes of the safety provisions, the Commissioners of Customs and Excise may authorise the disclosure to that person of any information obtained for the purposes of the exercise by the Commissioners of their functions in relation to imported goods.

(2) This subsection applies to an enforcement authority and to any officer of an enforcement authority.

(3) A disclosure of information made to any person under subsection (1) above shall be made in such manner as may be directed by the Commissioners of Customs and Excise and may be made throught such persons acting on behalf of that person as may be so directed.

(4) Information may be disclosed to a person under subsection (1) above whether or not the disclosure of the information has been requested by or on behalf of that person.

NOTE

1 This section contains powers formally within s 1 of the Consumer Safety (Amendment) Act 1986. It is important to note the recipient of any information pursuant to this section is subject to the restriction contained within s 38(1)(e) below.

38. Restrictions on disclosure of information[1]

(1) Subject to the following provisions of this section, a person shall be guilty of an offence if he discloses any information –

(a) which was obtained by him in consequence of its being given to any person in compliance with any requirement imposed by safety regulations or regulations under section 26 above;

(b) which consists in a secret manufacturing process or a trade secret and was obtained by him in consequence of the inclusion of the information–

(i) in written or oral representations made for the purposes of Part I or II of Schedule 2 to this Act; or

(ii) in a statement of a witness in connection with any such oral representations;

(c) which was obtained by him in consequence of the exercise by the Secretary of State of the power conferred by section 18 above;

(d) which was obtained by him in consequence of the exercise by any person of any power conferred by Part IV of this Act; or

(e) which was disclosed to or through him under section 37 above.

(2) Subsection (1) above shall not apply to a disclosure of information if the information is publicised information or the disclosure is made –

(a) for the purpose of facilitating the exercise of a relevant person's functions under this Act[2] or any enactment or subordinate legislation mentioned in subsection (3) below;

(b) for the purposes of compliance with a Community obligation; or

(c) in connection with the investigation of any criminal offence or for the purposes of any civil or criminal proceedings.

(3) The enactments and subordinate legislation referred to in subsection (2)(a) above are –

(a) the Trade Descriptions Act 1968;

(b) Parts II and III and section 125 of the Fair Trading Act 1973;

(c) the relevant statutory provisions within the meaning of Part 1 of the Health and Safety at Work etc Act 1974 or within the meaning of the Health and Safety at Work (Northern Ireland) Order 1978;

(d) the Consumer Credit Act 1974;

(e) the Restrictive Trade Practices Act 1976;

(f) the Resale Prices Act 1976;

(g) the Estate Agents Act 1979;

(h) the Competition Act 1980;

(i) the Telecommunications Act 1984;

(j) the Airports Act 1986;

(k) the Gas Act 1986;

(l) any subordinate legislation made (whether before or after the passing of this Act) for the purpose of securing compliance with the Directive of the Council of the European Communities, dated 10th September 1984 (No 84/450/EEC) on the approximation of the laws, regulations and administrative provisions of the member States concerning misleading advertising.

(4) In subsection (2)(a) above the reference to a person's functions shall include a reference to any function of making, amending or revoking any regulations or order.

(5) A person guilty of an offence under this section shall be liable –

(a) on summary conviction, to a fine not exceeding the statutory maximum;

(b) on conviction on indictment, to imprisonment for a term not exceeding two years or to a fine or to both.

(6) In this section –

'publicised information' means any information which has been disclosed in any civil or criminal proceedings or is or has been required to be contained in a warning published in pursuance of a notice to warn; and

'relevant person' means any of the following, that is to say –

(a) a Minister of the Crown, Government department or Northern Ireland department;
(b) the Monopolies and Mergers Commission, the Director General of Fair Trading, the Director General of Telecommunications or the Director General of Gas Supply;
(c) the Civil Aviation Authority;
(d) any weights and measures authority, and district council in Northern Ireland or any person on whom functions are conferred by regulations under section 27(2) above;
(e) any person who is an enforcing authority for the purposes of Part 1 of the Health and Safety at Work etc Act 1974 or for the purposes of Part II of the Health and Safety at Work (Northern Ireland) Order 1978.

NOTES

1 This section derives in part from the Consumer Safety (Amendment) Act 1986, s 11.

2 When the provisions of the Consumer Protection Bill were under debate in the House of Lords discussion took place as to whether the provisions of this section would prevent the giving of public warnings in relation to unsafe goods. It was stated on behalf of the Government that the section would not prevent a Trading Standards Officer from notifying or warning the public about unsafe goods. It appears that the power to do so stems from this sub-section.

39. Defence of due diligence[1]

(1) Subject to the following provisions of this section, in proceedings against any person for an offence to which this section applies[2] it shall be a defence for that person to show[3] that he took all reasonable steps and exercised all due diligence to avoid committing the offence[4].

(2) Where in any proceedings against any person for such an offence the defence provided by subsection (1) above involves an allegation that the commission of the offence was due –

(a) to the act or default of another[5]; or
(b) to reliance on information given by another,

that person shall not, without the leave of the court, be entitled to rely on the defence unless, not less than seven clear days before the hearing of the proceedings, he has served a notice under subsection (3) below on the person bringing the proceedings[6].

(3) A notice under this subsection shall give such information identifying or assisting in the identification of the person who committed the act or default or gave the information as is in the possession of the person serving the notice at the time he serves it.

(4) It is hereby declared that a person shall not be entitled to rely on the defence provided by subsection (1) above by reason of his reliance on information supplied by another, unless he shows that it was reasonable in all the circumstances for him to have relied on the information, having regard in particular –

(a) to the steps which he took, and those which might reasonably have been taken, for the purpose of verifying the information; and
(b) to whether he had any reason to disbelieve the information[7].

(5) This section shall apply to an offence under section 10, 12(1), (2) or (3), 13(4), 14(6) or 20(1) above.

NOTES
1 See generally chapter 10; para 10.6, *Due Diligence.*
2 See sub–s 5.
3 The burden of proof is on the Defendant, the standard is the balance of probabilities: see *R v Carr-Briant* [1943] KB 607; *R v Dunbar* [1958] 1 QB 1; *R v Hudson* [1966] 1 QB 448.
4 Whether or not the Defendant has exercised all due diligence is a question of fact, however, see the principles and cases at para 10(4) above for assistance. The duty to 'take all reasonable steps' adds little if anything to the duty to exercise all due diligence; see *Riverstone Meat Co Pty Ltd v Lancashire Shipping Co Ltd* [1960] 1 QB 536, CA.
5 See generally *Moore v Ray* [1951] 1 KB 98. This must be a wrongful act or default; see the footnotes to Section 40(1) and *Noss Farm Products Ltd v Lilico* [1945] 2 All ER 609; *Lamb v Sunderland and District Creamery Ltd* [1951] 1 All ER 923. However, neither mens rea nor negligence are necessary ingredients; see *Lindley v George W Horner & Co* [1950] 1 All ER 234 and *Fisher v Barrett & Pomeroy (Bakers) Ltd* [1954] 1 All ER 249.
6 See chapter 10(4), *Due Diligence* for discussion of the procedural requirements.
7 The existence of reasonable grounds and of the belief founded on them is a question of fact. However, the grounds must be such and sufficient as to induce in a reasonable person the required belief: see *McArdle v Egan* (1933) 98 JP 103, CA; *IRC v Rossminster Ltd* [1980] AC 952, HL.

40. Liability of persons other than principal offender[1]

(1) Where the commission by any person[2] of an offence to which section 39 above applies[3] is due to an act or default committed by some other person in the course of any business of his[4], the other person shall be guilty of the offence[5] and may be proceeded against and punished by virtue of this subsection whether or not proceedings are taken against the first–mentioned person.

(2) Where a body corporate is guilty of an offence[6] under this Act (including where it is so guilty by virtue of subsection (1) above) in respect of any act or default which is shown to have been committed with the consent[7] or connivance[8] or, of or to be attributable to any neglect[9] on the part of, any director, manager, secretary or other similar officer[10] of the body corporate or any person who was purporting to act in any such capacity he, as well as the body corporate, shall be guilty of that offence and shall be liable to be proceeded against and punished accordingly.

(3) Where the affairs of a body corporate are managed by its members, subsection (2) above shall apply in relation to the acts and defaults of a member in connection with his functions of management as if he were a director of the body corporate.

NOTES
1 This section allows the prosecution to pursue a 'person', eg company A, when its 'act or default' caused the commission of an offence by another person, eg company B. Both company A and company B may be convicted by virtue of this section; see *Lamb v Sunderland and District Creamery Ltd* [1951] 1 All ER 923. Further company A may be convicted whether or not proceedings are taken against company B. Frequently the cooperation of and evidence from company B will be required to secure a conviction against company A which, by reason of its higher status within the supply chain is more desirable for the general enforcement of the Act. If reliance is to be placed upon this section the prosecution should state that this is so; see *Atterton v Browne* [1945] KB 122. See also Reg 15 of the General Product Safety Regulations 1994.
2 See s 1, note 5. This includes a body of persons corporate or unincorporated.

3 See s 39(5) which refers to offences under ss 10, 12(1), (2) or (3), 13(4), 14(6) or 20(1). Although proceedings may be taken against company A notwithstanding that proceedings have not been taken against company B it is still necessary to show that company B has in fact been guilty of the primary defence; see *Cottee v Douglas Seaton (Used Cars) Ltd* [1972] 3 All ER 750; cf *Hollington v F Hewthorn & Co Ltd* [1943] KB 587. The 'act or default' must be 'wrongful'; see the note to s 39(2) and also *Noss Farm Products Ltd v Lilico* [1945] 2 All ER 609. In that case there was an alteration of the law after the manufacturer sold the item to a retail dealer. However the prosecution does not need to prove mens rea. See *Lamb v Sunderland and District Creamery Ltd* [1951] 1 All ER 923. 'In this case it was not necessary to prove mens rea. All that needed to be proved was that there was a sales to the prejudice of the purchaser of something which was not of the nature, substance, or quality demanded by him. The very fact of the article supplied being in that condition supplied the mens rea and constituted an offence'. Per Lord Goddard CJ. The case involved a wholesale milk dealer who purchased milk and then passed it on without testing. Lord Goddard further stated 'It is not a question of whether he knowingly or negligently sells the articles. He commits an offence if he sells it at all'. The following example constitutes a case where company A has *not* committed a 'wrongful act or default':

> Company A supplies toy rabbits on a wholesale basis to company B. The toy rabbits are each within individual plastic bags which if sold upon a retail basis fail to comply with the requirements of the Toy Safety Regulations 1989. However company A places several large labels on the carton, and also states upon the contractual information that the toy rabbits must be removed from the plastic bags before retail sale. Company B decides to ignore the warnings and for the purpose of keeping the rabbits clean sells them on in their bags without the accompanying warnings or notices. A retail sale of a rabbit in a plastic bag fails to comply with the Regulations and would therefore be due to the act of company A but not due to its wrongful act.

The necessary causal connection must in any event be proved by the prosecution to the normal standard ie beyond reasonable doubt. See *Tarleton Engineering Co Ltd v Nattrass* [1973] 3 All ER 699.

4 See *R v Warwickshire County Council, ex p Johnson* [1993] AC 583, [1993] 1 All ER 299, HL, where it was held that the Defendant had to have a proprietary or controlling interest and an ordinary employee does not fall into this category.

5 It is necessary for the prosecution to prove the relevant element of s 40(1) beyond reasonable doubt. See *Woolmington v DPP* [1935] AC 462.

6 A company may be convicted in respect of the criminal acts (including those requiring mens rea) of its Directors and Managers provided that they represent the directing mind and will of the corporation and have a requisite degree of power and control; see *DPP v Kent and Sussex Contractors Ltd* [1944] KB 146; *R v ICR Haulage Ltd* [1944] KB 551; *Tesco Supermarkets Ltd v Nattrass* [1972] AC 153. This means the company cannot be convicted for the criminal acts of simple employees unless the offence is one for which it should be held vicariously liable; see *Tesco Supermarkets Ltd v Nattrass* and also *R v Andrews Weatherfoil Ltd* [1972] 1 All ER 65 and *John Henshall (Quarries) Ltd v Harvey* [1965] 2 QB 233; *Ferguson v Weaving* [1951] 1 KB 814.

7 Knowledge will be an essential requirement of consent. See *Lamb v Wright & Co* [1924] 1 KB 857. In practice it will require express or implied approval of an action. See also *Huckerby v Elliott* [1970] 1 All ER 189.

8 This may mean passive consent or co-operation in relation to the action or omission. However it requires something more than mere negligence. See *Rogers v Rogers* (1830) 3 Hag Ecc 57; *Huckerby v Elliott* [1970] 1 All ER 189; *Mudge v Mudge* [1950] P 173.

9 This generally means a failure to perform a duty of which the person knows or ought to know; *Re Hughes, Rea v Black* [1943] Ch 296; *Crickitt v Kursaal Casino Ltd (No 2)* [1968] 1 All ER 139; *Huckerby v Elliott* [1970] 1 All ER 189; *Hirschler v Birch* (1987) 151 JP 396.

10 An Officer clearly means a person holding some relevant authority or with some 'say' in the control of the acts or omission of the company.

41. Civil proceedings[1]

(1) An obligation imposed by safety regulations shall be a duty owed to any person who may be affected by a contravention of the obligations and, subject to any provision to the contrary in the regulations and to the defences[2] and other incidents applying to actions for breach of statutory duty, a contravention of any such obligation[3] shall be actionable accordingly.

(2) This Act shall not be construed as conferring any other right of action in civil proceedings, apart from the right conferred by virtue of Part 1 of this Act, in respect of any loss or damage suffered in consequence of a contravention of a safety provision or of a provision made by or under Part III of this Act.

(3) Subject to any provision to the contrary in the agreement itself, an agreement shall not be void or unenforceable by reason only of a contravention of a safety provision or of a provision made by or under Part III of this Act.

(4) Liability by virtue of subsection (1) above shall not be limited or excluded by any contract term, by any notice or (subject to the power contained in subsection (1) above to limit or exclude it in safety regulations) by any other provision.

(5) Nothing in subsection (1) above shall prejudice the operation of section 12 of the Nuclear Installations Act 1965 (rights to compensation for certain breaches of duties confined to rights under this Act).

(6) In this section 'damage' includes personal injury and death.

NOTES

1 See the former provisions of the Consumer Safety Act 1978, s 6. It is important to note that the obligation under this section relates only to Safety Regulations under the Act and therefore not to either s 10 or the provisions of the General Product Safety Regulations 1994. The effect of this section as a whole is to make a breach of a provision of the Safety Regulations actionable as a breach of statutory duty.

2 See the former provisions of s 8 of the Consumer Safety Act 1978.

3 The burden of proof would be upon the plaintiff and the standard would be the ordinary civil standard.

42. Reports etc

(1) It shall be the duty of the Secretary of State at least once in every five years to lay before each House of Parliament a report on the exercise during the period to which the report relates of the functions which under Part II of this Act, or under Part IV of this Act in its application for the purposes of the safety provisions, are exercisable by the Secretary of State, weights and measures authorities, district councils in Northern Ireland and persons on whom functions are conferred by regulations made under section 27(2) above.

(2) The Secretary of State may from time to time prepare and lay before each House of Parliament such other reports on the exercise of those functions as he considers appropriate.

(3) Every weights and measures authority, every district council in Northern Ireland and every person on whom functions are conferred by regulations under subsection (2) of section 27 above shall, whenever the Secretary of State so directs, make a report to the Secretary of State on the exercise of the functions exercisable by that authority or council under that section or by that person by virtue of any such regulations.

(4) A report under subsection (3) above shall be laid before each House of Parliament not more than five years after the laying of the last report under section 8(2) of the Consumer Safety Act 1978.

43. Financial provisions

(1) There shall be paid out of money provided by Parliament –

(a) any expenses incurred or compensation payable by a Minister of the Crown or Government department in consequence of any provision of this Act; and

(b) any increase attributable to this Act in the sums payable out of money so provided under any other Act.

Any sums received by a Minister of the Crown or Government department by virtue of this Act shall be paid into the Consolidated Fund.

44. Service of documents etc

(1) Any document required or authorised by virtue of this Act to be served on a person may[1] be so served –

(a) by delivering it to him or by leaving it at his proper address or by sending it by post[2] to him at that address; or
(b) if the person is a body corporate, by serving it in accordance with paragraph (a) above on the secretary or clerk of that body; or
(c) if the person is a partnership, by serving it in accordance with that paragraph on a partner or on a person having control or management of the partnership business.

(2) For the purposes of subsection (1) above, and for the purposes of section 7 of the Interpretation Act 1978 (which relates to the service of documents by post) in its application to that subsection, the proper address of any person on whom a document is to be served by virtue of this Act shall be his last known address[3] except for –

(a) in the case of service on a body corporate or its secretary or clerk, it shall be the address of the registered or principal office[4] of the body corporate;
(b) in the case of service on a partnership or a partner or a person having the control or management of a partnership business, it shall be the principal office of the partnership;

and for the purposes of this subsection the principal officer of a company registered outside the United Kingdom or of a partnership carrying on business outside the United Kingdom is its principal office within the United Kingdom.

(3) The Secretary of State may by regulations make provisions for the manner in which any information is to be given to any person under any provision of Part IV of this Act.

(4) Without prejudice to the generality of subsection (3) above regulations made by the Secretary of State may prescribe the person, or manner of determining the person, who is to be treated for the purposes of section 28(2) or 30 above as the person from whom any goods were purchased or seized where the goods were purchased or seized from a vending machine.

(5) The power to make regulations under subsection (3) or (4) above shall be exercisable by statutory instrument subject to annulment in pursuance of a resolution of either House of Parliament and shall include powers –

(a) to make different provision for different cases; and
(b) to make such supplemental, consequential and transitional provision as the Secretary of State considers appropriate.

NOTES

1 This section is permissive only, therefore a document may be served in a different manner yet still constitute good service; see *Sharpley v Manby* [1942] 1 KB 217; *Stylo Shoes Ltd v Prices Tailors Ltd* [1960] Ch 396.

2 See s 7 of the Interpretation Act 1978. Service is deemed to be effected by properly addressing, prepaying and posting a letter containing the document and, unless the contrary is proved,

to have been effected at the time at which the letter would be delivered in the ordinary course of post. Service by post may be effected by ordinary or registered letter. *TO Supplies (London) Ltd v Jerry Creighton Ltd* [1952] 1 KB 42.

3 Service at the last known address is not good if a later address abroad is known. See *R v Farmer* [1892] 1 QB 637; *Stylo Shoes Ltd v Prices Tailors Ltd* above.

4 See the Companies Act 1985, s 287. The principal office is the place where the business of the company is managed and controlled; *Palmer v Caledonian Rly Co* [1892] 1 QB 823, CA.

45. Interpretation

(1) In this Act, except in so far as the context otherwise requires –

'aircraft' includes gliders, balloons and hovercraft;

'business' includes a trade or profession and the activities of a professional or trade association or of a local authority or other public authority;

'conditional sale agreement', 'credit–sale agreement' and 'hire–purchase agreement' have the same meanings as in the Consumer Credit Act 1974[1] but as if in that definition in that Act 'goods' had the same meaning as in this Act';

'contravention' includes a failure to comply and cognate expressions shall be construed accordingly;

'enforceable authority' means the Secretary of State, any other Minister of the Crown in charge of a Government department, any such department and any authority, council or other person on whom functions under this Act are conferred by or under section 27 above;

'gas' has the same meaning as in Part I of the Gas Act 1986[2];

'goods' includes substances, growing crops and things comprised in land by virtue of being attached to it and any ship, aircraft or vehicle;

'information' includes accounts, estimates and returns;

'magistrates' court', in relation to Northern Ireland, means a court of summary jurisdiction;

'mark' and 'trade mark' have the same meanings as in the Trade Marks Act 1938[3];

'modifications' includes additions, alterations and omissions, and cognate expressions shall be construed accordingly;

'motor vehicle' has the same meaning as in the Road Traffic Act 1972[4];

'notice' means a notice in writing;

'notice to warn' means a notice under section 13(1)(b) above;

'officer', in relation to an enforcement authority, means a person authorised in writing to assist the authority in carrying out its functions under or for the purposes of the enforcement of any of the safety provisions or of any of the provisions made by or under Part III of this Act';

'personal injury' includes any disease and any other impairment of a person's physical or mental condition;

'premises' includes any place and any ship, aircraft or vehicle;

'prohibition notice' means a notice under section 13(1)(a) above;

'records' includes any books or documents and any records in non-documentary form[5];

'safety provision' means the general safety requirement in section 10 above or any provision of safety regulations, a prohibition notice or a suspension notice[6];

'safety regulations' means regulations under section 11 above;

'ship' includes any boat or any other description of vessel used in navigation;

'subordinate legislation' has the same meaning as in the Interpretation Act 1978;

'substance' means any natural or artificial substance, whether in solid, liquid or gaseous form or in the form of a vapour, and includes substances that are comprised in or mixed with other goods;

'supply' and cognate expressions shall be construed in accordance with section 46 below;

'suspension notice' means a notice under section 14 above.

(2) Except in so far as the context otherwise requires, references in this Act to a contravention of a safety provision will, in relation to any goods, include references to anything which would constitute such a contravention if the goods were supplied to any person.

(3) References in this Act to any goods in relation to which any safety provision has been or may have been contravened shall include references to any goods which it is not reasonably practicable to separate from any such goods.

(4) Section 68(2) of the Trade Marks Act 1938 (construction of references to use of a mark) shall apply for the purposes of this Act as it applies for the purposes of that Act;

(5) (Applies to Scotland only).

NOTES

1 See s 189(1) of the Consumer Credit Act 1974.

2 See s 48(1) of the Gas Act 1986.

3 See s 68(1) of the Trade Marks Act 1938.

4 See s 190(1) of the Road Traffic Act 1972 and now s 185(1) of the Road Traffic Act 1988.

5 This may mean a letter, tape recording or video film. See *Carlish v East Ham Corpn and Edwards* [1948] 2 KB 380. *Grant v South Western and County Properties Ltd* [1975] Ch 185; *Senior v Holdsworth* [1976] QB 23.

6 See also Reg 11(B) of the General Product Safety Regulations 1994.

46. Meaning of 'supply'[1]

(1) Subject to the following provisions of this section, references in this Act to supplying goods[2] shall be construed as references to doing any of the following, whether as principal or agent, that is to say –

(a) selling hiring out or lending the goods;

(b) entering into a hire-purchase agreement to furnish the goods;

(c) the performance of any contract for work and materials to furnish the goods;

(d) providing the goods in exchange for any consideration (including trading stamps) other than money;

(e) providing the goods in or in connection with the performance of any statutory function; or

(f) giving the goods as a prize or otherwise making a gift of the goods;

and, in relation to gas or water, those references shall be construed as including references to providing the service by which the gas or water is made available for use.

(2) For the purposes of any reference in this Act to supplying goods, where a person ('the ostensible supplier') supplies goods to another person ('the customer') under a hire–purchase agreement, condition sale agreement or credit/sale agreement or under an agreement for the hiring of goods (other than a hire-purchase agreement) and the ostensible supplier –

(a) carries on the business of financing the provision of goods for others by means of such agreement; and

(b) in the course of that business acquired his interest in the goods supplied to the customer as a means of financing the provision of them for the customer by a further person ('the effective supplier')

the effective supplier and not the ostensible supplier shall be treated as supplying the goods to the customer[3].

(3) Subject to subsection (4) below, the performance of any contract by the erection of any building or structure on any land or by the carrying out of any other building works shall be treated for the purposes of this Act as a supply of goods in so far as, but only in so far as, it involves the provision of any goods to any person by means of their incorporation into the building, structure or works[4].

(4) Except for the purposes of, and in relation to, notices to warn or any provision made by or under Part III of this Act, references in this Act to supplying goods shall not include references to supplying goods comprised in land where the supply is effected by the creation or disposal of an interest in the land.

(5) Except in Part 1 of this Act references in this Act to a person supplying goods shall be confined to references to that person supplying goods in the course of a business of his, but for the purposes of this subsection it shall be immaterial whether the business is a business of dealing in the goods.

(6) For the purposes of subsection (5) above goods shall not be treated as supplied in the course of a business if they are supplied, in pursuance of an obligation arising under or in connection with the insurance of the goods, to the person with whom they were insured.

(7) Except for the purposes of, and in relation to, prohibition notices or suspension notices, references in Parts II to IV of this Act to supplying goods shall not include[5]–

(a) references to supplying goods where the person supplied carries on a business of buying goods of the same description as those goods and repairing or reconditioning them;

(b) references to supplying goods by a sale of articles as scrap (that is to say, for the value of materials included in the articles rather than for the value of the articles themselves).

(8) Where any goods have at any time been supplied by being hired out or lent to any person, neither a continuation or renewal of the hire or loan (whether on the same or different terms) nor any transaction for the transfer after that time of any interest in the goods to the person to whom they were hired or lent shall be treated for the purposes of this Act as a further supply of the goods to that person.

(9) A ship, aircraft or motor vehicle shall not be treated for the purposes of this Act as supplied to any person by reason only that services consisting in the carriage of goods or passengers in that ship, aircraft or vehicle, or in its use for any other purpose are provided to that person in pursuance of an agreement relating to the use of the ship, aircraft or vehicle for a particular period or for particular voyages, flights or journeys.

NOTES

1 This definition applies to both civil and criminal liability under Pts I and II.

2 'Supply' has been held to be confined to supply within the United Kingdom; *United States Tobacco International Inc v Secretary of State for Health* (1990) 155 JP 144.

3 The intention of this section is to treat the 'effective supplier' often the dealer or trader as the supplier for the purposes of the Act rather than anyone involved purely in the financing of the supply. Clearly a company solely involved in facilitating a supply by way of the provision of finance is not usually the 'true person to be aimed at' under the Act.

4 A combination of sub-s 3 and sub-s 4 is intended to cover the position of builders particularly in regard to potential liability under Pt I of the Act. See chapter 1 (para 1.1.3.). By sub-s 4 builders are not treated as supplying goods comprised in land where the supply is effected by the creation of a disposal of an interest but if goods are incorporated into a building and such an interest is not created or disposed of, then there is a relevant supply under the Act.

5 See also s 16(7)(a) above in relation to forfeiture.

47. Savings for certain privileges

(1) Nothing in this Act shall be taken as requiring any person to produce any records if he would be entitled to refuse to produce those records in any proceedings in any court on the grounds that they are the subject of legal professional privilege or, in Scotland, that they contain a confidential communication made by or to an advocate or solicitor in that capacity, or as authorising any person to take possession of any records which are in the possession of a person who would be so entitled.

(2) Nothing in this Act shall be construed as requiring a person to answer any question or give any information if to do so would incriminate that person or that person's spouse.

48. Minor and consequential amendments and repeals

(1) The enactments mentioned in Schedule 4 to this Act shall have effect subject to the amendments specified in that Schedule (being minor amendments and amendments consequential on the provisions of this Act).

(2) The following Acts shall cease to have effect, that is to say –

(a) the Trade Descriptions Act 1972, and
(b) the Fabrics (Misdescription) Act 1913.

(3) The enactments mentioned in Schedule 5 to this Act are hereby repealed to the content specified in the third column of that Schedule.

49. Northern Ireland

(1) This Act shall extent to Northern Ireland with the exception of –

(a) the provisions of Parts I and III[1];
(b) any provision amending or repealing an enactment which does not so extend; and
(c) any other provision so far is it has effect for the purposes of, or in relation to, a provision falling within paragraph (a) or (b) above.

(2) Subject to any Order in Council made by virtue of subsection (1)(a) of section 3 of the Northern Ireland Constitution Act 1973, consumer safety shall not be a transferred matter for the purposes of that Act but shall for the purposes of subsection (2) of that section be treated as specified in Schedule 3 to that Act.

(3) An Order in Council under paragraph 1(1)(b) of Schedule 1 to the Northern Ireland Act 1974 (exercise of legislative functions for Northern Ireland) which states that it is made only for purposes corresponding to any of the provisions of this Act mentioned in subsection (1)(a) to (c) above –

(a) shall not be subject to paragraph 1(4) and (5) of that Schedule (affirmative resolution procedure and procedure in cases of urgency); but

(b) shall be subject to annulment in pursuance of a resolution of either House of Parliament.

NOTES

1 Part 1 of the Act does not extend to Northern Ireland. However, the Consumer Protection (Northern Ireland) Order 1987 (SI 1987/2049 NI 20), (see additional materials) contains the provisions implementing the EEC Directive on Liability for Defective Products in Northern Ireland.

50. Short title, commencement and transitional provision

(1) This Act may be cited as the Consumer Protection Act 1987.

(2) This Act shall come into force on such day as the Secretary of State may by order made by statutory instrument appoint, and different days may be so appointed for different provisions or for different purposes.

(3) The Secretary of State shall not make an order under subsection (2) above bringing into force the repeal of the Trade Descriptions Act 1972, a repeal of any provision of that Act or a repeal of that Act or of any provisions of it for any purposes, unless a draft of the order has been laid before, and approved by a resolution of, each House of Parliament.

(4) An order under subsection (2) above bringing a provision into force may contain such transitional provision in connection with the coming into force of that provision as the Secretary of State considers appropriate.

(5) Without prejudice to the generality of the power conferred by subsection (4) above, the Secretary of State may by order provide for any regulations made under the Consumer Protection Act 1961 or the Consumer Protection Act (Northern Ireland) 1965 to have effect as if made under section 11 above and for any such regulations to have effect with such modifications as he considers appropriate for that purpose.

(6) The power of the Secretary of State by order to make such provision as is mentioned in subsection (5) above, shall, in so far as it is not exercised by an order under subsection (2) above, be exercisable by statutory instrument subject to annulment in pursuance of a resolution of either House of Parliament.

(7) Nothing in this Act or in any order under subsection (2) above shall make any person liable by virtue of Part I of this Act for any damage caused wholly or partly by a defect in a product which was supplied to any person by its producer before the coming into force of Part I of this Act.

(8) Expressions used in subsection (7) above and in Part I of this Act have the same meanings in that subsection as in that Part.

SCHEDULES

SCHEDULE 1

LIMITATION OF ACTIONS UNDER PART 1
PART 1
ENGLAND AND WALES

1. After section 11 of the Limitation Act 1980 (actions in respect of personal injuries) there shall be inserted the following section –

‘11A Actions in respect of defective products

(1) This section shall apply to an action for damages by virtue of any provision of Part 1 of the Consumer Protection Act 1987.

(2) None of the time limits given in the preceding provisions of this Act shall apply to an action to which this section applies.

(3) An action to which this section applies shall not be brought after the expiration of the period of ten years from the relevant time, within the meaning of section 4 of the said Act of 1987; and this subsection shall operate to extinguish a right of action and shall do so whether or not that right of action had accrued, or time under the following provisions of this Act had begun to run, at the end of the said period of ten years.

(4) Subject to subsection (5) below, an action to which this section applies in which the damages claimed by the plaintiff consist or include damages in respect of personal injuries to the plaintiff or any other person or loss of or damage to any property, shall not be brought after the expiration of the period of three years from[1] whichever is the later of –

(a) the date on which the cause of action accrued; and
(b) the date of knowledge of the injured person or, in the case of loss of or damage to property, the date of knowledge of the plaintiff or (if earlier) of any person in whom his cause of action was previously vested.

(5) If in a case where the damages claimed by the plaintiff consist of or include damages in respect of personal injuries to the plaintiff or any other person the injured person died before the expiration of the period mentioned in subsection (4) above, that subsection shall have effect as respects the cause of action surviving for the benefit of his estate by virtue of section 1 of the Law Reform (Miscellaneous Provisions) Act 1934 as if for the reference to that period there were substituted a reference to the period of three years from whichever is the later of –

(a) date of death; and
(b) the date of the personal representative's knowledge.

(6) For the purposes of this section 'personal representative' includes any person who is or has been a personal representative of the deceased, including an executor which has not proved the will (whether or not he has renounced probate) but not anyone appointed only as a special personal representative in relation to settled land; and regard shall be had to any knowledge acquired by any such person while a personal representative or previously.

(7) If there is more than one personal representative and their dates of knowledge are different, subsection (5)(b) above shall be read as referring to the earliest of those dates.

(8) Expressions used in this section or section 14 of this Act and in Part 1 of the Consumer Protection Act 1987 have the same meanings in this section or that section as in that Part; and section 1(1) of that Act (Part I to be construed as enacted for the purpose of complying with the product liability Directive) shall apply for the purpose of construing this section and the following provisions of this Act so

far as they relate to an action by virtue of any provision of that Part as it applies for the purpose of construing that Part.'

2. In section 12(1) of the said Act of 1980 (actions under the Fatal Accidents Act 1976), after the words 'section 11' there shall be inserted the words 'or 11A'.

3. In section 14 of the said Act of 1980 (definition of date of knowledge), in subsection (1), at the beginning there shall be inserted the words 'Subject to subsection (1A) below', and after that subsection there shall be inserted the following subsection –

'1(A) In section 11A of this Act and in section 12 of this Act so far as that section applies to an action by virtue of section 6(1) of the Consumer Protection Act 1987 (death caused by defective product) references to a person's date of knowledge are references to the date on which he first had knowledge of the following facts –

(a) such facts about the damage caused the defect as would lead a reasonable person who had suffered such damage to consider it sufficiently serious to justify his instituting proceedings[2] for damages against a defendant who did not dispute liability and was able to satisfy a judgement; and
(b) that the damage was wholly or partly attributable to the facts and circumstances alleged to constitute the defect; and
(c) the identity of the defendant[3].

but in determining the date on which a person first had such knowledge there shall be disregarded both the extent (if any) of that person's knowledge on any date of whether particular facts or circumstances would or would not, as a matter of law, constitute a defect and, in a case relating to loss of or damage to property, any knowledge which that person had on a date on which he had no right of action by virtue of Part I of that Act in respect of the loss or damage.'

4. In section 28 of the said Act of 1980 (extension of limitation in case of disability), after subsection (6) there shall be inserted the following subsection –

'(7) If the action is one to which section 11A of this Act applies or one by virtue of section 6(1)(a) of the Consumer Protection Act 1987 (death caused by defective product), subsection (1) above –
(a) shall not apply to the time limit prescribed by subsection (3) of the said section 11A or to that time limit as applied by virtue of section 12(1) of this Act; and
(b) in relation to any of the time limit prescribed by this Act shall have effect as if for the words 'six years' there were substituted the words 'three years'.

5. In section 32 of the said Act of 1980 (postponement of limitation period in case of fraud, concealment or mistake) –

(a) in subsection (1), for the words 'subsection (3)' there shall be substituted the words 'subsection (3) and (4A)'; and
(b) after subsection (4) there shall be inserted the following subsection –

'4(A) Subsection (1) above shall not apply in relation to the time limit prescribed by section 11 A(3) of this Act or in relation to that time limit as applied by virtue of section 12(1) of this Act'.

6. In section 33 of the said Act of 1980 (discretionary exclusion of time limit) –

(a) in subsection (1), after the words 'section 11' there shall be inserted the words 'or 11A';
(b) after the said subsection (1) there shall be inserted the following subsection –

'1(A) The court shall not under this section disapply –
(a) subsection (3) of section 11A; or
(b) where the damages claimed by the plaintiff are confined to damages for loss of or damage to any property, any other provision in its application to an action by virtue of Part 1 of the Consumer Protection Act 1987';

(c) in subsections (2) and (4), after the words 'section 11' there shall be inserted the words 'or subsection (4) of section 11A'
(d) in subsection (3)(b), after the words 'section 11' there shall be inserted the words 'by section 11A'; and
(e) in subsection (8), after the words 'section 11' there shall be inserted the words 'or 11A'

PART II APPLIES TO SCOTLAND

NOTES

1 In computing this period the day on which the cause of action accrued is excluded; see *Marren v Dawson Bentley & Co Ltd* [1961] 2 QB 135,[1961] 2 All ER 270 and *Pritam Kaur v S Russell & Sons Ltd* [1973] QB 336, [1973] 1 All ER 617, CA. When on the last day of the period the court office is closed all day, the time is extended to the first day on which the office reopens; see *Pritam Kaur v S Russell & Sons Ltd* above and *The Clifford Maersk* [1982] 3 All ER 905, [1982] 1 WLR 1292.

2 For relevant cases, see *Davies v British Insulated Callender's Cables Ltd* (1977) 121 Sol Jo 203 and *Buck v English Electric Co Ltd* [1978] 1 All ER 271, [1977] 1 WLR 806.

3 For a case in which it was held that the plaintiff had no knowledge of the defendant's identify and could not reasonably have been expected to acquire that knowledge, see *Simpson v Norwest Holst Southern Ltd* [1980] 2 All ER 471, [1980] 1 WLR 968, CA.

SCHEDULE 2

PROHIBITION NOTICES AND NOTICES TO WARN

PART I
PROHIBITION NOTICES

1. A prohibition notice in respect of any goods shall –

(a) state that the Secretary of State considers that the goods are unsafe;
(b) set out the reasons why the Secretary of State considers that the goods are unsafe;
(c) specify the day on which the notice is to come into force; and
(d) state that the trader may at any time make representations in writing to the Secretary of State for the purpose of establishing that the goods are safe.

2. (1) If representations in writing about a prohibition notice are made to the Secretary of State, it shall be the duty of the Secretary of State to consider whether to revoke the notice and –

(a) if he decides to revoke it, to do so;

(b) in any other case, to appoint a person to consider those representations, any further representations made (whether in writing or orally) by the trader about the notice and the statements of any witnesses examined under this Part of this Schedule.

(2) Where the Secretary of State has appointed a person to consider representations about a prohibition notice, he shall serve a notification on the trader which –

(a) states that the trader may make oral representations to the appointed person for the purpose of establishing that the goods to which the notice relates are safe; and

(b) specifies the place and time at which the oral representations may be made.

(3) The time specified in a notification served under sub–paragraph (2) above shall not be before the end of the period of twenty–one days beginning with the day on which the notification is served, unless the trader otherwise agrees.

(4) A person on whom a notification has been served under sub-paragraph (2) above or his representative may, at the place and time specified in the notification –

(a) make oral representations to the appointed person for the purpose of establishing that the goods in question are safe; and

(b) call and examine witnesses in connection with the representations.

3. (1) Where representations in writing about a prohibition notice are made by the trader to the Secretary of State at any time after a person has been appointed to consider representations about that notice, then whether or not the appointed person has made a report to the Secretary of State, the following provisions of this paragraph shall apply instead of paragraph 2 above.

(2) The Secretary of State shall, before the end of the period of one month beginning with the day on which he receives the representations, serve a notification on the trader which states –

(a) that the Secretary of State has decided to revoke the notice, has decided to vary it or, as the case may be, has decided neither to revoke nor to vary it; or

(b) that, a person having been appointed to consider representations about the notice, the trader may, at a place and time specified in the notification, make oral representations to the appointed person for the purpose of establishing that the goods to which the notice relates are safe.

(3) The time specified in a notification served for the purposes of sub–paragraph (2)(b) above shall not be before the end of the period of twenty–one days beginning with the day on which the notification is served, unless the trader otherwise agrees or the time is the time already specified for the purposes of paragraph 2(2)(b) above.

(4) A person on whom a notification has been served for the purposes of sub–paragraph (2)(b) above or his representative may, at the place and time specified in the notification –

(a) make oral representations to the appointed person for the purpose of establishing that the goods in question are safe; and
(b) call and examine witnesses in connection with the representations.

4. (1) Where a person is appointed to consider representations about a prohibition notice, it shall be his duty to consider –

(a) any written representations made by the trader about the notice, other than those in respect of which a notification is served under paragraph 3(2)(a) above;
(b) any oral representations made under paragraph 2(4) or 3(4) above; and
(c) any statements made by witnesses in connection with the oral representations,

and after considering any matters under this paragraph, to make a report (including recommendations) to the Secretary of State about the matters considered by him and the notice.

(2) It shall be the duty of the Secretary of State to consider any report made to him under sub–paragraph (1) above and, after considering the report, to inform the trader of his decision with respect to the prohibition notice to which the report relates.

5. (1) The Secretary of State may revoke or vary a prohibition notice by serving on the trader a notification stating that the notice is revoked or, as the case may be, is varied as specified in the notification.

(2) The Secretary of State shall not vary a prohibition notice so as to make the effect of the notice more restrictive for the trader.

(3) Without prejudice to the power conferred by section 13(2) of this Act, the service of a notification under sub–paragraph (1) above shall be sufficient to satisfy the requirement of paragraph 4(2) above that the trader shall be informed of the Secretary of State's decision.

PART II

NOTICES TO WARN

6. (1) If the Secretary of State proposes to serve a notice to warn on any person in respect of any goods, the Secretary of State, before he serves the notice, shall serve on that person a notification which –

(a) contains a draft of the proposed notice;
(b) states that the Secretary of State proposes to serve a notice in the form of the draft on that person;
(c) states that the Secretary of State considers that the goods described in the draft are unsafe;
(d) sets out the reasons why the Secretary of State considers that those goods are unsafe; and
(e) states that that person may make representations to the Secretary of State for the purpose of establishing that the goods are safe if, before the end of the period of fourteen days beginning with the day on which the notification is served, he informs the Secretary of State –
  (i) of his intention to make representations; and
  (ii) whether the representations will be made only in writing or both in writing and orally.

(2) Where the Secretary of State has served a notification containing a draft of a proposed notice to warn on any person, he shall not serve a notice to warn on that person in respect of the goods to which the proposed notice relates unless –

(a) the period of fourteen days beginning with the day on which the notification was served expires without the Secretary of State being informed as mentioned in sub–paragraph (1)(e) above;
(b) the period of twenty–eight days beginning with that day expires without any written representations being made by that person to the Secretary of State about the proposed notice; or
(c) the Secretary of State has considered a report about the proposed notice by a person appointed under paragraph 7(1) below.

7. (1) Where a person on whom a notification containing a draft of a proposed notice to warn has been served –

(a) informs the Secretary of State as mentioned in paragraph 6(1)(e) above before the end of the period of fourteen days beginning with the day on which the notification was served; and
(b) makes written representations to the Secretary of State about the proposed notice before the end of the period of twenty–eight days beginning with that day,

the Secretary of State shall appoint a person to consider those representations, any further representations made by that person about the draft notice and the statements of any witnesses examined under this Part of this Schedule.

(2) Where –

(a) the Secretary of State has appointed a person to consider representations about a proposed notice to warn; and
(b) the person whose representations are to be considered has informed the Secretary of State for the purposes of paragraph 6(1)(e) above that the representations he intends to make will include oral representations,

the Secretary of State shall inform the person intending to make the representations of the place and time at which oral representations may be made to the appointed person.

(3) Where a person on whom a notification containing a draft of a proposed notice to warn has been served is informed of a time for the purposes of sub–paragraph (2) above, that time shall not be –

(a) before the end of the period of twenty–eight days beginning with the day on which the notification was served; or
(b) before the end of the period of seven days beginning with the day on which that person is informed of the time.

(4) A person who has been informed of a place and time for the purposes of sub–paragraph (2) above or his representative may, at that place and time –

(a) make oral representations to the appointed person for the purpose of establishing that the goods to which the proposed notice relates are safe; and

(b) call and examine witnesses in connection with the representations.

8. (1) Where a person is appointed to consider representations about a proposed notice to warn, it shall be his duty to consider –

(a) any written representation made by the person on whom it is proposed to serve the notice; and

(b) in a case where a place and time has been appointed under paragraph 7(2) above for oral representations to be made by that person or his representative, any representations so made and any statements made by witnesses in connection with those representations,

and, after considering those matters, to make a report (including recommendations) to the Secretary of State about the matters considered by him and the proposal to serve the notice.

(2) It shall be the duty of the Secretary of State to consider any report made to him under sub-paragraph (1) above and, after considering the report, to inform the person on whom it was proposed that a notice to warn should be served of his decision with respect to the proposal.

(3) If at any time after serving a notification on a person under paragraph 6 above the Secretary of State decides not to serve on that person either the proposed notice to warn or that notice with modification, the Secretary of State shall inform that person of the decision; and nothing done for the purposes of any of the preceding provisions of this Part of this Schedule before that person was so informed shall –

(a) entitle the Secretary of State subsequently to serve the proposed notice or that notice with modification; or

(b) require the Secretary of State, or any person appointed to consider representations about the proposed notice, subsequently to do anything in respect of, or in consequence of, any such representations.

(4) Where a notification containing a draft of a proposed notice to warn is served on a person in respect of any goods, a notice to warn served on him in consequence, of a decision made under sub-paragraph (2) above shall either be in the form of the draft or shall be less onerous than the draft.

9. The Secretary of State may revoke a notice to warn by serving on the person on whom the notice was served a notification stating that the notice is revoked.

PART III
GENERAL

10. (1) Where in a notification served on any person under this Schedule the Secretary of State has appointed a time for the making of oral representations or the examination of witnesses, he may, by giving that person such notification as the Secretary of State considers appropriate, change that time to a later time or appoint further times at which further representations may be made or the examination of witnesses may be continued; and paragraphs 2(4), 3(4) and 7(4) above shall have effect accordingly.

(2) For the purposes of this Schedule the Secretary of State may appoint a person (instead of the appointed person) to consider any representations or statements, if the person originally appointed, or last appointed under this sub-paragraph, to consider those representations or statements has died or appears to the Secretary of State to be otherwise unable to act.

11. In this Schedule –

"the appointed person" in relation to a prohibition notice or a proposal to serve a notice to warn, means the person for the time being appointed under this Schedule to consider representations about the notice or, as the case may be, about the proposed notice;

"notification" means a notification in writing;

"trader", in relation to a prohibition notice, means the person on whom the notice is or was served.

SCHEDULE 3

(Amendments to the Health and Safety at Work Act 1974)

SCHEDULE 4

MINOR AND CONSEQUENTIAL AMENDMENTS

(i) The Explosives Act 1875: sections 31 and 80
(ii) The Trade Descriptions Act 1968: section 2 and section 28 (5A)
(iii) The Fair Trading Act 1973: Section 130(1)
(iv) The Consumer Credit Act 1974: Section 174(3)(a)
(v) The Torts (Interference with Goods) Act 1977: Section 1
(vi) The Estate Agents Act 1979: Section 10(3)(a)
(vii) The Competition Act 1980: Section 9(3)
(viii) The Employment Act 1982: Section 16(2)
(ix) The Telecommunications Act 1984: Sections 28(b) and 85(5)(b)
(x) The Airports Act 1986: Section 74(3)
(xi) The Gas Act 1986: Section 42
(xii) The Insolvency Act 1986: Section 281(5)(a)
(xiii) The Motor Cycle Noise Act 1987: Schedule paragraphs 3 and 5

SCHEDULE 5

Repeals of various Acts.

Part 4

OTHER MATERIALS

Chapter 18

EUROPEAN DIRECTIVE 85/374/EEC

Council Directive[1] of 25 July 1985 on the approximation of the laws, regulations and administrative provisions of the Member States concerning liability for defective products.

THE COUNCIL OF THE EUROPEAN COMMUNITIES

Having regard to the Treaty establishing the European Economic Community, and in particular Article 100 thereof,

Having regard to the proposal from the Commission[2],

Having regard to the opinion of the European Parliament[3],

Having regard to the opinion of the Economic and Social Committee[4],

Whereas approximation of the laws of the Member States concerning the liability of the producer for damage caused by the defectiveness of his products is necessary because the existing divergences may distort competition and affect the movement of goods within the common market and entail a differing degree of protection of the consumer against damage caused by a defective product to his health or property;

Whereas liability without fault on the part of the producer is the sole means of adequately solving the problem, peculiar to our age of increasing technicality, of a fair apportionment of the risks inherent in modern technological production;

Whereas liability without fault should apply only to movables which have been industrially produced; whereas, as a result, it is appropriate to exclude liability for agricultural products and game, except where they have undergone a processing of an industrial nature which could cause a defect in these products; whereas the liability provided for in this Directive should also apply to movables which are used in the construction of immovables or are installed in immovables;

Whereas protection of the consumer requires that all producers involved in the production process should be made liable, in so far as their finished product, component part or any raw material supplied by them was defective; whereas, for the same reason, liability should extend to importers of products into the Community and to persons who present themselves as producers by affixing their name, trade mark or other distinguishing feature or who supply a product the producer of which cannot be identified;

Whereas, in situations where several persons are liable for the same damage, the protection of the consumer requires that the injured person should be able to claim full compensation for the damage from any one of them;

Whereas, to protect the physical well-being and property of the consumer, the defectiveness of the product should be determined by reference not to its fitness for use but to the lack of the safety which the public at large is entitled to expect; whereas the safety is assessed by excluding any misuse of the product not reasonable under the circumstances;

Whereas a fair apportionment of risk between the injured person and the producer implies that the producer should be able to free himself from liability if he furnishes proof as to the existence of certain exonerating circumstances;

Whereas the protection of the consumer requires that the liability of the producer remains unaffected by acts or omissions of other persons having contributed to cause the damage; whereas, however, the contributory negligence of the injured person may be taken into account to reduce or disallow such liability;

Whereas the protection of the consumer requires compensation for death and personal injury as well as compensation for damage to property; whereas the latter should nevertheless be limited to goods for private use or consumption and be subject to a deduction of a lower threshold of a fixed amount in order to avoid litigation in an excessive number of cases; whereas this Directive should not prejudice compensation for pain and suffering and other non-material damages payable, where appropriate, under the law applicable to the case;

Whereas a uniform period of limitation for the bringing of action for compensation is in the interests both of the injured person and of the producer;

Whereas products age in the course of time, higher safety standards are developed and the state of science and technology progresses; whereas, therefore, it would not be reasonable to make the producer liable for an unlimited period for the defectiveness of his product; whereas, therefore, liability should expire after a reasonable length of time, without prejudice to claims pending at law;

Whereas, to achieve effective protection of consumers, no contractual derogation should be permitted as regards the liability of the producer in relation to the injured person;

Whereas under the legal systems of the Member States an injured party may have a claim for damages based on grounds of contractual liability or on grounds of non-contractual liability other than that provided for in this Directive; in so far as these provisions also serve to attain the objective of effective protection of consumers, they should remain unaffected by this Directive; whereas, in so far as effective protection of consumers in the sector of pharmaceutical products is already also attained in a Member State under a special liability system, claims based on this system should similarly remain possible;

Whereas, to the extent that liability for nuclear injury or damage is already covered in all Member States by adequate special rules, it has been possible to exclude damage of this type from the scope of this Directive;

Whereas, since the exclusion of primary agricultural products and game from the scope of this Directive may be felt, in certain Member States, in view of what is expected for the protection of consumers, to restrict unduly such protection, it should be possible for a Member State to extend liability to such products;

Whereas, for similar reasons, the possibility offered to a producer to free himself from liability if he proves that the state of scientific and technical knowledge at the time when he put the product into circulation was not such as to enable the existence of a defect to be discovered may be felt in certain Member States to restrict unduly the protection of the consumer; whereas it should therefore be possible for a Member State to maintain in its legislation or to provide by new legislation that this exonerating circumstance is not admitted; whereas, in the case of new legislation, making use of this derogation should, however, be subject to a Community stand-still procedure, in order to raise, if possible, the level of protection in a uniform manner throughout the Community;

Whereas, taking into account the legal traditions in most of the Member States, it is inappropriate to set any financial ceiling on the producer's liability without fault; whereas, in so far as there are, however, differing traditions, it seems possible to admit that a Member State may derogate from the principle of unlimited liability by providing a limit for the total liability of the producer for damage resulting from a death or personal injury and caused by identical items with the same defect, provided that this limit is established at a level sufficiently high to guarantee adequate protection of the consumer and the correct functioning of the common market;

Whereas the harmonization resulting from this cannot be total at the present stage, but opens the way towards greater harmonization; whereas it is therefore necessary that the Council receive at regular intervals, reports from the Commission on the application of this Directive, accompanied, as the case may be, by appropriate proposals;

Whereas it is particularly important in this respect that a re-examination be carried out of those parts of the Directive relating to the derogations open to the Member States, at the expiry of a period of sufficient length to gather practical experience on the effects of these derogations on the protection of consumers and on the functioning of the common market;

HAS ADOPTED THIS DIRECTIVE

NOTES
1 OJ L 210/29.
2 OJ No C 241, 14, 10, 1976, p 9 and OJ No C 271, 26, 10, 1979, p 3.
3 OJ No C 127, 21, 5, 1979, p 61.
4 OJ No C 114, 7, 5, 1979, p 15.

Article 1

The producer shall be liable for damage caused by a defect in his product.

Article 2

For the purpose of this Directive 'product' means all movables, with the exception of primary agricultural products and game, even though incorporated into another movable or into an immovable. 'Primary agricultural products' means the products of the soil, of stock-farming and of fisheries, excluding products which have undergone initial processing. 'Product' includes electricity.

Article 3

1. 'Producer' means the manufacturer of a finished product, the producer of any raw material or the manufacturer of a component part and

any person who, by putting his name, trade mark or other distinguishing feature on the product presents himself as its producer.

2. Without prejudice to the liability of the producer, any person who imports into the Community a product for sale, hire, leasing or any form of distribution in the course of his business shall be deemed to be a producer within the meaning of this Directive and shall be responsible as a producer.

3. Where the producer of the product cannot be identified, each supplier of the product shall be treated as its producer unless he informs the injured person, within a reasonable time, of the identity of the producer or of the person who supplied him with the product. The same shall apply, in the case of any imported product, if this product does not indicate the identity of the importer referred to in paragraph 2, even if the name of the producer is indicated.

Article 4

The injured person shall be required to prove the damage, the defect and the causal relationship between defect and damage.

Article 5

Where, as a result of the provisions of this Directive, two or more persons are liable for the same damage, they shall be liable jointly and severally, without prejudice to the provisions of national law concerning the rights of contribution or recourse.

Article 6

1. A product is defective when it does not provide the safety which a person is entitled to expect, taking all circumstances into account, including:

(a) the presentation of the product;

(b) the use to which it could reasonably be expected that the product would be put;

(c) the time when the product was put into circulation.

2. A product shall not be considered defective for the sole reason that a better product is subsequently put into circulation.

Article 7

The producer shall not be liable as a result of this Directive if he proves:

(a) that he did not put the product into circulation; or

(b) that, having regard to the circumstances, it is probable that the defect which caused the damage did not exist at the time when the product was put into circulation by him or that this defect came into being afterwards; or

(c) that the product was neither manufactured by him for sale or any form of distribution for economic purpose nor manufactured or distributed by him in the course of his business; or

(d) that the defect is due to compliance of the product with mandatory regulations issued by the public authorities; or

(e) that the state of scientific and technical knowledge at the time when he put the product into circulation was not such as to enable the existence of the defect to be discovered; or

(f) in the case of a manufacturer of a component, that the defect is attributable to the design of the product in which the component has been fitted or to the instructions given by the manufacturer of the product.

Article 8

1. Without prejudice to the provisions of national law concerning the right of contribution or recourse, the liability of the producer shall not be reduced when the damage is caused both by a defect in product and by the act or omission of a third party.

2. The liability of the producer may be reduced or disallowed when, having regard to all the circumstances, the damage is caused both by a defect in the product and by the fault of the injured person or any person for whom the injured person is responsible.

Article 9

For the purpose of Article 1, 'damage' means:

(a) damage caused by death or by personal injuries;

(b) damage to, or destruction of, any item of property other than the defective product itself, with a lower threshold of 500 ECU, provided that the item of property:

  (i) is of a type ordinarily intended for private use or consumption, and

  (ii) was used by the injured person mainly for his own private use or consumption.

This Article shall be without prejudice to national provisions relating to non-material damage.

Article 10

1. Member States shall provide in their legislation that a limitation period of three years shall apply to proceedings for the recovery of damages as provided for in this Directive. The limitation period shall begin to run from the day on which the plaintiff became aware, or should reasonably have become aware, of the damage, the defect and the identity of the producer.

2. The laws of Member States regulating suspension or interruption of the limitation period shall not be affected by this Directive.

Article 11

Member States shall provide in their legislation that the rights conferred upon the injured person pursuant to this Directive shall be extinguished upon the expiry of a period of 10 years from the date on which the producer put into circulation the actual product which caused the damage, unless the injured person has in the meantime instituted proceedings against the producer.

Article 12

The liability of the producer arising from this Directive may not, in relation to the injured person, be limited or excluded by a provision limiting his liability or exempting him from liability.

Article 13

This Directive shall not affect any rights which an injured person may have according to the rules of the law of contractual or non-contractual liability or a special liability system existing at the moment when this Directive is notified.

Article 14

This Directive shall not apply to injury or damage arising from nuclear accidents and covered by international conventions ratified by the Member States.

Article 15

1. Each Member State may:

(a) by way of derogation from Article 2, provide in its legislation that within the meaning of Article 1 of this Directive 'product' also means primary agricultural products and game;

(b) by way of derogation from Article 7 (e), maintain or, subject to the procedure set out in paragraph 2 of this Article, provide in this legislation that the producer shall be liable even if he proves that the state of scientific and technical knowledge at the time when he put the product into circulation was not such as to enable the existence of a defect to be discovered.

2. A Member State wishing to introduce the measure specified in paragraph 1 (b) shall communicate the text of the proposed measure to the Commission. The Commission shall inform the other Member States thereof.

The Member State concerned shall hold the proposed measure in abeyance for nine months after the Commission is informed and provided that in the meantime the Commission has not submitted to the Council a proposal amending this Directive on the relevant matter. However, if within three months of receiving the said information, the Commission does not advise the Member State concerned that it intends submitting such a proposal to the Council, the Member State may take the proposed measure immediately.

If the Commission does submit to the Council such a proposal amending this Directive within the aforementioned nine months, the Member State concerned shall hold the proposed measure in abeyance for a further period of 18 months from the date on which the proposal is submitted.

3. Ten years after the date of notification of this Directive, the Commission shall submit to the Council a report on the effect that rulings by the courts as to the application of Article 7 (e) and of paragraph 1 (b) of this Article have on consumer protection and the functioning of the common market. In the light of this report the Council, acting on a proposal from the Commission and pursuant to the terms of Article 100 of the Treaty, shall decide whether to repeal Article 7(e).

Article 16

1. Any Member State may provide that a producer's total liability for damage resulting from a death or personal injury and caused by identical items with the same defect shall be limited to an amount which may not be less than 70 million ECU.

2. Ten years after the date of notification of this Directive, the Commission shall submit to the Council a report on the effect on consumer protection and the functioning of the common market of the implementation of the financial limit on liability by those Member States which have used the option provided for in paragraph 1. In the light of this report the Council, acting on a proposal from the Commission and pursuant to the terms of Article 100 of the Treaty, shall decide whether to repeal paragraph 1.

Article 17

This Directive shall not apply to products put into circulation before the date on which the provisions referred to in Article 19 enter into force.

Article 18

1. For the purposes of this Directive, the ECU shall be that defined by Regulation (EEC) No 3180/78[1], as amended by Regulation (EEC) No 2626/84[2]. The equivalent in national currency shall initially be calculated at the rate obtaining on the date of adoption of this Directive.

2. Every five years the Council, acting on a proposal from the Commission, shall examine and, if need be, revise the amounts in this Directive, in the light of economic and monetary trends in the Community.

NOTES

1 OJ No L 379, 30, 12, 1978, p 1.

2 OJ No L 247, 16, 9, 1984, p 1.

Article 19

1. Member States shall bring into force, not later than three years from the date of notification of this Directive, the laws, regulations and administrative provisions necessary to comply with this Directive. They shall forthwith inform the Commission thereof[1].

2. The procedure set out in Article 15 (2) shall apply from the date of notification of this Directive.

NOTE
1 This Directive was notified to the Member States on 30 July 1985.

Article 20

Member States shall communicate to the Commission the texts of the main provisions of national law which they subsequently adopt in the field governed by this Directive.

Article 21

Every five years the Commission shall present a report to the Council on the application of this Directive and, if necessary, shall submit appropriate proposals to it.

Article 22

This Directive is addressed to the Member States.

Done at Brussels, 25 July 1985.

For the Council

The President

J POOS

Chapter 19

COUNCIL DIRECTIVE 92/59/EEC OF 29 JUNE 1992 ON GENERAL PRODUCT SAFETY

Introductory note This Council Directive on general product safety was done at Luxembourg on 29 June 1992. It must be complied with by 29 June 1994 at the latest.

THE COUNCIL OF THE EUROPEAN COMMUNITIES

Having regard to the Treaty establishing the European Economic Community, and in particular Article 100a thereof,

Having regard to the proposal from the Commission,

In co-operation with the European Parliament,

Having regard to the opinion of the Economic and Social Committee;

Whereas it is important to adopt measures with the aim of progressively establishing the internal market over a period expiring on 31 December 1992; whereas the internal market is to comprise an area without internal frontiers on which the free movement of goods, persons, services and capital is ensured;

Whereas some Member States have adopted horizontal legislation on product safety, imposing, in particular, a general obligation on economic operators to market only safe products; whereas those legislations differ in the level of protection afforded to persons; whereas such disparities and the absence of horizontal legislation in other Member States are liable to create barriers to trade and distortions of competition within the internal market;

Whereas it is very difficult to adopt Community legislation for every product which exists or may be developed; whereas there is a need for a broadly-based, legislative framework of a horizontal nature to deal with those products, and also to cover lacunae in existing or forthcoming specific legislation, in particular with a view to ensuring a high level of protection of safety and health of persons, as required by Article 100a(3) of the Treaty;

Whereas it is therefore necessary to establish on a Community level a general safety requirement for any product placed on the market that is intended for consumers or likely to be used by consumers; whereas certain second-hand goods should nevertheless be excluded by their nature;

Whereas production equipment, capital goods and other products used exclusively in the context of a trade or business are not covered by this Directive;

Whereas, in the absence of more specific safety provisions, within the frame-work of Community regulations, covering the products concerned, the provisions of this Directive are to apply;

Whereas when there are specific rules of Community law, of the total harmonization type, and in particular rules adopted on the basis of the new approach, which lay down obligations regarding product safety, further obligations should not be imposed on economic operators as regards the placing on the market of products covered by such rules;

Whereas, when the provisions of specific Community regulations cover only certain aspects of safety or categories of risks in respect of the product concerned, the obligations of economic operators in respect of such aspects are determined solely by those provisions;

Whereas it is appropriate to supplement the duty to observe the general safety requirement by an obligation on economic operators to supply consumers with relevant information and adopt measures commensurate with the characteristics of the products, enabling them to be informed of the risks that these products might present;

Whereas in the absence of specific regulations, criteria should be defined whereby product safety can be assessed;

Whereas Member States must establish authorities responsible for monitoring product safety and with powers to take the appropriate measures;

Whereas it is necessary in particular for the appropriate measures to include the power for Member States to organize, immediately and efficiently, the withdrawal of dangerous products already placed on the market;

Whereas it is necessary for the preservation of the unity of the market to inform the Commission of any measure restricting the placing on the market of a product or requiring its withdrawal from the market except for those relating to an event which is local in effect and in any case limited to the territory of the Member State concerned; whereas such measures can be taken only in compliance with the provisions of the Treaty, and in particular Articles 30 and 36;

Whereas this Directive applies without prejudice to the notification procedures in Council Directive 83/189/EEC of 28 March 1983 laying down a procedure for the provision of information in the field of technical standards and regulations and in Commission Decision 88/383 EEC of 24 February 1988 providing for the improvement of information on safety, hygiene and health at work.

Whereas effective supervision of product safety requires the setting-up at national and Community levels of a system of rapid exchange of information in emergency situations in respect of the safety of a product and whereas the procedure laid down by Council Decision 89/45/EEC of 21 December 1988 on a Community system for the rapid exchange of information on dangers arising from the use of consumer products should therefore be incorporated into this Directive and the above Decision should be repealed; whereas it is also advisable for this Directive to take over the detailed procedures adopted under the above Decision and to give the Commission, assisted by a committee, power to adapt them;

Whereas, moreover, equivalent notification procedures already exist for pharmaceuticals, which come under Directives 75/319/EEC and 81/851/EEC concerning animal diseases referred to in Directive 89/662/EEC and in the form of the system for the rapid exchange of information in radiological emergencies under Decision 87/600/Euratom.

Whereas it is primarily for Member States in compliance with the Treaty and in particular with Articles 30 to 36 thereof, to take appropriate measures with regard to dangerous products located within their territory;

Whereas in such a situation the decision taken on a particular product could differ from Member State to another; whereas such a difference may entail unacceptable disparities in consumer protection and constitute a barrier to intra-Community trade;

Whereas it may be necessary to cope with serious product-safety problems which affect or could affect, in the immediate future, all or a large part of the Community and which, in view of the nature of the safety problem posed by the product cannot be dealt with effectively in a manner commensurate with the urgency of the problem under the procedures laid down in the specific rules of Community law applicable to the products or category of products in question;

Whereas it is therefore necessary to provide for an adequate mechanism allowing, in the last resort, for the adoption of measures applicable throughout the Community, in the form of a decision addressed to the Member States, in order to cope with emergency situations as mentioned above; whereas such a decision is not of direct application to economic operators and must be incorporated into a national instrument; whereas measures adopted under such a procedure can be no more than interim measures that have to be taken by the Commission assisted by a committee of representatives of the Member States; whereas for reasons of cooperation with the Member States, it is appropriate to provide for a regulatory committee according to procedure III(b) of Decision 87/373/EEC.

Whereas this Directive does not affect victims rights within the meaning of Council Directive 85/374/EEC of 25 July 1985 on the approximation of the laws, regulations and administration provisions of the Member States concerning liability for defective products;

Whereas it is necessary that Member States provide for appropriate means of address before the competent courts in respect of measures taken by the competent authorities which restrict the placing on the market of a product or require its withdrawal;

Whereas it is appropriate to consider, in the light of experience, possible adaptation of this Directive, particularly as regards extension of its scope and provisions on emergency situations and intervention at Community level;

Whereas, in addition, the adoption measures concerning imported products with a view to preventing risks to the safety and health of persons must comply with the Community's international obligations.

TITLE 1 OBJECTIVE-SCOPE-DEFINITIONS

Article 1

1. The purpose of the provisions of this Directive is to ensure that products placed on the market are safe.

2. The provisions of this Directive shall apply in so far as there are no specific provisions in rules of Community law governing the safety of the products concerned.

In particular, where specific rules of Community law contain provisions imposing safety requirements on the products which they govern, the provisions of Articles 2 to 4 of this Directive shall not, in any event, apply to those products.

Where specific rules of Community law contain provisions governing certain aspects of product safety or categories of risks for the products concerned, those are the provisions which shall apply to the products concerned with regard to the relevant safety aspects or risks.

Article 2

For the purposes of this Directive:

(a) product shall mean any product intended for consumers or likely to be used by consumers, supplied whether for consideration or not in the course of a commercial activity and whether new, used or reconditioned.

However, this Directive shall not apply to second-hand products supplied as antiques or as products to be repaired or reconditioned prior to being used, provided that the supplier clearly informs the person to whom he supplies the product to that effect;

(b) safe product shall mean any product which, under normal or reasonably foreseeable conditions of use, including duration, does not present any risk or only the minimum risks compatible with the product's use, considered as acceptable and consistent with a high level of protection for the safety and health of persons, taking into account the following points in particular:

- the characteristics of the product, including its composition, packaging, instructions for assembly and maintenance,
- the effect on other products, where it is reasonably foreseeable that it will be used with other products,
- the presentation of the product, the labelling, any instructions for its use and disposal and any other indication or information provided by the producer,
- the categories of consumers at serious risk when using the product, in particular children.

The feasibility of obtaining higher levels of safety or the availability of other products presenting a lesser degree of risk shall not constitute grounds for considering a product to be 'unsafe' or 'dangerous';

(c) dangerous product shall mean any product which does not meet the definition of 'safe product' according to point (b) hereof;

(d) producer shall mean:

- the manufacturer of the product, when he is established in the Community, and any other person presenting himself as the manufacturer by affixing to the product his name, trade mark or other distinctive mark, or the person who reconditions the product,
- the manufacturer's representative, when the manufacturer is not established in the Community or, if there is no representative established in the Community, the importer of the product,
- other professionals in the supply chain, insofar as their activities may affect the safety properties of a product placed on the market.

(e) distributor shall mean any professional in the supply chain whose activity does not affect the safety properties of a product.

TITLE II GENERAL SAFETY REQUIREMENT

Article 3

1. Producers shall be obliged to place only safe products on the market.

2. Within the limits of their respective activities, producers shall

– provide consumers with the relevant information to enable them to assess the risks inherent in a product throughout the normal or reasonably foreseeable period of its use, where such risks are not immediately obvious without adequate warnings, and to take precautions against those risks.

Provision of such warnings does not, however, exempt any person from compliance with the other requirements laid down in this Directive.

– adopt measures commensurate with the characteristics of the products which they supply, to enable them to be informed of risks which these products might present and to take appropriate action including, if necessary, withdrawing the product in question from the market to avoid these risks.

The above measures shall for example include, whenever appropriate, marking of the products or product batches in such a way that they can be identified, sample testing of marketed products, investigating complaints made and keeping distributors informed of such monitoring.

3. Distributors shall be required to act with due care in order to help to ensure compliance with the general safety requirement, in particular by not supplying products which they know or should have presumed, on the basis of the information in their possession and as professionals, do not comply with this requirement. In particular, within the limits of their respective activities, they shall participate in monitoring the safety of products placed on the market, especially by passing on information on product risks and cooperating in the action taken to avoid these risks.

Article 4

1. Where there are no specific Community provisions governing the safety of the products in question, a product shall be deemed safe when it conforms to the specific rules of national law of the Member State in whose territory the product is in circulation, such rules being drawn up in conformity with the Treaty, and in particular Articles 30 and 36 thereof, and laying down the health and safety requirements which the product must satisfy in order to be marketed.

2. In the absence of specific rules as referred to in paragraph 1, the conformity of a product to the general safety requirement shall be assessed having regard to voluntary national standards giving effect to a European standard or, where they exist, to Community technical specifications or, failing these, to standards drawn up in the Member State in which the product is in

circulation, or to the codes of good practice in respect of health and safety in the sector concerned or to the state of the art and technology and to the safety which consumers may reasonably expect.

3. Conformity of a product with the provisions mentioned in paragraphs 1 or 2 shall not bar the competent authorities of the Member States from taking appropriate measures to impose restrictions on its being placed on the market or to require its withdrawal from the market where there is evidence that, despite such conformity, it is dangerous to the health and safety of consumers.

TITLE III OBLIGATIONS AND POWERS OF THE MEMBER STATES

Article 5

Member States shall adopt the necessary laws, regulations and administrative provisions to make producers and distributors comply with their obligations under this Directive in such a way that products placed on the market are safe. In particular, Member States shall establish or nominate authorities to monitor the compliance of products with the obligation to place only safe products on the market and arrange for such authorities to have the necessary powers to take the appropriate measures incumbent upon them under this Directive, including the possibility of imposing suitable penalties in the event of failure to comply with the obligations deriving from this Directive. They shall notify the Commission of the said authorities; the Commission shall pass on the information to the other Member States.

Article 6

1. For the purposes of Article 5, Member States shall have the necessary powers, acting in accordance with the degree of risk and in conformity with the Treaty, and in particular Articles 30 and 36 thereof, to adopt appropriate measures with a view, inter alia, to:

(a) organizing appropriate checks on the safety properties of products, even after their being placed on the market as being safe, on an adequate scale, up to the final stage of use or consumption;

(b) requiring all necessary information from the parties concerned;

(c) taking samples of a product or a product line and subjecting them to safety checks;

(d) subjecting product marketing to prior conditions designed to ensure product safety and requiring that suitable warnings be affixed regarding the risks which the product may present;

(e) making arrangements to ensure that persons who might be exposed to a risk from a product are informed in good time and in a suitable manner of the said risk by, inter alia, the publication of special warnings;

(f) temporarily prohibiting, for the period required to carry out the various checks, anyone from supplying, offering to supply or exhibiting a product or product batch, whenever there are precise and consistent indications that they are dangerous;

(g) prohibiting the placing on the market of a product or product batch which has proved dangerous and establishing the accompanying measures needed to ensure that the ban is complied with;

(h) organizing the effective and immediate withdrawal of a dangerous product or product batch already on the market and, if necessary, its destruction under appropriate conditions;

2. The measures to be taken by the competent authorities of the Member States under this Article shall be addressed, as appropriate, to

(a) the producer;

(b) within the limits of their respective activities, distributors and in particular the party responsible for the first stage of distribution on the national market;

(c) any other persons, where necessary, with regard to cooperation in action taken to avoid risks arising from a product.

TITLE IV NOTIFICATION AND EXCHANGES OF INFORMATION

Article 7

1. Where a Member State takes measures which restrict the placing of a product or a product batch on the market or require its withdrawal from the market, such as provided for in Article 6(1)(d) to (h), the Member State shall, to the extent that such notification is not required under any specific Community legislation, inform the Commission of the said measures, specifying its reasons for adopting them. This obligation shall not apply where the measures relate to an event which is local in effect and in any case limited to the territory of the Member State concerned.

2. The Commission shall enter into consultations with the parties concerned as quickly as possible. Where the Commission concludes, after such consultations, that the measure is justified, it shall immediately inform the Member State which initiated the action and the other Member States. Where the Commission concludes, after such consultations, that the measure is not justified, it shall immediately inform the Member State which initiated the action.

TITLE V EMERGENCY SITUATIONS AND ACTION AT COMMUNITY LEVEL

Article 8

1. Where a Member State adopts or decides to adopt emergency measures to prevent, restrict or impose specific conditions on the possible marketing or use, within its own territory, of a product or product batch to the health and safety of consumers, it shall forthwith inform the Commission

thereof, unless provision is made for this obligation in procedures of a similar nature in the context of other Community instruments.

This obligation shall not apply if the effects of the risk do not, or cannot, go beyond the territory of the Member State concerned.

Without prejudice to the provisions of the first subparagraph, Member States may pass on to the Commission any information in their possession regarding the existence of a serious and immediate risk before deciding to adopt the measures in question.

2. On receiving this information, the Commission shall check to see whether it complies with the provisions of this Directive and shall forward it to the other Member States, which, in turn, shall immediately inform the Commission of any measures adopted.

3. Detailed procedures for the Community information system described in this Article are set out in the Annex. They shall be adapted by the Commission in accordance with the procedure laid down in Article 11.

Article 9

If the Commission becomes aware, through notification given by the Member States or through information provided by them, in particular under Article 7 or Article 8, of the existence of a serious and immediate risk from a product to the health and safety of consumers in various Member States and if:

(a) one or more Member States have adopted measures entailing restrictions on the marketing of the product or requiring its withdrawal from the market, such as those provided for in Article 6(1)(d) to (h);

(b) Member States differ on the adoption of measures to deal with the risk in question;

(c) the risk cannot be dealt with, in view of the nature of the safety issue posed by the product and in a manner compatible with the urgency of the case, under the other procedures laid down by the specific Community legislation applicable to the product or category of products concerned; and

(d) the risk can be eliminated effectively only by adopting appropriate measures applicable at Community level, in order to ensure the protection of health and safety of consumers and the proper functioning of the common market,

the Commission, after consulting the Member States and at the request of at least one of them, may adopt a decision, in accordance with the procedure laid down in Article 11, requiring Member States to take temporary measures from among those listed in Article 6(1)(d) to (h).

Article 10

1. The Commission shall be assisted by a Committee on Product Safety Emergencies, hereinafter referred to as 'the Committee', composed of the representatives of the Member States and chaired by a representative of the Commission.

2. Without prejudice to Article 9(c), there shall be close cooperation between the Committee referred to in paragraph 1 and the other Committees established by specific rules of Community law to assist the Commission as regards the health and safety aspects of the product concerned.

Article 11

1. The Commission representative shall submit to the Committee a draft of the measures to be taken. The Committee, having verified that the conditions listed in Article 9 are fulfilled, shall deliver its opinion on the draft within a time limit which the Chairman may lay down according to the urgency of the matter but which may not exceed one month. The opinion shall be delivered by the majority laid down in Article 148(2) of the Treaty for adoption of decisions by the Council on a proposal from the Commission. The votes of the representatives of the Member States within the Committee shall be weighted in the manner set out in that Article. The Chairman shall not vote.

The Commission shall adopt the measures in question, if they are in accordance with the opinion of the Committee. If the measures proposed are not in accordance with the Committee's opinion, or in the absence of an opinion, the Commission shall forthwith submit to the Council a proposal regarding the measures to be taken. The Council shall act by a qualified majority.

If the Council has not acted within 15 days of the date on which the proposal was submitted to it, the measures proposed shall be adopted by the Commission unless the Council has decided against them by a simple majority.

2. Any measure adopted under this procedure shall be valid for no longer than three months. That period may be prolonged under the same procedure.

3. Member States shall take all necessary measures to implement the decisions adopted under this procedure within less than 10 days.

4. The competent authorities of the Member States responsible for carrying out measures adopted under this procedure shall, within one month, give the parties concerned an opportunity to submit their views and shall inform the Commission accordingly.

Article 12

The Member States and the Commission shall take steps necessary to ensure that their officials and agents are required not to disclose information obtained for the purposes of this Directive which, by its nature, is covered by professional secrecy, except for information relating to the safety properties of a given product which must be made public if circumstances so require, in order to protect the health and safety of persons.

TITLE VI MISCELLANEOUS AND FINAL PROVISIONS

Article 13

This Directive shall be without prejudice to Directive 85/374/EEC.

Article 14

1. Any decision adopted under this Directive and involving restrictions on the placing of a product on the market, or requiring its

withdrawal from the market, must state the appropriate reasons on which it is based. It shall be notified as soon as possible to the party concerned and shall indicate the remedies available under the provisions in force in the Member State in question and the time limits applying to such remedies.

The parties concerned shall, whenever feasible, be given an opportunity to submit their views before the adoption of the measure. If this had not been done in advance because of the urgency of the measures to be taken, such opportunity shall be given in due course after the measure has been implemented. Measures requiring the withdrawal of a product from the market shall take into consideration the need to encourage distributors, users and consumers to contribute to the implementation of such measures.

2. Member States shall ensure that any measure taken by the competent authorities involving restrictions on the placing of a product on the market or requiring its withdrawal from the market can be challenged before the competent courts.

3. Any decision taken by virtue of this Directive and involving restrictions on the placing of a product on the market or requiring its withdrawal from the market shall be entirely without prejudice to assessment of the liability of the party concerned, in the light of the national criminal law applying in the case in question.

Article 15

Every two years following the date of adoption, the Commission shall submit a report on the implementation of this Directive to the European Parliament and the Council.

Article 16

Four years from the date referred to in Article 17(1), on the basis of a Commission report on the experience acquired, together with appropriate proposals, the Council shall decide whether to adjust this Directive, in particular with a view to extending its scope as laid down in Article 1(1) and Article 2(a), and whether the provisions of Title V should be amended.

Article 17

1. Member States shall adopt the laws, regulations and administrative provisions necessary to comply with this Directive by 29 June 1994 at the latest. They shall forthwith inform the Commission thereof. The provisions adopted shall apply with effect from 29 June 1994.

2. When these measures are adopted by the Member States, they shall contain a reference to this Directive or be accompanied by such a reference on the occasion of their official publication. The methods of making such a reference shall be laid down by the Member States.

3. Member States shall communicate to the Commission the text of the provisions of national law which they adopt in the area covered by this Directive.

Article 18

Decision 89/45/EEC is hereby repealed on the date referred to in Article 17(1).

Article 19

This Directive is addressed to the Member States.
Done at Luxembourg, 29 June 1992.

ANNEX

Detailed procedures for the application of the Community system for the rapid exchange of information provided for in article 8

1. The system covers products placed on the market as defined in Article 29(a) of this Directive.

Pharmaceuticals, which come under Directive 75/319/EEC and 81/851/EEC, and animals, to which Directive 82/894/EEC applies and products of animal origin, as far as they are covered by Directive 89/662/EEC, and the system for radiological emergencies which covers widespread contamination of products (Decision 87/600/Euratom), are excluded, since they are covered by equivalent notification procedures.

2. The system is essentially aimed at a rapid exchange of information in the event of a serious and immediate risk to the health and safety of consumers. It is impossible to lay down specific criteria as to what, precisely, constitutes an immediate and serious risk; in this regard, the national authorities will therefore judge each individual case on its merits. It should be noted that, as Article 8 of this Directive relates to immediate threats posed by a product to consumers, products involving possible long-term risks, which call for a study of possible technical changes by means of directives or standards are not concerned.

3. As soon as serious and immediate risk is detected, the national authority shall consult, insofar as possible and appropriate, the producer or distributor of the product concerned. Their point of view and the details which they supply may be useful both to the administrations of the Member States and to the Commission in determining what action should be taken to ensure that the consumer is protected with a minimum of commercial disruption. To these ends the Member States should endeavour to obtain the maximum of information on the products and the nature of the danger, without compromising the need for rapidity.

4. As soon as a Member State has detected a serious and immediate risk, the effects of which extend beyond its territory, and measures have been taken or decided on, it shall immediately inform the Commission under Article 8 of this Directive. All available details shall be given, in particular on:

(a) information to identify the product;

(b) the danger involved, including the results of any tests/analyses which are referred to assessing the level of risk;

(c) the nature of the measures taken or decided on;

(d) information on supply chains where such information is possible.

Such information must be transmitted in writing, preferably by telex or fax, but may be preceded by a telephone call to the Commission. It should be remembered that the speed with which the information is communicated is crucial.

5. Without prejudice to point 4, Member States may, where appropriate, pass information to the Commission at the stage preceding the decision on the measures to be taken. Immediate contact, as soon as a risk is discovered or suspected, can in fact facilitate preventive action.

6. If the Member State considers certain information to be confidential, it should specify this and justify its request for confidentiality, bearing in mind that the need to take effective measures to protect consumers normally outweighs considerations of confidentiality. It should also be remembered that precautions are taken in all cases, both by the Commission and by the members of the network responsible in the various Member States, to avoid any unnecessary disclosure of information likely to harm the reputation of a product or series of products.

7. The Commission shall verify the conformity of the information received with Article 8 of this Directive, contact the notifying country, if necessary, and forward the information immediately by telex or fax to the relevant authorities in the other Member States with a copy of each permanent representation; these authorities may, at the same time as the transmission of the telex, be contacted by telephone. The Commission may also contact the Member State presumed to be the country of origin of the product to carry out the necessary verifications.

8. At the same time the Commission, when it considers it to be necessary, and in order to supplement the information received, can in exceptional circumstances institute an investigation of its own motion (and/or convene the Committee on Emergencies provided for in Article 10(1) of this Directive.

In the case of such an investigation Member States shall supply the Commission with the requested information to the best of their ability.

9. The other Member States are requested, wherever possible, to inform the Commission without delay of the following:

(a) whether the product has been marketed in its territory;

(b) supplementary information it has obtained on the danger involved, including the results of any test/analyses carried out to assess the level of risk,

and in any case must inform the Commission as soon as possible of the following;

(c) the measures taken or decided on, of the type mentioned in Article 8(1) of this Directive;

(d) when the product mentioned in this information has been found within their territory but no measures have been taken or decided on and the reasons why no measures are to be taken.

10. The Commission may, in the light of the evolution of a case and the information received from Member States under point 9 above, convene the above Committee on Emergencies in order to exchange views on the results obtained and to evaluate the measures taken. The Committee on Emergencies may also be convened at the request of a representative of a Member State.

11. The Commission shall, by means of its internal coordination procedures, endeavour to:

(a) avoid unnecessary duplication in dealing with notifications;
(b) make full use of the expertise available within the Commission;
(c) keep the other services concerned fully informed;
(d) ensure that discussion in the various relevant committees are held in accordance with Article 10 of this Directive.

12. When a Member State intends, apart from any specific measures taken because of serious and immediate risks, to modify its legislation by adopting technical specifications, the latter must be notified to the Commission at the draft stage, in accordance with Directive 83/189/EEC, if necessary, quoting the urgent reasons set out in Article 9(3) of that Directive.

13. To allow it to have an overview of the situation, the Committee on Emergencies shall be periodically informed of all the notifications received and of the follow-up. With regard to points 8 and 10 above, and in those cases which fall within the scope of procedures and/or committees provided for by Community legislation governing specific products or product sectors, those committees shall be involved. In cases where the Committee on Emergencies is not involved and no provisions are made under 11(d) the contact points shall be informed of any exchange of views within other committees.

14. At present there are two networks of contact points: the food products network and the non-food products network. The list of contact points and officials responsible for the networks with telephone, telex and fax numbers and addresses is confidential and distributed to the members of the network only. This list enables contact to be established with the Commission and between Member States in order to facilitate clarification of points of detail. When such contacts between Member States give rise to new information of general interest, the Member States which initiated the bilateral contact shall inform the Commission. Only information received or confirmed through contact points in Member States may be considered as received through the rapid exchange of information procedure.

Every year the Commission shall carry out a review of the effectiveness of the network, of any necessary improvements and of the progress made in the communications technology between the authorities responsible for its operation.

Chapter 20

GENERAL PRODUCT SAFETY REGULATIONS 1994 (1994 NO 2328) CONSUMER PROTECTION

Made	5th September 1994
Laid before Parliament	8th September 1994
Coming into force	3rd October 1994

Whereas the Secretary of State is a Minister designated (a) for the purposes of Section 2(2) of the European Communities Act 1972 (b) in relation to measures to consumer protection as regards general product safety;

Now, the Secretary of State, in exercise of the powers conferred on him by Section 2(2) of that Act and of all other powers enabling him in that behalf hereby makes the following Regulations:-

Citation and commencement

1. These Regulations may be cited as the General Product Safety Regulations 1994 and shall come into force on 3rd October 1994[1].

NOTE

1 The Council Directive on General Product Safety: 92/59/EEC was to be complied with by 29 June 1994 at the latest, for the effects of the delay see chapter 4, *European Perspective*.

Interpretation

2. (1) In these Regulations

"the 1968 Act" mean the Medicines Act 1968(c);

"the 1987 Act" means the Consumer Protection Act 1987(d);

"the 1990 Act" means the Food Safety Act 1990(e);

"commercial activity" includes a business and a trade[1];

"consumer" means a consumer acting otherwise than in the course of a commercial activity;

"dangerous product" means any product other than a safe product;

"distributor" means any professional in the supply chain whose activity does not affect the safety properties of a product[2];

"enforcement authority" means the Secretary of State, any other Minister of the Crown in charge of a Government Department, any such department and any authority, council and other person on whom functions under these Regulations are imposed by or under Regulation 11;

"general safety requirement" means the requirement in Regulation 7;

"the GPS Directive" means Council Directive 92/59/EEC on general product safety (a)[3];

"the 1991 Order" means the Food Safety (Northern Ireland) Order 1991(b);

"producer"[4] means

(a) the manufacturer of the product, when he is established in the Community, and includes any person presenting himself as the manufacturer by affixing to the product his name, trade mark or other distinctive mark, or the person who reconditions[5] the product;

(b) when the manufacturer is not established[6] in the Community

(i) if the manufacturer does not have a representative[7] established in the Community, the importer of the product[8];

(ii) in all other cases, the manufacturer's representatives; and

(c) other professionals in the supply chain, insofar as their activities may affect the safety properties of a product placed on the market;

"product"[9] means any product[10] intended for consumers or likely to be used by consumers, supplied whether for consideration or not in the course of a commercial activity and whether new, used or reconditioned[11]; provided, however, a product which is used exclusively in the context of a commercial activity even if it is used for or by[12] a consumer shall not be regarded as a product for the purposes of these Regulations provided always and for the avoidance of doubt this exception shall not extend to the supply[13] of such a product to a consumer.

"safe product"[14] means any product which under normal or reasonably foreseeable conditions of use[15], including duration[16], does not present any risk[17] or only the minimum risks compatible with the product's use[18], considered as acceptable and consistent with a high level of protection for the safety and health of persons[19], taking into account in particular[20] –

(a) the characteristics of the product, including its composition, packaging instructions for assembly and maintenance[21];

(b) the effect on other products, where it is reasonably foreseeable that it will be used with other products[22];

(c) the presentation of the product[23], the labelling, any instructions for its use and disposal and any other indication or information provided by the producer; and

(d) the categories of consumers at serious risk when using the product, in particular children[24],

and the fact that higher levels of safety may be obtained[25] or other products presenting a lesser degree of risk may be available shall not of itself cause the product to be considered other than a safe product[26].

(2) References in these Regulations to the "Community" are references to the European Economic Area established under the Agreement signed at Oporto on 2nd May 1992 as adjusted by the Protocol signed at Brussels on 17th March 1993(c).

NOTES

1 It is interesting to note that the Directive refers to 'economic operators' within the preamble. See also the notes to s 2(2) of the Act.

2 See the definition of 'producer' and sub-s (c) which states that if a professional in the supply chain carries out activities which do affect the safety properties of a product that person is deemed to be a 'producer'. The definition throws up two new concepts for consideration:

(i) *Professional*
See *IR V v Maxse* [1919] 1KB 647. A profession is usually held to mean an occupation which requires skill. The definition is likely to be seen in the light of the fact that a product whether supplied for consideration or not has to be supplied in the course of a commercial activity, and in practice those who ordinarily stand to be affected are retailers or wholesalers. The Consumer Safety Unit (DTI) May 1995 Guidance Notes state that "professional" is considered to refer to a person carrying on a commercial activity.

(ii) *Activity affecting the safety properties of a product*
This will catch any person within the supply chain who alters the condition or state of the goods for example by assembly or of fixing some form of new or additional labelling or packaging.

3 Article 92/59/EEC is expressly stated to be without prejudice to Directive 85/374/EEC.

4 See Art 2(d). The definition within the Regulation closely mirrors that within the Directive. It is to be compared with the definition of 'Producer' contained within s 1(2) of the Act.

5 See the notes to s 1(2)(a). There is a distinction between those who recondition, re-fit or renovate goods and those who merely service or repair. This is particularly important in the light of the fact that the definition of product includes used or reconditioned goods. However, it is to be noted that if a person does not recondition a product it is still possible to affect its safety properties by virtue of servicing or repair and hence to be caught by the definition of a producer within sub-s (c).

6 This is likely to be defined as the setting up or managing of an undertaking within the EEC. See for example the Treaty of Rome 1957 Article 52, Directive 75/363; *Patrick v Ministry of Cultural Affairs*: 11/77 [1977] 2 CMLR 523.

7 The most obvious example of a representative is an agent.

8 Neither the Regulations nor the Articles expressly state whether the relevant importer is the first importer into the Community or any subsequent importer into the relevant Member State. (This is to be compared with s 2(2)(c) of the Act where only the person who imports 'into the Community' is caught by the section. Hence, movement within the Community does not create additional liability.) This may be of considerable practical importance. It is submitted that when taken in context this definition should also mean the importer of a product into the Community. See also differing requirements under specific Regulations such as the Toys (Safety) Regulations 1989, Regs 9 and 10. Under Reg 9 reference is made to the importer into the Community whereas under Reg 10 the duty is upon the person who 'supplies a toy on the first occasion on which it is supplied in the Community provided that he is established in the United Kingdom'. The effect of defining the importer of the product as the importer of the product into the Community means that Reg 8 will apply to this person whereas any subsequent importer to a Member State, provided that the importation does not include affixing to the product any name, trade mark or other distinctive mark or indeed any activity that may affect the safety properties of the product, will be deemed to be a distributor.

9 It is important to note the definition of product under Art 2 which refers to 'any product intended for consumers or likely to be used by consumers, supplied whether for consideration or not in the course of a commercial activity and whether new, used or reconditioned (but not applying to) second-hand products supplied as antiques or as products to be repaired or reconditioned prior to being used, provided that the supplier clearly informs the person to whom he supplies the product to that effect.' Within the preamble to the Directive it is stated that it is necessary to establish a Community level requirement 'for any product placed on the market that is intended for consumers or likely to be used by consumers, whereas certain second-hand goods should nevertheless be excluded by their nature; whereas production equipment, capital goods and other products used exclusively in the context of a trade or business are not covered by this Directive.' The Regulations work by the interaction of the definition of product and also Reg 3 which restricts the ambit of the definition. However it is difficult to see how the exclusion for 'a product which is used exclusively in the context of a commercial activity' can be justified upon the basis of the Directive; see *Davis* [1994] Consum LJ, Current Survey 26. It can be strongly argued that the definition of product is too restrictive and that the specific exemption for products used exclusively in the context of a commercial activity should be seen as inconsistent with the Article; see also chapter 4, *European Perspective*. The exemption leaves an area to be covered by s 10 of the 1987 Act. As an example, some car garages now supply a microwave oven for use by customers who

purchase food at the station shop. If a microwave was for some reason unsafe it would be supplied to the customer within the meaning of 'supply' in s 46(1)(a), and hence potentially caught by s 10(1)(a) of the Consumer Protection Act which covers the supply of consumer goods which fail to comply with the General Safety requirement. It would be likely to be considered a product which is used exclusively in the context of a commercial activity although it is used by a consumer and thus be excluded from the provisions of these regulations.

Further, difficulty is caused by the interaction of the phrase 'used for or by' and 'supplied to' particularly having regard to the meaning of supply within s 46 of the Consumer Protection Act 1987. Supply is not further defined within the Regulations. One interpretation may be that if supply is defined as it is within s 46 of the Act then definition of 'used for or by a consumer' will be very narrow indeed. Unfortunately this could fall foul of the argument that the Directive refers to 'other products used exclusively in the context of a trade or business' and these products would be caught by the regulations when the Directive intended that they should not be covered. In any event regard must be had to the fact that Member States should not create barriers to trade and distortions of competition within the internal market. Applying the different statutory test under s 10 of the 1987 Act to products which should be caught by the General Product Safety Regulations or applying the regulations to products which should be exempt, may fall foul of this requirement. One rationale for the exclusion is that it is designed to exclude the Public Transport Sector: See Cartwright 'Product Safety and Consumer Protection' [1995] MLR 222. See also generally Davies [1994] Consum LJ, Current Survey 22 and Howells 'the general duty to market safer products in the United Kingdom' [1994] LMCLQ 479.

10 The goods excluded from the effect of s 10 by sub-s 10(7) including, significantly, food and motor vehicles are not excluded from this definition. In relation to food the DTI Guidance Notes (May 1995) seek to clarify the situation at para 48:

> "The Food Safety Act 1990 (and regulations made under that Act) is recognised as dealing with the significant safety issues relating to food (and is enforced by Food Authorities). Thus the 1990 Act (and regulations made under that Act) will prevail in the case of food safety and food satisfying those requirements should be presumed to satisfy the requirements of the Regulations. Relevant enforcement action should be taken under the provisions of the 1990 Act (or regulations made under that Act as appropriate) and businesses should not be placed under double jeopardy by parallel action for the same matter also being taken under the Regulations. (In Northern Ireland the equivalent food safety legislation is the Food Safety (Northern Ireland) Order 1991)."

This statement is based upon an argument that the 'product' (food) is covered by national legislation; see Reg 10(1). However, note Reg 11(c)(ii)(bb).

11 Section 10(4)(c) provided a defence for 'second-hand' goods. On behalf of the Government it was stated that 'to require all second-hand consumer goods to comply would really not be reasonable. The change, and improving standards, would make it difficult to assess the level of safety that second-hand goods should reach. The inclusion of second-hand goods would place a heavy burden on retailers. It would also put a heavy burden on the buyers, because there are two problems; first many of these goods which are supplied at a low price so that the purchase may repair or renovate them – and this may well include increasing their level of safety – could no longer be supplied. Secondly, it is possible that retailers who supply perfectly sound second-hand items at low prices to those on perhaps lower incomes may feel that the risk of supplying a product which, with the General Safety requirement, might fail does not warrant the continuation of their business'. HOLOR Vol 483. In fact the availability of the defence provided by s 104(c) did not depend upon the goods actually being second-hand but upon them being described as such. It is submitted that when used or reconditioned goods are considered with regard to their 'safety' for the purposes of these Regulations considerable weight must be attached to a description that the goods are used or second-hand. The term 'reconditioned' tends to imply a higher level of safety because repair, servicing and other remedial processes have already taken place.

12 Cf supply. See note 10 above.

13 There is an outstanding question as to how supply will be defined; see s 46 of the Consumer Protection Act 1987, and note 10 above.

14 See Art 2(b). The definition within the Regulations closely follows that within the Article.

15 This will include a degree of misuse; see the footnote to s 3(2)(b) of the Act. However, it is very important to note that *reasonably* foreseeable is a far less strict test than would have been the case if merely the word 'foreseeable' had been used. It is submitted that the objective test should consider conditions of use arising naturally (ie according to the usual course of things or such as should have been *reasonably* contemplated). The market will contain

unreasonable, careless and idiosyncratic consumers who may be highly susceptible to injury. Further, many products will present a risk if all *possibly* foreseeable conditions of use are considered. However it is quite clear that the test concerns only the normal use of the product and when there is reasonably foreseeable abnormal use or misuse. As has been stated earlier with reference to the definition of a 'defect' (see footnotes to s 3(2)(b)) the concept of reasonably foreseeable degrees of misuse or abnormal use may be a particularly difficult one for those engaged within the manufacture or supply of some consumer products.

16 Section 10 did not contain any express reference to consideration of safety throughout the product's lifetime. Certainly this will add force to the argument that many warnings which are printed upon packaging (which is usually instantly discarded once the item is opened) have very limited effect and that consideration should be given to permanent warnings on the item itself. Further specific reference to duration will mean that items which may not present any real risk of injury at the time of supply which are clearly and obviously going to disintegrate to present such a risk, will be caused.

17 It is important to distinguish between risk and hazard. A hazard is a method of injury or potential source of harm, whereas the risk is the likelihood of the hazard occurring. For example a hazard may be being run over by a car whilst on any pedestrian journey within a town (which of course could have potentially very serious consequences), but the risk is the likelihood of that happening which upon an ordinary daily basis would be very small. Hence, if the elimination of a hazard was to be considered then centres of towns would have to be completely pedestrianised. However in practice the hazard is accepted but the risk managed, for example by the imposition of a speed restriction; s 19(1).

18 The Consumer Protection Act 1987 contained a definition of safe within s 19(1) which was 'no risk, or no risk apart from one reduced to a minimum of death or personal injury being caused by the goods, the keeping, use or consumption of the goods, the assembly of any of the goods which are or are to be supplied unassembled, any emission or leakage from the goods or as a result of the keeping, use or consumption of the goods, from anything else; or reliance on the accuracy of any measurement, calculation or other reading made by or by means of the goods'. Section 10 required consumer goods to be *reasonably* safe and hence qualified the definition of safe. The Regulations contain no such dilution of what is a very similar requirement for safety (ie no risk or only a minimum risk compatible with the product's use). The requirement under Reg 7 is not to place any product on the market unless the product is safe (as opposed to reasonably safe). It is likely that many cases will focus around the phrase 'minimum risks compatible with the product's use'. It is clear from the balance of the definition of a safe product that consumers are allowed to have a degree choice as to the level of risk inherent in the product. If the Regulations did not allow a range of products with relative degrees of safety then many items would disappear from the market or the prices become prohibitively expensive. The level of safety of products needs to reflect the requirements of society generally and also to accept that 'accidents happen'. Products are not therefore necessarily to be free from risk but free from 'unacceptable' risk.

19 See s 3(1). It is submitted that the word 'persons' should be read as persons generally. A population possesses a great inherent diversity of physical and mental attributes and it is submitted that the objective test should apply to a representative cross-section of the target population.

20 See s 3(2). All relevant circumstances should be considered but the matters set out at (a) to (d) must be considered. See *R v Walsall Magistrates, ex p PMS* (17 March 1994, unreported), DC.

21 Compare (a) and (c) with s 3(2)(a). See also s 10(2)(a). Recently there has been considerable concern about the adequacy of instructions provided for assembly or maintenance. Such instructions must be comprehensive and bear in mind reasonably foreseeable use including misuse. Whilst it is not necessary to give 'an idiot's guide' it is also not permissable to assume a particularly high degree of expertise. Coventry Magistrates Court, in a case which concerned a 'French Maid' laundry holder rejected the argument that a higher degree of familiarity with the type of screw attachment required to secure an item to the wall could be assumed because the type of item would be sold in DIY shops leaving the consumer to choose the type of screw attachment. It was held that it was necessary within the instructions to specify the length of screw required including the reference to particular surfaces (the particular consumer did not use a long enough screw and the item detached from the wall causing personal injury).

22 See *Whirpool (UK) Ltd and Magnet Ltd v Gloucestershire County Council* (1993) 159 JP 123.

23 See s 10(2)(a), (and notes) with reference to Art 6(1)(a) of the 1985 Directive. It is submitted that the presentation of the product (or its labelling) will be of vital importance when considering used, second-hand or reconditioned goods particularly in the light of legitimate expectation of consumers. Presentation will also include 'marketing'. In relation to instructions and warnings, see *Coventry City Council v Ackerman Group plc* [1995] Crim LR 140.

24 This phrase could mean either:
(i) the categories of people at an increased or higher risk of the hazard occurring by virtue of ignorance or lack of knowledge; or
(ii) the risk of more serious personal injury; for example the risk of choking upon a peanut may be relatively similar for all those above the age of 18 months but the risk of serious personal injury as a result is far higher for those below the age of 3 years due to the size of the airways.

In practice however this distinction may be of little more than academic interest as regard may be had to all relevant circumstances.

25 Article 2 states that 'the *feasibility* of obtaining higher levels of safety or the availability of other products presenting a lesser degree of risk shall not constitute grounds for considering a product to be 'unsafe' or 'dangerous'. Hence the phrase 'may be obtained' means not only may be obtained within the market place from other products but also may theoretically be obtained by an alteration to the product which is not reflected within other products within the market place.

26 See s 10(2)(c). There is no specific reference to the cost of an item but clearly this may be of considerable importance as often the item that a prosecuting authority will seek to put up in comparison with the item subject to prosecution will be more expensive. The problem has been that Courts have a tendency to set standards as against the safest item on the market so as to preclude the sale of cheaper articles which although presenting a slightly higher level of risk do not 'possess undue risk'. The hidden effect is the regulation and restriction of consumer choice for which there is frequently no justification. (See the notes above).

Application and revocation

3. These Regulations do not apply to –
(a) second-hand products which are antiques[1];
(b) products supplied for repair or reconditioning before use, provided the supplier clearly informs the person to whom he supplies the product to that effect[2]; or
(c) any product where there are specific provisions in rules of Community law governing all aspects of the safety of the product.[3]

NOTES

1 Article 2(a) states that the directive shall not apply to second-hand products supplied as antiques. Bearing in mind the fact that other products which are used, second-hand or reconditioned are caught by the Regulations it will be wise to ensure that the products are 'supplied as' antiques, ie stated to be such or obviously such by virtue of presentation amongst other items so described.

2 See Art 2(a). The method of passing on such 'information' is not specified save that it should be clear. This may allow arguments that oral statements were made at the time of supply to the effect that the item required repair or re-conditioning before use. It should be noted that some products are subject to national safety regulations made under the 1987 Act which require that both new and secondhand items must satisfy the relevant safety requirements. Examples are toys, electrical and gas cookers and heaters, upholstered furniture (flammability), prams and pushchairs. Secondhand goods covered by regulations made under the 1987 Act which do not satisfy the relevant safety requirements set out in such regulations can be supplied to a person carrying on a business repairing or reconditioning such goods or sold as scrap but *cannot* be sold to consumers for repair or reconditioning.

3 The vital word is 'all'. This means that there must be a comprehensive coverage by the relevant Directive for this sub-section to have effect.

4. The requirements of these Regulations apply to a product where the product is the subject of provisions of Community law other than the GPS Directive insofar as those provisions do not make specific provision governing an aspect of the safety of the product[1].

NOTE

1 The effect of this Regulation is to mean that if a Directive covering aspects of the safety of a particular product fails to cover an aspect of safety, possibly by virtue of the fact that the

hazard arises out of a new development or type of such a product, then the Regulations will apply in relation to the said aspect of safety. This is potentially important particularly in areas where the market is fast developing. The argument cannot be run that if the Directive must be considered to be all encompassing whether or not a particular hazard is catered for within the Directive the exclusion shall only be taken to mean that it was not intended to be covered.

5. For the purposes of these Regulations the provisions of section 10 of the 1987 Act to the extent that they impose general safety requirements which must be complied with if products are to be –

(i) placed on the market, offered or agreed to be placed on the market or exposed or possessed to be placed on the market by producers; or

(ii) supplied, offered or agreed to be supplied or exposed or possessed to be supplied by distributors,

are hereby disapplied[1].

NOTE

1 The scope of sub-ss (1) and (2) are extremely wide and effectively cover all usual types of supply. If s 10 continues to have any application it will be in individual and peculiar circumstances; see the notes above in relation to the definition of product.) However, s 10 (save in relation to s 10(3)(b)(ii)) has *not* been repealed.

6. (1) Sub-paragraph (ii) of paragraph (b) of sub-section (3) of Section 10 of the 1987 Act is hereby repealed[1].

(2) The Approval of Safety Standards Regulations 1987 (SI 1987/1911) are hereby revoked.

NOTE

1 This sub-section states that consumer goods should not be regarded as failing to comply with the General Safety Requirements in respect of any failure to do more in relation to any matter than is required by any standard of safety approved for the purposes of this sub-section by or under any such Regulations and imposing requirements with respect to that matter. The revocation of the approval of Safety Standards Regulations 1987 now means that such standards are effectively devalued in terms of the ability to rely solely upon strict compliance with them. There is now only the ability to assess safety referred to in Reg 10(2)(1) below.

General safety requirement

7. No producer shall place a product on the market unless the product is a safe product[1].

NOTE

1 See Art 3(1) and Reg 14 (the defence of due diligence). Article 1 of the Directive states that the purpose of the provision of the Directive is to ensure that products placed on the market are safe. There is no due diligence defence included in the Directive which therefore provides for strict criminal liability. The fact that the Regulations do not follow the Directive leaves open an argument that there is a failure to properly implement at national level. See chapter 4, *European Perspective*.

Requirement as to information

8. (1) Within the limits of his activity[1], a producer shall[2] –

(a) provide consumers with the relevant information to enable them to assess the risks inherent in a product throughout the normal or reasonably foreseeable period of its use, where such risks are not immediately obvious without adequate warnings, and to take precautions against those risks[3]; and

(b) adopt measures commensurate with the characteristics of the products which he supplies[4], to enable him to be informed of the risks which these products might present[5] and to take appropriate action[6], including, if necessary, withdrawing the product in question from the market[7] to avoid those risks.

(2) The measures referred to in sub-paragraph (b) of paragraph (1) above may include, whenever appropriate –

(i) marking of the products or product batches in such a way that they can be identified[8];
(ii) sample testing of marketed products[9];
(iii) investigating complaints[10]; and
(iv) keeping distributors informed of such monitoring[11].

NOTES

1 Note the requirements of a distributor within the limit of his activities under Reg 9(b). It is submitted that the phrase 'the limits of his activity' leaves open an argument based upon the nature, extent or scale of production and the economic resources of the producer. The phrase is lifted from Art 3(2) which refers to the limits of 'their respective activities'. The preamble states 'whereas it is appropriate to supplement the duty to observe the general safety requirements by an obligation on *economic operators* to supply customers with relevant information and adopt measures commensurate with the characteristics of the products, enabling them to be informed of the risks that these products might present'. The requirements within the Regulations are both product specific and regulatory in terms of general systems. However whilst there may be an argument that having regard to the size and administrative resources of a producer certain steps would mean that economic supply could no longer continue, 'the limits of activity' may well be interpreted to mean solely the nature and type of supply regardless of the financial resources or individual position of the producer involved; see *Riley v Webb* (1987) 151 JP 372. Certainly (1)(a) is likely to be held to be a duty regardless of the size or scale of the producer. With regard to (1)(b) the position is a little less clear. The fact that the measures required are stated to be 'commensurate with the characteristic of the product' would support an argument that anyone who wishes to produce a particular type of product must set up adequate and proper systems and that economic arguments will not be permitted. In reality there is considerable risk that all producers' systems will be compared as against the 'Rolls Royce system' of a large producer within the field. A practical example can be seen with regard to product recall. In 1994 a large chemicals company imported some soft toy dogs as part of a promotion. After the dogs were distributed throughout the country through large scale DIY wholesalers it was discovered that the percentage of those imported had dangerous detachable eyes. The company, fearing a public relations disaster, immediately recalled the item using, inter alia:

(i) Articles in all daily newspapers and using other news media providing (according to monitored results) over an 80% opportunity for the general public to view;
(ii) Used its sophisticated computer and sales system to immediately trace all batches and thereafter sent its employees to track down the products;
(iii) encouraged any consumer to return a dog by agreeing to pay postage and package and to substitute a safe alternative dog.

The product recall had the full involvement and cooperation of the Trading Standards Department and was in practical terms beyond criticism: the cost was considerable. The type of toy in question is regularly imported by many companies into this country and supplied in a similar fashion to wholesalers or large retail outlets. Hence the 'limits of the activity' in terms of the objective nature of supply and distribution is the same albeit that numbers may be considerably smaller. Virtually all of the importers would not have the economic resources to match the nature and extent of the recall carried out by the company. If the phrase 'limits of activity' is to be strictly confined to the objective nature of supply and distribution then Regulation 8 may in practice produce an intolerably high burden upon some small producers. See also with regard to the approach of the Courts to different standards for different businesses depending upon size; *Garrett v Boots Ltd* (16 July 1980, unreported), DC.

2 This means that the duties are obligatory. Note the contents of Regs 12 and 13. Breach of

Reg 8 is not therefore an offence. However this is a safety provision for the purposes of s 14 (Suspension Notices), see Reg 11.

3 See also the definition of a 'safe product' in Reg 2 and sub-paras (a) and (b) above. Hence the existence, nature, extent and effectiveness of information or warnings supplied are relevant in considering whether a product is a safe product for the purposes of the requirements under s 7 *and* also relevant when considering if the producer has complied with the requirements under Reg 8(1)(a). The Council Resolution of the 5 April 1993; [1993] OJ C 110/1 stated that 'labelling is one important means of achieving better information and transparency for the consumer and of ensuring that the internal market functions harmoniously.' Hence the giving of information enabling a consumer to take appropriate action is seen as a vital component part within European consumer law. See Weatherill 'The Role of the Informed Consumer in European Community Law and Policy' (1994) Consum LJ, 49 at 50 and Cartwright: Product Safety and Consumer Protection (1995) MLR 222. The duty to provide information under Reg 8(1)(a) may well prove significant when a 'hidden' aspect presents only a minimum risk or a risk to only a small proportion of the population. In such circumstances if a producer fails to provide information about any inherent risk there may not be a breach of Reg 7 but may still be a breach of Reg 8(a). For example an item may be covered in paint which contains a relatively high level of lead. However when considering whether the product is 'safe' it may not have been previously arguable that it was necessary to provide a specific warning about the lead because the product was only likely to come into the hands of children over 36 months and hence there was a very low risk of a child ingesting sufficient of the paint to cause a difficulty. Hence although the level of lead was not known a warning 'Not Suitable for Children under 36 months' may have been thought to be sufficient. Under Reg 8(a) it will arguably be necessary to go further and to indicate the nature of the hazard so as to allow the consumer to assess the risk inherent (for example a mother of a 3 year old child who has behavioural difficulties and tends to chew items). Under certain Regulations (for example the Toys (Safety) Regulations 1989) there is now a requirement to indicate the likely hazard. This should now be considered as possibly applying to all products with inherent and hidden dangers.

4 Note the linking of the duty to the characteristics of the products.

5 This is likely to tie in with Reg 9(b) and the duty upon distributors to pass on information on product risks. Further this phrase is likely to encompass the requirement for comprehensive analysis and testing, including by responsible external experts, market testing of the products and liaison with suitable bodies such as the Child Accident Prevention Trust, ROSPA and any relevant trade association. The aim is to produce a harmonised genus of 'informed' producers and to exclude those who manufacture or import then supply onto the market without adequate research, testing or analysis.

6 Appropriate action in practice (in decending order of effect) is likely to involve recall, or ensuring removal from sale by contacting relevant wholesalers or retailers or discontinuing supply in the relevant form. Clearly, the date of supply and the likely shelf-life of the product will be relevant considerations together with the nature and extent of risks imposed by the product remaining on the market. This may be a particularly fine and difficult balancing act and cooperation with a local Enforcement Officer, ie a Trading Standards Officer may well be advisable. In this respect there is likely to be little or no prospect of establishing a 'due diligence defence' under Reg 14 in respect of a subsequent supply if appropriate action has not been taken.

7 See chapter 10, *Section 39* above in respect of recall. It is important to note that recall letters should be mandatory rather than advisory. See *Coventry City Council v Ackerman Group plc* [1995] Crim LR 140 in which letters sent to wholesalers advised that they 'should consider' removing items from sale rather than stating that they 'must' remove from sale.

8 Since the introduction of British Standard 5750 many companies are able to identify the relevant consignment or batch when a complaint is made in respect of a defective and unsafe product. See now BSEN/ISO 9000. However it now seems clear that the duties upon producers are such that every company should consider the implementation of such a system where large numbers of products are concerned.

9 This is the method that Trading Standards Departments regularly use to identify unsafe products (the other main method being by virtue of complaints). A major element of this Regulation is the requirement that producers have an ongoing evaluation of the safety of their products. However, few companies go as far as sample testing of items already on the market. Indeed if adequate systems have been set up to ensure that only safe products are put upon the market the only real advantage of sample testing thereafter when the products are actually on the market is to obtain consumer information and responses. However there is an argument that this should already have been properly investigated by a pre-launch market test (as is often the case in the United States).

10 Companies can no longer simply rely upon what one Judge referred to as the 'box of chocolates' response. A proper system will thoroughly investigate the complaint so as to determine whether the individual circumstances give rise to concern as to the safety of the product on the market. Producers will therefore be asked as to whether they have a complaints record or procedure and in any sizable concern it will be difficult to justify the absence of some form of system.

11 It is the clear intention of the Regulations that there be considerable interaction between producers and distributors; see Reg 9(b). Certainly one good method of monitoring the risks which products might present is to periodically enquire of distributors as to whether there have been any complaints or problems concerning the item. If this is stated to be part of the ongoing monitoring procedure the distributor *has a duty* to participate and hence to answer such enquiries. It is of course very difficult for a distributor to comply with the requirements of Regulation 9 unless he has been informed of the producer's relevant system and how information is to be communicated. This is the likely rationale behind this sub-section.

Requirements of distributors

9. A distributor shall act with due care[1] in order to help ensure compliance with the requirements of Regulation 7 above, and in particular, without limiting the generality of the foregoing –

(a) a distributor shall not supply products to any person which he knows, or should have presumed, on the basis of the information in his possession and as a professional, are dangerous products[2]; and

(b) within the limits of his activities[3], a distributor shall participate in monitoring[4] the safety of products placed on the market, in particular by passing on information on the product risks and cooperating in the action taken to avoid those risks[5].

NOTES

1 See Art 3(3). This is likely to be held to mean 'adequate caution in all the circumstances' and in effect is likely to amount to the exercise of all reasonable steps and due diligence to avoid contravention; See *Milkins v Roberts* [1949] SASR 251. This general duty is particularly wide and will therefore encompass a huge range of possible scenarios whereby a distributor has acted, in effect, negligently thus allowing a product which is not safe onto the market. See also chapter 10, *Section 39*, Due Diligence.

2 See also s 10(4)(b). The test is both subjective and objective. In respect of the objective test there is also a degree of knowledge which the distributor should possess 'as a professional' (ie as a skilled economic operator). A distributor must therefore not only have regard to the information in his possession but also to information which could be obtained from relevant trade associations or other 'professional sources'. Further, when acting as a professional, a distributor must take some steps to satisfy himself that the products are indeed safe and comply with the contractual description. Reliance upon a blanket assurance by the producer will not be likely to exonerate him; see chapter 10, *Section 39*. See also *Riley v Webb*; *Taylor v Lawrence Fraser (Bristol) Ltd* (1977) 121 Sol Jo 757; *Sherratt v Geralds the American Jewellers Ltd* (1970) 68 LGR 256. It has long been the regular practice of Trading Standards Departments to seek to regulate the potential supply of unsafe products onto the market by concentrating criminal prosecutions upon the actions of manufacturers or importers of items. However, it is clear that the express requirements of both the Directive and the Regulations mean that the actions of the distributor must be scrutinised.

3 See note 34 and Cartwright [1995] MLR 222 where it is suggested that this is a question of fact for each case and what is reasonable to expect of a large retailer may be unreasonable for a small distributor. However, the DTI Notes for Guidance define the phrase as referring 'to the capacity of a person, given his position in the supply chain, to influence the safety of a product'. See the notes to Reg 8(1) above.

4 Unlike Reg 8(2) there are no further details as to what forms such 'monitoring' should take. However it is submitted that at the very least there should be a system for the investigation, analysis and communication onto the producer of all relevant complaints.

5 It has often been the complaint of Manufacturers' or Importers' Associations that it is frequently impossible to have a constructive dialogue with a distributor. Further when letters

are sent concerning products and, for example, asking the distributor to tear off a slip and return it, that such information is not returned. This could be vitally important when considering a recall or a request that products be either temporarily or permanently taken off 'the shelves'. Further, in circumstances such as those in *Coventry City Council v Ackerman Group plc* [1995] Crim LR 140, where the producer sends labels to a distributor and suggests by letter that they should be fixed to the item by way of additional warning, although the letter is not in mandatory terms it would be likely that the distributor would be in great difficulty in arguing that he did not think the extra expense justified. This would be likely to be seen as a failure to *cooperate* in action taken to avoid risks.

It is not a defence to contravention of this section that the distributor exercised due diligence; see Reg 14(5).

Presumption of conformity and product assessment

10. (1) Where in relation to any product such product conforms to the specific rules of the law of the United Kingdom laying down the health and safety requirements which the product must satisfy in order to be marketed there shall be a presumption that, until the contrary is proved, the product is a safe product[1].

(2) Where no specific rules as are mentioned or referred to in paragraph (1) exist, the conformity of a product to the general safety requirement shall be assessed taking into account[2] –

- (i) voluntary national standards of the United Kingdom giving effect to a European standard; or
- (ii) Community technical specifications; or
- (iii) if there are no such voluntary national standards of the United Kingdom or Community technical specifications –
  - (aa) standards drawn up in the United Kingdom[3]; or
  - (bb) the codes of good practice in respect of health and safety in the product sector concerned[4]; or
  - (cc) the state or the art and technology,[5]

and the safety which consumers may reasonably expect[6].

NOTES

1 See Art 4(1) and compare with s 10(3)(b)(iii).

2 If any of the following types of requirement are in existence they *must* be taken into account in assessing conformity of the product to the General Safety Requirement.

3 The effect of the two sub-sections of Reg 6 means that published standards of safety no longer provide an absolute defence for compliance. Indeed there is not even a presumption that compliance with a standard means that the product is safe. This is a considerable change as formerly the approved Safety Standards regime formed an integral part of the system of the assessment of the safety of a great number of products. However the standards were in practice frequently difficult to interpret and failed to address certain matters which were considered by many to be obvious hazards. Sometimes the rationale was as simple as the inability to easily establish a harmonised test procedure.

4 See chapter 6, *Evidential Sources*. When considering a product there are often a number of associations in existence some of which produce Codes of Practice. See generally *R v Walsall Magistrates, ex p PMS* (17 March 1994, unreported), DC, per Laws J.

5 See s 3(2)(c) and s 4(1)(e).

6 See s 3(1). Note the word 'reasonably'.

Enforcement

11. For the purposes of providing the enforcement of these Regulations –

(a) Section 13 of the 1987 Act (prohibition notices and notices to warn) shall (to the extent that it does not already do so) apply to products as it applies to relevant goods under that section;

(b) the requirements of these Regulations shall constitute safety provisions for the purposes of Section 14 (suspension notices), 15 (appeals against suspension notices), 16 (forfeiture: England, Wales and Northern Ireland), 17 (forfeiture: Scotland) and 18 (power to obtain information) of the 1987 Act;

(c) (i) subject to paragraph (ii) below a weights and measures authority in Great Britain and a district council in Northern Ireland shall have the same duty to enforce these Regulations as they have in relation to Part II of the 1987 Act, and Part IV, Section 37 and 38 and subsections (3) and (4) of Section 42 of that Act shall apply accordingly;

(ii) without prejudice to the provisions of paragraphs (a) and (b) above and sub-paragraph (i) above, insofar as these Regulations apply –

(aa) to products licensed in accordance with the provisions of the 1968 Act, it shall be the duty of the enforcement authority as defined in Section 132(1) of the 1968 Act to enforce or to secure the enforcement of these Regulations and sections 108 to 115 and Section 119 of and Schedule 3 to that Act shall apply accordingly as if these Regulations were regulations made under the said Act;

(bb) in relation to food within the meaning of Section 1 of the 1990 Act, it shall be the duty of each food authority as defined in Section 5 of the 1990 Act to enforce or to secure the enforcement of these Regulations, within its area, in Great Britain and Sections 9, 29, 30 and 32 of that Act shall apply accordingly as if these Regulations were food safety requirements made under the said Act and Section 10 of that Act shall apply as if these Regulations were regulations made under Part II of that Act; and

(cc) in relation to food within the meaning of article 2 of the 1991 Order, it shall be the duty of the relevant enforcement authority as provided for in article 26 of that Order to enforce or to secure enforcement of these Regulations in Northern Ireland and articles 8, 29, 30, 31, and 33 of that Order shall apply accordingly as if these Regulations were food safety requirements made under that Order and article 9 of that Order shall apply as if these Regulations were regulations made under Part II of that Order;

(d) in sections 13(4) and 14(6) of the 1987 Act for the words "six months" there shall be substituted "three months"[1]; and

(e) nothing in this Regulation shall authorise any enforcement authority to bring proceedings in Scotland for an offence.

NOTE

1 Section 13(4) relates to contravention of a Prohibition Notice or a Notice to Warn and s 14 (6) relates to contravention of Suspension Notice.

Offences and preparatory acts

12. Any person who contravenes Regulation 7 or 9(a) shall be guilty of an offence.

13. No producer or distributor shall[1] –

(a) offer or agree to place on the market any dangerous product or expose or possess any such product for placing on the market[2]; or

(b) offer or agree to supply any dangerous product or expose or possess any such product for supply[3],

and any person who contravenes the requirements of this Regulation shall be guilty of an offence.

NOTES

1 This sub-section relates to the 'preparatory acts'. It is important to note that when considering distributors to compare this section with Reg 9(a).

2 See chapter 9, para 9.5.

3 See generally s 46 of the Consumer Protection Act for the definition of 'supply'. This section refers to four separate categories:

(a) offer to supply;
(b) agree to supply;
(c) expose for supply;
(d) possess for supply.

All are preparatory in that there has been no execution of an agreement.

Offer

Goods placed in a shop window are not necessarily 'offered for sale' see *Fisher v Bell* [1961] 1 QB 394 and in respect of a supermarket; *Pharmaceutical Society of Great Britain v Boots Cash Chemists (Southern) Ltd* [1953] 1 QB 401. See also *Haggard v Mason* [1976] 1 All ER 337 where the item in fact supplied was different from that which was the subject of the 'offer to supply'. In practical terms if there are any difficulties little is lost by the allegation of possession for supply.

Agrees

A concluded agreement will be required see *Lacis v Cashmarts* [1969] 2 QB 400.

Exposes

The goods must be visible see *Crane v Lawrence* (1890) 25 QBD 152.

Possesses

This will involve an element of knowledge and control but not necessarily close proximity see *Sullivan v Earl of Caithness* [1976] QB 966; *Bellerby v Carle* [1983] 2 AC 101, HL. Further there is a requirement to prove that the possession was 'for supply' see *Birkett v McGlassons Ltd* [1957] 1 All ER 369.

Defence of due diligence[1]

14. (1) Subject to the following paragraphs of this Regulation, in proceedings against any person for an offence under these Regulations it shall be a defence for that person to show that he took all reasonable steps and exercised all due diligence to avoid committing the offence.

(2) Where in any proceedings against any person for such an offence the defence provided by paragraph (1) above involves an allegation that the commission of the offence was due–

(a) to the act or default of another, or

(b) to reliance on information given by another,

that person shall not, without leave of the court, be entitled to rely on the defence unless, not less than seven days before, in England, Wales and Northern Ireland, the hearing of the proceedings or, in Scotland, the trial diet, he has served a notice under paragraph (3) below on the person bringing the proceedings.

(3) A notice under this paragraph shall give such information identifying or assisting in the identification of the person who committed the act or default or gave the information as is in the possession of the person serving the notice at the time he serves it.

(4) It is hereby declared that a person shall not be entitled to rely on the defence provided in paragraph (1) above by reason of his reliance on information supplied by another, unless he shows that it was reasonable in all the circumstances for him to have relied on the information, having regard in particular –

(a) to the steps which he took, and those which might reasonably have been taken, for the purpose of verifying the information; and

(b) to whether he had any reason to disbelieve the information.

(5) It is hereby declared that a person[2] shall not be entitled to rely on the defence provided by paragraph (1) above or by Section 39(1) of the 1987 Act (defence of due diligence) if he has contravened regulation 9(b).

NOTES

1 See chapter 10(4). Regulation 14 follows the wordings of s 39 in respect of sub-ss 1 to 4. It is important to note that the Directive does not contain provision for such a defence and hence it may be properly argued that there is a failure to fully implement the Directive as the inclusion of the Defence may not adequately ensure that only safe products are placed upon the market. See Art 1(1). See further chapter 4, *European Perspective*. However by virtue of the requirements of Reg 8 with regard to due care and Reg 9(a), if a prosecutor can establish the relevant facts it is highly unlikely that such a defence could be successful.

2 A distributor.

Liability of persons other than principal offender[1]

15. (1) Where the commission by any person of an offence to which Regulation 14 above applies is due to the act or default committed by some other person in the course of a commercial activity of his, the other person shall be guilty of an offence and may be proceeded against and punished by virtue of this paragraph whether or not proceedings are taken against the first-mentioned person.

(2) Where a body corporate is guilty of an offence under the Regulations (including where it is so guilty by virtue of paragraph (1) above) in respect of any act or default which is shown to have been committed with the consent or connivance of, or to be attributable to any neglect on the part of any director, manager, secretary or other similar officer of the body corporate or any person who was purporting to act in any such capacity he, as well as the body corporate, shall be guilty of that offence and shall be liable to be proceeded against and punished accordingly.

(3) Where the affairs of a body corporate are managed by its members, paragraph (2) above shall apply in relation to the acts and defaults of a member in connection with his functions of management as if he were a director of the body corporate.

(4) Where a Scottish partnership is guilty of an offence under regulation 14 above (including where it is so guilty by virtue of paragraph (1) above) in respect of any act or default which is shown to have been committed with the consent or connivance of, or to be attributable to any neglect on the part of, a partner in the partnership, he, as well as the partnership, shall be guilty of that offence and shall be liable to be proceeded against and punished accordingly.

NOTE
1 See s 40 and the notes thereto.

Extension of the time for bringing summary proceedings

16. (1) Notwithstanding Section 127 of the Magistrates' Court Act 1980(a) and article 19 of the Magistrates' Courts (Northern Ireland) Order 1981(b) in England, Wales and Northern Ireland a Magistrates' Court may try an information (in the case of England and Wales) or a complaint (in the case of Northern Ireland) in respect of proceedings for an offence under Regulation 12 or 13 above if (in the case of England and Wales) the information is laid or (in the case of Northern Ireland) the complaint is made within twelve months from the date of the offence.[1]

(2) Notwithstanding section 331 of the Criminal Procedure (Scotland) Act 1975(c), in Scotland summary proceedings for an offence under Regulation 12 or 13 above may be commenced at any time within twelve months from the date of the offence.

(3) For the purposes of paragraph (2) above, section 331(3) of the Criminal Procedure (Scotland) Act 1975 shall apply as it applies for the purposes of that section.

NOTE
1 When considering an allegation of contravention of s 10 of the Consumer Protection Act 1987 the relevant period is 6 months.

Penalties

17. A person guilty of an offence under Regulation 12 or 13 above shall be liable on summary conviction to –

(a) imprisonment for a term not exceeding three months; or
(b) a fine not exceeding level 5 on the standard scale; or to both.

Duties of enforcement authorities

18. (1) Every enforcement authority shall give immediate notice to the Secretary of State of any action taken by it to prohibit or restrict the supply of any product or forfeit or do any other thing in respect of any product for the purposes of these Regulations.

(2) The requirements of paragraph (1) above shall not apply in the case of any action taken in respect of any second-hand product.

5th September 1994

Minister of State
Department of Trade and Industry

Chapter 21

THE CONSUMER PROTECTION (NORTHERN IRELAND) ORDER 1987 (SI 1987/2049: NI 20)

Made	26th November 1987
Laid before Parliament	15th December 1987
Coming into operation in accordance with Article 1	

Whereas this Order is made only for purposes corresponding to the provisions of the Consumer Protection Act 1987 mentioned in section 49(1)(a) to (c) of that Act:

Now, therefore, Her Majesty, in exercise of the powers conferred by paragraph 1 of Schedule 1 to the Northern Ireland Act 1974 (as modified by section 49(3) of that Act of 1987) and of all other powers enabling Her in that behalf, is pleased, by and with the advice of Her Privy Council, to order, and it is hereby ordered, as follows:–

PART I INTRODUCTORY

1. Title, commencement and transitional provision

(1) This Order may be cited as the Consumer Protection (Northern Ireland) Order 1987.

(2) The following provisions, namely –

(a) Part I;

(b) Part II and Schedule I;

(c) Article 28 and Schedule 2;

(d) paragraphs 3 and 7 of Schedule 3, and Article 35(1) in so far as it relates to those paragraphs of that Schedule; and

(e) Article 35(2) and Schedule 4;

shall come into operation on 1 March 1988.

(3) The remaining provisions of this Order shall come into operation on such day or days as the Head of the Department may by order appoint.

(4) An order under paragraph (3) may contain such transitional provisions as the Head of the Department considers appropriate.

(5) Nothing in this Order shall make any person liable by virtue of Part II for any damage caused wholly or partly by a defect in a product which was supplied to any person by its producer before the coming into operation of Part II.

(6) Expressions used in paragraph (5) and in Part II have the same meanings in that paragraph as in that Part.

2. Interpretation

(1) The Interpretation Act (Northern Ireland) 1954 shall apply to Article 1 and the following provisions of this Order as it applies to a Measure of the Northern Ireland Assembly.

(2) In this Order –

"aircraft" includes gliders, balloons and hovercraft;

"business" includes a trade or profession and the activities of a professional or trade association or of a district council or other public authority;

"conditional sale agreement", "credit sale agreement" and "hire–purchase agreement" have the same meanings as in the Consumer Credit Act 1974 but as if in the definitions in that Act "goods" had the same meaning as in this Order;

"the Department" means the Department of Economic Development;

"gas" means –

(a) any substance in a gaseous state which consists wholly or mainly of methane, ethane, propane, butane, hydrogen or carbon monoxide;
  (i) a mixture of two or more of those gases; or
  (ii) a combustible mixture of one or more of those gases and air; and

(b) any other substance in a gaseous state which is gaseous at a temperature of 15°C and a pressure of 1013.25 millibars and is specified in an order made by the Department subject to negative resolution;

"goods" includes substances, growing crops and things comprised in land by virtue of being attached to it and any ship, aircraft or vehicle;

"information" includes accounts, estimates and returns;

"mark" and "trade mark" have the same meanings as in the Trade Marks Act 1938;

"modifications" includes additions, alteration and omissions;

"motor vehicle" has the same meaning as in the Road Traffic (Northern Ireland) Order 1981;

"notice" means a notice in writing;

"officer" in relation to the Department, means a person authorised in writing to assist the Department in carrying out its functions under or for the purposes of the enforcement of any of the provisions made by or under Part III;

"personal injury" includes any disease and any other impairment of a person's physical or mental condition;

"premises" includes any place and any ship, aircraft or vehicle;

"records" includes any books or documents and any records in non-documentary form;

"ship" includes any boat and any other description of vessel used in navigation;

"subordinate legislation" means a statutory instrument as defined in section 1(d) of the Interpretation Act (Northern Ireland) 1954;

"substance" means any natural or artificial substance, whether in solid, liquid or gaseous form or in the form of a vapour, and includes substances that are comprised in or mixed with other goods;

"supply" shall be construed in accordance with Article 3.

(3) Section 68(2) of the Trade Marks Act 1938 (construction of references to use of a mark) shall apply for the purposes of this Order as it applies for the purposes of that Act.

3. Meaning of "supply"

(1) Subject to the following provisions of this Article, references in this Order to supplying goods shall be construed as references to doing any of the following, whether as principal or agent, that is to say –

(a) selling, hiring out or lending the goods;

(b) entering into a hire-purchase agreement to furnish the goods;

(c) the performance of any contract for work and materials to furnish the goods;

(d) providing the goods in exchange for any consideration (including trading stamps) other than money;

(e) providing the goods in or connection with the performance of any statutory function; or

(f) giving the goods as a prize or otherwise making a gift of the goods;

and, in relation to gas or water, those references shall be construed as including references to providing the service by which the gas or water is made available for use.

(2) For the purpose of any reference in this Order to supplying goods, where a person ("the ostensible supplier") supplies goods to another person ("the customer") under a hire-purchase agreement, conditional sale agreement or credit–sale agreement or under an agreement for the hiring of goods (other than a hire-purchase agreement) and the ostensible supplier –

(a) carries on the business of financing the provision of goods for others by means of such agreements; and

(b) in the course of that business acquired his interest in the goods supplied to the customer as a means of financing the provision of them for the customer by a further person ("the effective supplier"),

the effective supplier and not the ostensible supplier shall be treated as supplying the goods to the customer.

(3) Subject to paragraph (4), the performance of any contract by the erection of any building or structure on any land or by the carrying out of any other building works shall be treated for the purposes of this Order as a supply of goods in so far as, but only so far as, it involves the provision of any goods to any person by means of their incorporation into the building, structure or works.

(4) Except for the purposes of, and in relation to, any provision made by or under Part III, references in this Order to supplying goods shall not include references to supplying goods comprised in land where the supply is effected by the creation or disposal of an interest in the land.

(5) Except in Part II, references in this Order to a person's supplying goods shall be confined to references to that person's supplying goods in the course of a business of his, but for the purposes of this paragraph it shall be immaterial whether the business is a business of dealing in the goods.

(6) For the purposes of paragraph (5) goods shall not be treated as supplied in the course of a business if they are supplied, in pursuance of an obligation arising under or in connection with the insurance of the goods, to the person with whom they were insured.

(7) References in Parts III and IV to supplying goods shall not include –

(a) references to supplying goods where the persons supplied carries on a business of buying goods of the same description as those goods and repairing or reconditioning them;

(b) references to supplying goods by a sale of articles as scrap (that is to say, for the value of materials included in the articles rather than for the value of the articles themselves).

(8) Where any goods that have at any time been supplied by being hired out or lent to any person, neither a continuation or renewal of the hire or loan (whether on the same or different terms) nor any transaction for the transfer after that time of any interest in the goods to the person to whom they were hired or lent shall be treated for the purposes of this Order as a further supply of the goods to that person.

(9) A ship, aircraft or motor vehicle shall not be treated for the purposes of this Order as supplied to any persons by reason only that services consisting in the carriage of goods or passengers in that ship, aircraft or vehicle, or in its use for any other purpose, are provided to that person in pursuance of any agreement relating to the use of the ship, aircraft or vehicle for a particular period or for particular voyages, flights or journeys.

PART II PRODUCT LIABILITY

4. Purpose and construction of Part II

(1) This Part shall have effect for the purpose of making such provision as is necessary in order to comply with the product liability Directive and shall be construed accordingly,

(2) In this Part –

"agricultural produce" means any produce of the soil, of stock–farming or of fisheries;

"dependant" and "relative" have the same meaning as they have in the Fatal Accidents (Northern Ireland) Order 1977;

"producer", in relation to a product, means –

(a) the persons who manufactured it;

(b) in the case of a substance which has not been manufactured but has been won or abstracted, the person who won or abstracted it;

(c) in the case of a product which has not been manufactured, won or abstracted but essential characteristics of which are attributable to an industrial or other process having been carried out (for example, in relation to agriculture produce), the person who carried out that process;

"product" means any goods or electricity and (subject to paragraph (3)) includes a product which is comprised in another product, whether by virtue of being a component part of raw material or otherwise; and

"the product liability Directive" means the Directive of the Council of the European Communities, dated 25 July 1985 (No 85/374/EEC) on the approximation of the laws, regulations and administrative provisions of the member States concerning liability for defective products.

(3) For the purposes of this Part, a person who supplies any product in which products are comprised, whether by virtue of being component parts of raw materials or otherwise, shall not be treated by reason only of his supply of that product as supplying any of the products so comprised.

5. Liability for defective products

(1) Subject to this Part, where any damage is caused wholly or partly by a defect in a product, every person to whom paragraph (2) applies shall be liable for the damage.

(2) This paragraph applies to –

(a) the producer of the product;

(b) any person who, by putting his name on the product or using a trade mark or other distinguishing mark in relation to the product, has held himself out to be the producer of the product;

(c) any person who has imported the product into a member State from a place outside the member States in order, in the course of any business of his, to supply it to another.

(3) Subject to this Part, where any damage is caused wholly or partly by a defect in a product, any person who supplied the product (whether to the person who suffered the damage, to the producer of any product in which the product in question is comprised or to any other person) shall be liable for the damage if –

(a) the person who suffered the damage requests the supplier to identify one or more of the persons (whether still in existence or not) to whom paragraph (2) applies in relation to the product;

(b) that request is made within a reasonable period after the damage occurs and at a time when it is not reasonably practicable for the person making the request to identify all those persons; and

(c) the supplier fails, within a reasonable period after receiving the request, either to comply with the request or to identify the person who supplied the product to him.

(4) Neither paragraph (2) nor paragraph (3) shall apply to a person in respect of any defect in any game or agricultural produce if the only supply of the game or produce by that person to another was at a time when it had not undergone an industrial process.

(5) Where two or more persons are liable by virtue of this Part for the same damage, their liability shall be joint and several.

(6) This Article shall be without prejudice to any liability arising otherwise than by virtue of this Part.

6. Meaning of "defect"

(1) Subject to the following provisions of this Article, there is a defect in a product for the purposes of this Part if the safety of the product is not such as persons generally are entitled to expect; and for those purposes "safety" , in relation to a product, shall include safety with respect to products comprised in that product and safety in the context of risks of damage to property, as well as in the context of death or personal injury.

(2) In determining for the purposes of paragraph (1) what persons generally are entitled to expect in relation to a product all the circumstances shall be taken into account, including –

(a) the manner in which, and purposes for which, the product has been marketed, its get–up, the use of any mark in relation to the product and any instructions for, or warnings with respect to, doing or refraining from doing anything with or in relation to the product;

(b) what might reasonably be expected to be done with or in relation to the product; and

(c) the time when the product was supplied by its producer to another; and nothing in this Article shall require a defect to be inferred from the fact alone that the safety of a product which is supplied after that time is greater than the safety of the product in question.

7. Defences

(1) In any civil proceedings by virtue of this Part against any person ("the person proceeded against") in respect of a defect in a product it shall be a defence for him to show –

(a) that the defect is attributable to compliance with any requirement imposed by or under any enactment or with any Community obligation; or

(b) that the person proceeded against did not at any time supply the product to another; or

(c) that the following conditions are satisfied, that is to say –

(i) that the only supply of the product to another by the person proceeded against was otherwise than in the course of a business of that person's; and

(ii) that Article 5(2) does not apply to that person or applies to him by virtue only of things done otherwise than with a view to profit; or

(d) that the defect did not exist in the product at the relevant time; or

(e) that the state of scientific and technical knowledge at the relevant time was not such that a producer of products of the same description as the product in question might be expected to have discovered the defect if it had existed in his products while they were under his control; or

(f) that the defect –

(i) constituted a defect in a product ("the subsequent product") in which the product in question had been comprised; and

(ii) was wholly attributable to the design of the subsequent product or to compliance by the producer of the product in question with instructions given by the producer of the subsequent product.

(2) In this Article "the relevant time", in relation to electricity, means the time at which it was generated, being a time before it was transmitted or distributed, and in relation to any other product, means –

(a) if the person proceeded against is a person to whom paragraph (2) of Article 5 applies in relation to the product, the time when he supplied the product to another;

(b) if that paragraph does not apply to that person in relation to the product, the time when the product was last supplied by a person to whom that paragraph does apply in relation to the product.

8. Damage giving rise to liability

(1) Subject to this Article, in this Part "damage" means death or personal injury or loss of or damage to any property (including land).

(2) A person shall not be liable under Article 5 in respect of any defect in a product for the loss of or any damage to the product itself or for the loss of or any damage to the whole or any part of any product which has been supplied with the product in question comprised in it.

(3) A person shall not be liable under Article 5 for any loss of or damage to any property which, at the time it is lost or damaged, is not –

(a) of a description of property ordinarily intended for private use, occupation or consumption; and

(b) intended by the person suffering the loss or damage mainly for his own private use, occupation or consumption.

(4) No damages shall be awarded to any person by virtue of this Part in respect of any loss of or damage to any property if the amount which would fall to be so awarded to that person, apart from this paragraph and any liability for interest, does not exceed £275.

(5) In determining for the purposes of this Part who has suffered any loss of or damage to property and when any such loss or damage occurred, the loss or damage shall be regarded as having occurred at the earliest time at which a person with an interest in the property had knowledge of the material facts about the loss or damage.

(6) For the purposes of paragraph (5) the material facts about any loss or damage to any property are such facts about the loss or damage as would lead a reasonable person with an interest in the property to consider the loss or damage sufficiently serious to justify his instituting proceedings for damages against a defendant who did not dispute liability and was able to satisfy as judgment.

(7) For the purposes of paragraph (5) a person's knowledge includes knowledge which he might reasonably have been expected to acquire –

(a) from facts observable or ascertainable by him; or

(b) from facts ascertainable by him with the help of appropriate expert advice which it is reasonable for him to seek;

but a person shall not be taken by virtue of this paragraph to have knowledge of a fact ascertainable by him only with the help of expert advice unless he has failed to take all reasonable steps to obtain (and, where appropriate, to act on) that advice.

9. Application of certain enactments etc

(1) Any damage for which a person is liable under Article 5 shall be deemed to have been caused for the purposes of the Fatal Accidents (Northern Ireland) Order 1977, by that person's wrongful act, neglect or default.

(2) Where –

(a) a person's death is caused wholly or partly by a defect in a product, or a person dies after suffering damage which has been so caused;
(b) a request such as mentioned in sub-paragraph (a) of paragraph (3) of Article 5 is made to a supplier of the product by that person's personal representatives or, in the case of a person whose death is caused wholly or partly by the defect, by any dependant or relative of that person; and
(c) the conditions specified in sub-paragraphs (b) and (c) of that paragraph are satisfied in relation to that request,

this Part shall have effect for the purposes of Part III of the Law Reform (Miscellaneous Provisions) Act (Northern Ireland) 1937 and the Fatal Accidents (Northern Ireland) Order 1977 as if liability of the supplier to that person under that paragraph did not depend on that person having requested the supplier to identify certain persons or on the said conditions having been satisfied in relation to a request made by that person.

(3) Section 1 of the Congenital Disabilities (Civil Liability) Act 1976 shall have effect for the purposes of this Part as if –

(a) a person were answerable to a child in respect of an occurrence caused wholly or partly by a defect in a product if he is or has been liable under Article 5 in respect of any effect of the occurrence on a parent of the child, or would be so liable if the occurrence caused a parent of the child to suffer damage;
(b) the provisions of this Part relating to liability under Article 5 applied in relation to liability by virtue of sub-paragraph (a) under the said section 1; and
(c) sub-section (6) of the said section 1 (exclusion of liability) were omitted.

(4) Where any damage is caused partly by a defect in a product and partly by the fault of the person suffering the damage, the Law Reform (Miscellaneous Provisions) Act (Northern Ireland) 1948 and Article 7 of the Fatal Accidents (Northern Ireland) Order 1977 (contributory negligence) shall have effect as if the defect were the fault of every person liable by virtue of this Part for the damage caused by the defect.

(5) In paragraph (4) "fault" has the same meaning as in the said Act of 1948.

(6) Schedule 1 shall have effect for the purpose of amending the Statute of Limitations (Northern Ireland) 1958 in its application in relation to the bringing of actions by virtue of this Part.

(7) It is hereby declared that liability by virtue of this Part is to be treated as liability in tort for the purposes of any enactment conferring jurisdiction on any court with respect to any matter.

(8) Nothing in this Part shall prejudice the operation of section 12 of the Nuclear Installations Act 1965 (rights to compensation for certain breaches of duties confined to rights under that Act).

10. Prohibition on exclusions from liability

The liability of a person by virtue of this Part to a person who has suffered damage caused wholly or partly by a defect in a product, or to a dependant or relative of such a person, shall not be limited or excluded by any contract term, by any notice or by any other provision.

11. Power to modify enactments

(1) The Secretary of State may by order make such modifications of this Part and of any other enactment (including an enactment contained in Part I and the following Parts, or in an Order, Measure or Act made or passed after this Order) as appear to him to be necessary or expedient in consequence of any modification of the product liability Directive which is made at any time after the making of this Order.

(2) An order under paragraph (1) shall be subject to affirmative resolution.

12. Application of Part II to Crown

(1) Subject to paragraph (2), this Part shall bind the Crown; including the Crown in right of Her Majesty's Government in the United Kingdom.

(2) The Crown shall not, as regards the Crown's liability by virtue of this Part, be bound by this Part further than the Crown is made liable in tort under the Crown Proceedings Act 1947.

SCHEDULES

Schedule 1 Limitation of actions under Part II

1. In subsection (6) (definition of date of knowledge) of section 9A of the Statute of Limitations (Northern Ireland) 1958 (in this Schedule referred to as "the 1958 Act"), at the beginning there shall be inserted the words "Subject to sub-section (6A)," and after that subsection there shall be inserted the following sub-section –

"(6A) In section 9A and in section 9B so far as that section applies to an action by virtue of Article 9(1) of the Consumer Protection (Northern Ireland) Order 1987 (death caused by defective product) references to a person's date of knowledge are references to the date on which he first had knowledge of the following facts –

(a) such facts about the damage caused by the defect as would lead a reasonable person who had suffered such damage to consider it sufficiently serious to justify his instituting proceedings for damages against a defendant who did not dispute liability and was able to satisfy a judgement; and

(b) that the damage was wholly or partly attributable to the facts and circumstances alleged to constitute the defect; and

(c) the identify of the defendant;

but, in determining the date on which a person first had such knowledge there shall be disregarded both the extent (if any) of that person's knowledge on any date of whether particular facts or circumstances would or would not, as a matter of law, constitute a defect and, in a case relating to loss of or damage to property, any knowledge which that person had on a date on which he had no right of action by virtue of Part II of that Order in respect of the loss or damage".

2. After section 9A of the 1958 Act there shall be inserted the following section –

"Action in respect of defective products.

9AA.–(1) This section shall apply to an action for damages by virtue of any provision of Part II of the Consumer Protection (Northern Ireland) Order 1987.

(2) None of the time limits given in sections 8 to 9A shall apply to an action to which this section applies.

(3) An action to which this section applies shall not be brought after the expiration of the period of ten years from the relevant time, within the meaning of Article 7 of the said Order of 1987; and this subsection shall operate to extinguish a right of action and shall do so whether or not that right of action had accrued, or time under the following provisions of this Act had begun to run, at the end of that period of ten years.

(4) Subject to subsection (5), an action to which this section applies in which the damages claimed by the plaintiff consist of or include damages in respect of personal injuries to the plaintiff or any other person or loss of or damage to any property, shall not be brought after the expiration of the period of three years from whichever is the later of –

(a) The date on which the cause of action accrued; and
(b) the date of knowledge of the injured person or, in the case of loss of or damage to property, the date of knowledge of the plaintiff or (if earlier) of any person in whom his cause of action was previously vested.

(5) If, in a case where the damages claimed by the plaintiff consist of or include damages in respect of personal injuries to the plaintiff or any other person, the injured person died before the expiration of the period mentioned in subsection (4), that subsection shall have effect as respects the cause of action surviving for the benefit of his estate by virtue of section 14 of the Law Reform (Miscellaneous Provisions) Act (Northern Ireland) 1937 as if for the reference to that period there were substituted a reference to the period of three years from whichever is the later of –

(a) the date of death; and
(b) the date of the personal representative's knowledge.

(6) For the purposes of this section 'personal representative' is any person who is or has been a personal representative of the deceased, including an executor who has not proved the will (whether or not he has renounced probate); and regard shall be had to any knowledge acquired by any such person while a personal representative or previously.

(7) If there is more than one personal representative and their dates of knowledge are different, subsection (5)(b) shall be read as referring to the earliest of those dates.

(8) Expressions used in this section or section 9A(6) to (9) and in Part II of the Consumer Protection (Northern Ireland) Order 1987 have the same meanings in this section or that section as in that Part; and Article 4(1) of that Order (Part II to be construed as enacted for the purpose of complying with the product liability Directive) shall apply for the purpose of construing this section and following provisions of this Act so far as they relate to an action by virtue of any provision of that Part (as it applies for the purpose of construing that Part."

3. In section 9B(2) of the 1958 Act (actions under the Fatal Accidents (Northern Ireland) Order 1977), after the words "section 9A" there shall be inserted the words "or 9AA".

4. In section 9D of the 1958 Act (discretionary exclusion of time limit) –

(a) in sub-section (1), after the words "section 9A" there shall be inserted the words "or 9AA".

(b) after sub-section (1) there shall be inserted the following subsection –

"(1A) The court shall not under this section disapply –

(a) sub-section (3) of section 9AA; or

(b) where the damages claimed by the plaintiff are confined to damages for loss of or damage to any property, any other provision in its application to an action by virtue of Part II of the Consumer Protection (Northern Ireland) Order 1987".

(c) in sub-sections (2) and (4), after the words "section 9A" there shall be inserted the words "or sub-section (4) of section 9AA";

(d) in subsection (3)(b), after "section 9A" there shall be inserted ",9AA"; and

(e) in sub-section (8), after "section 9A" there shall be inserted ", 9AA".

5. In section 50 of the 1958 Act (extension of limitation period in case of disability), after sub-section (6) there shall be inserted the following sub-section –

"(6A) In the case of an action which section 9AA applies or one by virtue of Article 9(1) of the Consumer Protection (Northern Ireland) Order 1987 (death caused by defective product), sub-section (1) –

(a) shall not apply to the time limit prescribed by sub-section (3) of section 9AA or to that time limit as applied by virtue of section 9B(2); and

(b) in relation to any other time limit prescribed by this Act, shall have effect as if for the words 'six years' there were substituted the words 'three years'.".

6. In section 70 of the 1958 Act (postponement of limitation period in case of fraud, concealment or mistake) –

(a) in sub-section (1), for the words "sub-section (3)" there shall be substituted the words "sub-sections (3) and (4A)"; and

(b) after subsection (4) there shall be inserted the following sub-section –

"(4A) Sub-section (1) shall not apply in relation to the time limit prescribed by section 9AA(3) or in relation to that time limit as applied by virtue of section 9B(2).".

Chapter 22

UNFAIR TERMS IN CONSUMER CONTRACTS REGULATIONS 1994 SI 1994/3159

Whereas the Secretary of State is a Minister designated (a) for the purposes of section 2(2) of the European Communities Act 1972, (b) in relation to measures relating to consumer protection;

Now, the Secretary of State, in exercise of the powers conferred upon him by section 2(2) of that Act and of all other powers enabling him in that behalf hereby makes the following Regulations:

1. Citation and commencement

These Regulations may be cited as the Unfair Terms in Consumer Contracts Regulations 1994 and shall come into force on 1st July 1995.

2. Interpretation

(1) In these Regulations –

'business' includes a trade or profession and the activities of any government department or local or public authority;

'the Community' means the European Economic Community and the other States in the European Economic Area;

'consumer' means a natural person who, in making a contract to which these Regulations apply, is acting for purposes which are outside his business;

'court' in relation to England and Wales and Northern Ireland means the High Court, and in relation to Scotland, the Court of Session;

'Director' means the Director General of Fair Trading;

'EEA Agreement' means the Agreement on the European Economic Area signed at Oporto on 2nd May 1992 as adjusted by the protocol signed at Brussels on 17 March 1993;

'seller' means a person who sells goods and who, in making a contract to which these Regulations apply, is acting for purposes relating to his business; and

'supplier' means a person who supplies goods or services and who, in making a contract to which these Regulations apply is acting for purposes relating to his business.

(2) In the application of these Regulations to Scotland for references to an 'injunction' or an 'interlocutory injunction' there shall be substituted references to an 'interdict' or 'interim interdict' respectively.

3. Terms to which these Regulations apply

(1) Subject to the provisions of Schedule 1, these Regulations apply to any term in a contact concluded between a seller or supplier and a consumer where the said term has not been individually negotiated.

(2) In so far as it is in plain, intelligible language, no assessment shall be made of the fairness of any term which –

(a) defines the main subject matter of the contract, or

(b) concerns the adequacy of the price or remuneration, as against the goods or services sold or supplied.

(3) For the purposes of these Regulations, a term shall always be regarded as not having been individually negotiated where it has been drafted in advance and the consumer has not been able to influence the substance of the term.

(4) Notwithstanding that a specific term or certain aspects of it in a contract has been individually negotiated, these Regulations shall apply to the rest of a contract if an overall assessment of the contract indicates that it is a pre–formulated standard contract.

(5) It shall be for any seller or supplier who claims that a term was individually negotiated to show that it was.

4. Unfair terms

(1) In these Regulations, subject to paragraphs (2) and (3) below, 'unfair term' means any term which contrary to the requirement of good faith causes a significant imbalance in the parties' rights and obligations under the contract to the detriment of the consumer.

(2) An assessment of the unfair nature of a term shall be made taking into account the nature of the goods or services for which the contract was concluded and referring, as at the time of the conclusion of the contact, to all circumstances attending the conclusion of the contract and to all the other terms of the contract or of another contract on which it is dependent.

(3) In determining whether a term satisfies the requirement of good faith, regard shall be had in particular to the matters specified in Schedule 2 to these Regulations.

(4) Schedule 3 to these Regulations contains an indicative and non–exhaustive list of the terms which may be regarded as unfair.

5. Consequence of inclusion of unfair terms in contracts

(1) An unfair term in a contract concluded with a consumer by a seller or supplier shall not be binding on the consumer.

(2) The contract shall continue to bind the parties it if is capable of continuing in existence without the unfair term.

6. Construction of written contracts

A seller or supplier shall ensure that any written term of a contract is expressed in plain, intelligible language, and if there is doubt about the meaning of a written term, the interpretation most favourable to the consumer shall prevail.

7. Choice of law clauses

These Regulations shall apply notwithstanding any contact term which applies or purports to apply the law of a non Member State, if the contract has a close connection with the territory of the Member States.

8. Prevention of continued use of unfair terms

(1) It shall be the duty of the Director to consider any complaint made to him that any contract term drawn up for general use is unfair, unless the complaint appears to the Director to be frivolous or vexatious.

(2) If having considered a complaint about any contract term pursuant to paragraph (1) above the Director considers that the contract term is unfair he may, if he considers it appropriate to do so, bring proceedings for an injunction (in which proceedings he may also apply for an interlocutory injunction) against any person appearing to him to be using or recommending use of such a term in contracts concluded with consumers.

(3) The Director may, if he considers it appropriate to do so, have regard to any undertakings given to him by or on behalf of any person as to the continued use of such a term in contracts concluded with consumers.

(4) The Director shall give reasons for his decision to apply or not to apply, as the case may be, for an injunction in relation to any complaint which these Regulations require him to consider.

(5) The court on an application by the Director may grant an injunction on such terms as it thinks fit.

(6) An injunction may relate not only to use of a particular contract term drawn up for general use but to any similar term, or a term having like effect, used or recommended for use by any party to the proceedings.

(7) The Director may arrange for the dissemination in such form and manner as he considers appropriate of such information and advice concerning the operation of these Regulations as may appear to him to be expedient to give to the public and to all persons likely to be affected by these Regulations.

4 December 1994 Department of Trade and Industry

SCHEDULE 1 REGULATION 3(1)

Contracts and particular terms excluded from the scope of these Regulations

These Regulations do not apply to –

(a) any contact relating to employment;
(b) any contract relating to succession rights;
(c) any contract relating to rights under family law;
(d) any contract relating to the incorporation and organisation of companies or partnerships; and
(e) any term incorporated in order to comply with or which reflects –
  (i) statutory or regulatory provisions of the United Kingdom; or
  (ii) the provisions or principles of international conventions to which the member States or the Community are party.

SCHEDULE 2 REGULATION 4(3)

Assessment of good faith

In making an assessment of good faith, regard shall be had in particular to–
- (a) the strength of the bargaining positions of the parties;
- (b) whether the consumer had an inducement to agree to the term;
- (c) whether the goods or services were sold or supplied to the special order of the consumer, and
- (d) the extent to which the seller or supplier has dealt fairly and equitably with the consumer.

SCHEDULE 3 REGULATION 4(4)

Indicative and illustrative list of terms which may be regarded as unfair

1. Terms which have the object or effect of –
   - (a) excluding or limiting the legal liability of a seller or supplier in the event of the death of a consumer or personal injury to the latter resulting from an act or omission of that seller or supplier.
   - (b) inappropriately excluding or limiting the legal rights of the consumer vis–à–vis the seller or supplier or another party in the event of total or partial non–performance or inadequate performance by the seller or supplier of any of the contractual obligations, including the option of offsetting a debt owed to the seller or supplier against any claim which the consumer may have against him;
   - (c) making an agreement binding on the consumer whereas provision of services by the seller or supplier is subject to a condition whose realisation depends on his own will alone;
   - (d) permitting the seller or supplier to retain sums paid by the consumer where the latter decides not to conclude or perform the contract, without providing for the consumer to receive compensation of an equivalent amount for the seller supplier where the latter is the party cancelling the contract;
   - (e) requiring the consumer who fails to fulfil his obligation to pay a disproportionably high sum in compensation;
   - (f) authorising the seller or supplier to dissolve the contract on a discretionary basis where the same facility is not granted to the consumer, or permitting the seller or supplier to retain the sums paid for services not yet supplied by him where it is the seller or supplier himself who dissolves the contract;
   - (g) enabling the seller or supplier to terminate a contract of indeterminate duration without reasonable notice except where there are serious grounds for doing so;
   - (h) automatically extending a contract of fixed duration where the consumer does not indicate otherwise, when the deadline fixed for the consumer to express this desire not to extend the contract is unreasonably early;

(i) irrevocably binding the consumer to terms with which he had no real opportunity of becoming acquainted before the conclusion of the contract;

(j) enabling the seller or supplier to alter the terms of the contract unilaterally without a valid reason which is specified in the contract;

(k) enabling the seller or supplier to alter unilaterally without a valid reason any characteristics of the product or service to be provided;

(l) providing for the price of goods to be determined at the time of delivery or allowing a seller of goods or supplier of series to increase their price without in both cases giving the consumer the corresponding right to cancel the contract if the final price is too high in relation to the price agreed when the contract was concluded;

(m) giving the seller or supplier the right to determine whether the goods or services supplied are in conformity with the contract, or giving him the exclusive right to interpret any term of the contract;

(n) limiting the seller's or supplier's obligation to respect commitments undertaken by his agents or making his commitments subject to compliance with a particular formality;

(o) obliging the consumer to fulfil all his obligations where the seller or supplier does not perform his obligations;

(p) giving the seller or supplier the possibility of transferring his rights and obligations under the contract, where this may serve to reduce the guarantees for the consumer, without the latter's agreement;

(q) excluding or hindering the consumer's right to take legal action or exercise any other legal remedy, particulary by requiring the consumer to take disputes exclusively to arbitration not covered by legal provisions, unduly restricting the evidence available to him or imposing on him a burden of proof which, according to the applicable law, should lie with another party to the contract.

2. Scope of subparagraphs 1(g), (j) and (l)

(a) Subparagraph 1(g) is without hindrance to terms by which a supplier of financial services reserves the right to terminate unilaterally a contract of indeterminate duration without notice where there is a valid reason, provided that the supplier is required to inform the other contacting party or parties thereof immediately.

(b) Subparagraph 1(j) is without hindrance to terms under which a supplier of financial services reserves the right to alter the rate of interest payable by the consumer or due to the latter, or the amount of other charges for financial services without notice where there is a valid reason, provided that the supplier is required to inform the other contacting party or parties thereof at the earliest opportunity and that the latter are free to dissolve the contract immediately.

Subparagraph 1(j) is also without hindrance to terms under which a seller or supplier reserves the right to alter unilaterally the conditions of a contact of indeterminate duration, provided that he is required to inform the consumer with reasonable notice and that the consumer is free to dissolve the contract.

(c) Subparagraphs 1(g), (j) and (l) do not apply to:

(i) transactions in transferable securities, financial instruments and other products or services where the price is linked to fluctuations in a stock exchange quotation or index or a financial market rate that the seller or supplier does not control;

(ii) contracts for the purchase or sale of foreign currency, traveller's cheques or international money orders denominated in foreign currency;

(d) Subparagraph 1(l) is without hindrance to price indexation clauses, where lawful, provided that the method by which prices vary is explicitly described.

Chapter 23

SALE AND SUPPLY OF GOODS ACT 1994 (1994 C 35)

An act to amend the law relating to the sale of goods; to make provision as to the terms to be implied in certain agreements for the transfer of property in or the hire of goods, in hire-purchase agreements and on the exchange of goods for trading stamps and as to the remedies for breach of the terms of such agreements; and for connected purposes [3 November 1994].

Northern Ireland. This Act applies; see s8(4) post.

PROVISIONS RELATING TO THE UNITED KINGDOM

1. Implied term about quality

(1) In section 14 of the Sale of Goods Act 1979 (implied terms about quality or fitness) for subsection (2) there is substituted –

'(2) Where the seller sells goods in the course of a business, there is an implied term that the goods supplied under the contact are of satisfactory quality.

(2A) For the purposes of this Act, goods are of satisfactory quality if they meet the standard that a reasonable person would regard as satisfactory, taking account of any description of the goods, the price (if relevant) and all the other relevant circumstances.

(2B) For the purposes of this Act, the quality of goods includes their state and condition and the following (among others) are in appropriate cases aspects of the quality of goods –

(a) fitness for all the purposes for which goods of the kind in question are commonly supplied,

(b) appearance and finish,

(c) freedom from minor defects,

(d) safety, and

(e) durability.

(2C) The term implied by subsection (2) above does not extend to any matter making the quality of goods unsatisfactory –

(a) which is specifically drawn to the buyer's attention before the contract is made,

(b) where the buyer examines the goods before the contract is made, which that examination ought to reveal, or

(c) in the case of a contract for sale by sample, which would have been apparent on a reasonable examination of the sample'.

(2) In section 15 of that Act (sale by sample) in subsection (2)(c) for 'rendering them unmerchantable' this is substituted 'making their quality unsatisfactory'.

2. Acceptance of goods and opportunity to examine them

(1) In section 35 of the Sale of Goods Act 1979 (acceptance) for the words from 'when he intimates' to '(2)' there is substituted –

'subject to subsection (2) below –

(a) when he intimates to the seller that he has accepted them, or

(b) when the goods have been delivered to him and he does any act in relation to them which is inconsistent with the ownership of the seller.

(2) Where goods are delivered to the buyer, and he has not previously examined them, he is not deemed to have accepted them under subsection (1) above until he has had a reasonable opportunity of examining them for the purpose –

(a) of ascertaining whether they are in conformity with the contract, and

(b) in the case of a contract for sale by sample, of comparing the bulk with the sample.

(3) Where the buyer deals as consumer or (in Scotland) the contract of sale is a consumer contract, the buyer cannot lose his right to rely on subsection (2) above by agreement, waiver or otherwise.

(4) The buyer is also deemed to have accepted the goods when after the lapse of a reasonable time he retains the goods without intimating to the seller that he has rejected them.

(5) The questions that are material in determining for the purposes of subsection (4) above whether a reasonable time has elapsed include whether the buyer has had a reasonable opportunity of examining the goods for the purpose mentioned in subsection (2) above.

(6) The buyer is not by virtue of this section deemed to have accepted the goods merely because –

(a) he asks for, or agrees to, their repair by or under an arrangement with the seller, or

(b) the goods are delivered to another under a sub-sale or other disposition.

(7) Where the contact is for the sale of goods making one or more commercial units, a buyer accepting any goods included in a unit is deemed to have accepted all the goods making the unit; and in this subsection 'commercial unit' means a unit division of which would materially impair the value of the goods or the character of the unit.

(8),'

(2) In section 34 of that Act (buyer to have opportunity to examine goods) –

(a) the words from the beginning to '(2)' are repealed; and
(b) at the end of that section there is inserted 'and, in the case of a contract for sale by sample, of comparing the bulk with the sample'.

3. Right of partial rejection

(1) After section 35 of the Sale of Goods Act 1979 there is inserted the following section –

'35A Right of partial rejection

(1) If the buyer –
  (a) has the right to reject the goods by reason of a breach on the part of the seller that affects some or all of them, but
  (b) accepts some of the goods, including, where there are any goods unaffected by the breach, all such goods,

he does not by accepting them lose his right to reject the rest.

(2) In the case of a buyer having the right to reject an instalment of goods, subsection (1) above applies as if references to the goods were references to the goods comprised in the instalment.

(3) For the purposes of subsection (1) above, goods are affected by a breach if by reason of the breach they are not in conformity with the contract.

(4) This section applies unless a contrary intention appears in, or is to be implied from, the contract.'

(2) At the beginning of section 11(4) of that Act (effect of accepting goods) there in inserted 'Subject to section 35A below'.

(3) Section 30(4) of that Act (rejection of goods not within contract description) is repealed.

PROVISIONS RELATING TO ENGLAND AND WALES AND NORTHERN IRELAND

4. Modification of remedies in non-consumer cases

(1) After section 15 of the Sale of Goods Act 1979 there is inserted the following –

'MISCELLANEOUS

15A Modifications of remedies for breach of condition in non-consumer cases

(1) Where in the case of a contract of sale –
  (a) the buyer would, apart from this subsection, have the right to reject goods by reason of a breach on the part of the seller of a term implied by section 13, 14 or 15 above, but
  (b) the breach is so slight that it would be unreasonable for him to reject them,

then, if the buyer does not deal as consumer, the breach is not to be treated as a breach of condition but may be treated as a breach of warranty.

(2) This section applies unless a contrary intention appears in, or is to be implied from, the contract.

(3) It is for the seller to show that a breach fell within subsection (1)(b) above.

(4) This section does not apply to Scotland.'

(2) In section 30 of that Act (delivery of shortfall or excess) after subsection (2) there is inserted –

'(2A)' A buyer who does not deal as a consumer may not –

(a) where the seller delivers a quantity of goods less than he contracted to sell, reject the goods under subsection (1) above, or

(b) where the seller delivers a quantity of goods larger than he contracted to sell, reject the whole under subsection (2) above,

if the shortfall or, as the case may be, excess is so slight that it would be unreasonable for him to do so.

(2B) It is for the seller to show that a shortfall or excess fell within subsection (2A) above.

(2C) Subsections (2A) and (2B) above do not apply to Scotland.'

5.,6. (Apply to Scotland only)

GENERAL

7. Amendments and repeals

(1) Schedule 2 to this Act (which makes minor and consequential amendments of the Sale of Goods Act 1979 and the Uniform Laws on International Sales Act 1967, and makes amendments of enactments relating to the supplyof goods corresponding to the amendments of that Act of 1979 made by this Act) shall have effect.

(2) The enactments mentioned in Schedule 3 to this Act are repealed to the extent specified in Column 3 of that Schedule.

8. Short title, commencement and extent

(1) This Act may be cited as the Sale and Supply of Goods Act 1994.

(2) This Act shall come into force at the end of the two months beginning with the day on which it is passed.

(3) This Act has effect in relation to contracts of sale of goods, hire purchase agreements, contracts for the transfer of goods, contracts for the hire of goods and redemptions of trading stamps for goods (as the case may be) made after this Act comes into force.

(4) This Act extends to Northern Ireland.

INDEX